DATE DUE

POINT LOMA NAZARENE COLLEGE

Ryan Library

3900 Lomaland Drive, San Diego, CA 92106-2899

Call Number

339.22
I61

Accession Number

196988

INTERNATIONAL COMPARISONS OF THE
DISTRIBUTION OF HOUSEHOLD WEALTH

INTERNATIONAL COMPARISONS OF
THE DISTRIBUTION OF
HOUSEHOLD WEALTH

INTERNATIONAL COMPARISONS OF THE DISTRIBUTION OF HOUSEHOLD WEALTH

edited by

EDWARD N. WOLFF

339.22
I61

CLARENDON PRESS · OXFORD
1987

POINT LOMA NAZARENE COLLEGE
196988
RYAN LIBRARY

Oxford University Press, Walton Street, Oxford OX2 6DP

Oxford New York Toronto
Delhi Bombay Calcutta Madras Karachi
Petaling Jaya Singapore Hong Kong Tokyo
Nairobi Dar es Salaam Cape Town
Melbourne Auckland

and associated companies in
Beirut Berlin Ibadan Nicosia

Oxford is a trade mark of Oxford University Press

Published in the United States
by Oxford University Press, New York

© Edward Wolff 1987

All rights reserved. No part of this publication may be reproduced,
stored in a retrieval system, or transmitted, in any form or by any means,
electronic, mechanical, photocopying, recording, or otherwise, without
the prior permission of Oxford University Press

British Library Cataloguing in Publication Data
International comparisons of the distribution of household wealth.
1. Wealth   2. Income distribution
I. Wolff, Edward N.
339.2'2   HC79.W4
ISBN 0-19-828511-6

Library of Congress Cataloging in Publication Data
International comparisons of the distribution of household wealth.
Papers originally presented at the Conference on International Comparisons of the Distribution
of Household Wealth, November 11-12, 1983 in New York City.
Bibliography: p.
1. Income distribution—Europe—Congresses.
2. Income distribution—United States—Congresses.
3. Income distribution—Canada—Congresses.   4. Wealth—
Europe—Congresses.   5. Wealth—United States—
Congresses.   6. Wealth—Canada—Congresses.   I. Wolff,
Edward N.   II. Conference on International Comparisons of the Distribution of
Household Wealth (1983: New York, N.Y.)
HC240.9.15156   1987   339.2'2'094   86-31241
ISBN 0-19-828511-6

Set by Colset Private Limited, Singapore
Printed in Great Britain
at the University Printing House, Oxford
by David Stanford
Printer to the University

To
my mother, Ethel, and my father, Arthur

PREFACE

The papers that are included in this book were originally presented at the C.V. Starr Center Conference on International Comparisons of the Distribution of Household Wealth. The conference was held 11–12 November 1983, in New York City and sponsored by the C.V. Starr Center for Applied Economics at New York University. Many others, besides the authors whose papers are included in this work, participated and made valued contributions to the sessions. Dominique Strauss-Kahn (Université de Paris X), Joseph Quinn (Boston College), André Babeau (Université de Paris), Meinhard Miegel (Institut fur Wirtschaft- und Gesellschaftspolitik in Bonn), T. Cameron Whiteman (Department of Health and Human Services in Washington), Leo J.M. Aarts (Leyden University), and Clyde Browning (University of North Carolina at Chapel Hill) all presented papers, which because of their preliminary nature or other publication commitments, are not included here. Patricia Ruggles (the Urban Institute in Washington DC), Thomas Juster (Institute for Social Research at the University of Michigan), Richard Ruggles (Yale University), Michael O'Higgins (University of Bath), Lars Osberg (Dalhousie University), Roger Gordon (University of Michigan), and Paul Menchik (Michigan State University) all served as formal discussants and made valuable comments on the papers. Raymond Goldsmith (Yale University), R. Robert Russell (New York University), and Alois Wenig (University of Bielefeld, West Germany) chaired the various sessions of the conference. Finally, Marcia Marley ably reviewed the papers for the volume.

The conference's focus was on empirical work on household wealth distribution. Six countries were represented at the conference: Canada, the Federal Republic of Germany, France, Sweden, the United Kingdom, and the United States. The primary goal of the conference was to provide a survey of the latest data and information available on the size distribution of household wealth in North America and Europe. Authors were also asked to report on time trends on wealth inequality in their country. Statistical issues received special attention at the conference. These included

(a) sampling problems, (b) asset coverage, (c) underreporting biases, (d) the unit of observation, (e) the treatment of retirement assets, (f) institutional differences in wealth ownership across countries, (g) relative price effects, and (h) the statistical measurement of wealth distributions.

Several more substantive issues also attracted particular interest at the conference, which were as follows: (a) Has there been any historical movement towards greater equality in the distribution of household wealth? (b) What factors are responsible for time trends in wealth inequality? (c) How has retirement wealth affected overall inequality in the size distribution of household wealth? (d) How have demographic factors affected wealth inequality? (e) What is the relation between the distribution of income and the distribution of wealth? (f) What effect have changes in household behaviour had on the inequality of wealth?

The results reported in this volume should appeal to a broad audience. For economists, there are several findings that shed new light on the competing hypotheses regarding household savings, wealth formation, and wealth distribution. For a more general readership, results regarding the level and distribution of household wealth bear directly on social issues regarding the level of well-being and the degree of equity and fairness in society. In this regard, cross-national comparisons of wealth inequality may be of particular interest. Finally, for those concerned about social policy, findings on changes in household wealth inequality over time allow an evaluation of the effectiveness of government programme, particularly income and wealth taxation and income transfers, in reducing inequality. Of particular relevance here is the role of public pension systems and retirement wealth in reducing overall wealth concentration. It should be noted that the papers in the volume focus primarily on 'facts', rather than explanations. However, these facts provide the starting-point for the proper analysis of the effects of household behaviour and social policy on household wealth accumulation.

CONTENTS

ABBREVIATIONS

API	Asset Price Index
CPS	Current Population Survey
C/QPP	Canada and Quebec Pensions Plan
CREP	Centre de Recherche sur L'Épargne
CSO	Central Statistical Office
ESRC	Economic and Social Research Council
FAD	Financial assets less unsecured debt
FT	Financial Times
FIX	FT/Actuaries index of fixed interest securities
GIS	Guaranteed income supplement
GNP	Gross National Product
GSSLW	Gross Social Security Lifetime Wealth
HDW	Household disposable wealth
HK	Human capital wealth
HLW	Household lifetime wealth
HOUS	Department of the Environment second-hand house price index
HRW	Household reserve wealth
IRS	Internal Revenue Service
ISDP	Income Survey Development Program
LAND	Ministry of Agriculture and Fisheries total land price index
LIDW	Life insurance death wealth
LIRW	Life insurance reserve wealth
NW	Net Worth
NWCH	Net worth less consumer durables and home equity
OAS	Old Age Security
OTA	Office of Tax Analysis
PB	Pension benefits
PDW	Pension disposable wealth
PRW	Pension reserve wealth
RCDIW	Royal Commission on the Distribution of Income and Wealth
RPI	Retail Price Index
RPP	Registered pension plan

RRSP	Registered Retirement Savings Plan
RWI	Relative Wealth Index
SCF	Statistics Canada Survey of Consumer Finances
SFCC	Survey of Financial Characteristics of Consumers
SHAR	FT/Actuaries index of ordinary shares
SIC	Standard Industrial Classification
SSA	Social security accumulations
SSLW	Social security lifetime wealth
SSMAX	Maximum taxable wage base
SSW	Social security wealth
SSWAGE	Social security wage base
WAIS	Wisconsin Asset and Income Study
YMPE	Year's maximum pensionable earnings
YPI	Yield Price Index

1

Introduction and Overview

Edward N. Wolff and Marcia Marley

I. Introduction

Originally presented at a conference sponsored by the C.V. Starr Center for Applied Economics at New York University in November 1983, the chapters included in this volume report some of the latest evidence available on inequality in household wealth in Canada, France, Sweden, the United Kingdom, and the United States. Six major themes emerge in this volume.

1. Time Trends

Perhaps the most important finding is the gradual but persistent decline in the degree of wealth inequality among households during the twentieth century. This observation is based on data for Sweden, the UK, and the US, the only countries for which such long time-series information is available. According to the Spånt chapter, the share of total household wealth held by the top 1 per cent of wealth holders declined from 50 per cent in 1920 to 21 per cent in 1975 in Sweden. As shown in the Shorrocks paper, the share of the top 1 per cent in the United Kingdom fell from 61 per cent in 1923 to 23 per cent in 1980. The decline in wealth inequality in the United States was less dramatic. Previous work by Robert Lampman (1962) indicates that the share of the top 1 per cent of individuals fell from a peak of 36 per cent in 1929 to 26 per cent in 1956. The Smith chapter contained in this volume shows a further decline to 19 per cent in 1976.[1] It is interesting to note that these three countries differ quite considerably in tax policy, the extent of social transfers, macroeconomic performance, and in other social and political institutions. Shorrocks argues that the magnitude of these trends potentially represents a 'major social revolution' in the industrialized world.

2. Cross-Sectional Evidence

Despite this significant downward trend in inequality, household wealth is still highly concentrated today. In the mid-1970s, the richest 1 per cent held a quarter of all household wealth in France and the US, over 30 per cent in the UK, and about a sixth in Sweden. Moreover, household wealth is considerably more concentrated than household income. Greenwood, for example, calculated that the top 1 per cent of wealthholders owned 24 per cent of total wealth in the US in 1973, while the richest 1 per cent of families with regard to income received 11 per cent of all income.

3. The Role of Retirement Systems

Another major concern of the chapters in this volume is the role of retirement systems in household wealth accumulation. One of the major developments in the post-war period has been the enormous growth in both public and private pension systems. Even though such pension funds are not in the direct control of individuals or families, they are a source of future income to families and thus may be perceived as a form of family wealth. Moreover, as Feldstein (1974) has argued, insofar as families accumulate 'traditional' wealth to provide for future consumption needs, the growth of such pension funds may have offset private savings and hence traditional wealth accumulation.

Two different treatments of pensions are represented in the chapters included in this volume.[2] The first is a 'wealth' approach, where various attempts are made to estimate both public and private pension wealth. These imputations are based on varying assumptions about the future growth in earnings and pension benefits. Such estimates are then included as part of household wealth (see below for a discussion of alternative concepts of household wealth). In some analyses, cross-sectional comparisons are provided of the distribution of such wider notions of wealth and of traditional measures of household wealth. In other analyses, time-series trends are compared for the concentration of expanded household wealth and for conventional wealth measures. The second is an 'annuity' approach, where retirement income flows from both public and private pensions are projected on the basis of varying assumptions regarding future benefit growth. These estimated benefits are then included along with expected income flows from traditional household wealth to compute post-retirement income. Analyses are then possible regarding the 'adequacy' of retirement income with respect to pre-retirement income.

4. Definition of Wealth

Another theme that emerges in these chapters is that there is no unique concept or definition of wealth that is satisfactory for all purposes. As Shorrocks notes, a 'proper' definition of wealth can reflect: (a) the potential future consumption represented by the stock of wealth; (b) ability to circumvent financial constraints that would otherwise bind; (c) the power and influence that can be exercised; or (d) the potential advantages transmitted to future generations of heirs.

In the chapters in this volume, various measures of wealth are used.[3] The conventional or traditional definition of household wealth includes assets and liabilities that have a current market value and that are directly or indirectly marketable (fungible). A typical list of assets includes owner-occupied housing and other real estate; consumer durables and household inventories; cash, checking and savings accounts, bonds, and other financial instruments; corporate stocks or shares; the equity in unincorporated businesses; trust funds; and the cash surrender value of life insurance policies and pension plans. This measure is often referred to as 'disposable' wealth, since it represents those assets over which the family or individual has control.

A wider definition of household wealth will often add some valuation of pension rights, from both public and private sources, to disposable wealth. Such a measure provides a better gauge of potential future consumption. A still wider definition will also include human capital or some comparable measure of future earnings possibilities, since this also adds to future consumption possibilities. The major drawback with this approach is that many simplifying assumptions are required in order to estimate expected income paths. For example, the researcher must project the discount rate, the future growth of earnings, and future retirement transfers. Moreover, tractibility entails limiting such projections to representative population groups, thus underestimating the true variance in the distribution of future income flows.

Some authors have also proposed definitions that are narrower than disposable wealth. One measure subtracts from conventional wealth the value of home equity, consumer durables, and household inventories. By eliminating assets held primarily for service flows, this measure probably more accurately reflects the economic and social power of a family than traditional wealth measures. Another measure, defined as financial assets less unsecured debt, is probably the most useful for assessing a family's liquidity. Another concept of wealth includes assets held primarily for their income-producing potential. This form of wealth includes business equity, stocks and shares, bonds and other securities, and investment real estate. It is primarily held by the upper wealth classes and is often transmitted to succeeding generations.

Another definitional issue revolves around the proper unit of observation. As we shall discuss below, there are three basic units of observation in primary wealth data: the family (or household), the individual, and the tax-paying unit. However, in general, the proper unit for either welfare or behavioural analysis will not directly correspond to the observational unit. In regard to welfare, family wealth, family per capita wealth, and some combination of the two have each been used as a measure of welfare in the various chapters in this volume. Family wealth is employed most frequently, since families are the primary unit of consumption. However, smaller families are probably better off than larger families who have the same level of family wealth. This recommends a family per capita wealth measure. Greenwood, for example, adjusts her inequality measure for household size. Yet, there are economies of consumption, so that family per capita wealth may actually understate the welfare level of large families. An alternative approach is to divide household wealth by an 'equivalence scale' which adjusts family size for actual consumption needs. Radner and Vaughan, for example, use the US poverty line levels as an equivalence scale to obtain a household wealth welfare measure.

From a behavioural point of view, the family is used most often as the unit of analysis, since families tend to make wealth decisions jointly and accumulate wealth over time for future consumption needs. Yet, over time, the family is not a stable unit. Children leave families to set up independent family units. Moreover, it is quite common for married couples to separate or divorce, and, as a result, for family wealth to be split. From this standpoint, it may also be appropriate to base behavioural models on individual wealth accumulation decisions.[4]

5. Data Sources

There is extensive discussion in this volume concerning the measurement problems and biases inherent in the various sources of household wealth data.[5] Five principal sources are identified in these chapters. The first is estate tax records, which are actual tax returns filed for probate. Such data have a great degree of reliability, since they are subject to scrutiny and audit by the state. Their main limitation, in the US at least, is that the threshold for filing is relatively high, so that only a small proportion of estates (typically, 1 per cent or so) are required to file returns.[6] Another difficulty with these data is that the sample consists of decedents. As a result, various assumptions must be used to construct 'estate multipliers' in order to infer the distribution of wealth among the living. Insofar as mortality rates are inversely correlated with wealth (that is, the rich tend to live longer), the resulting multipliers can be biased. Moreover, the resulting estimated distribution of wealth is by individual, rather than by family. Changing ownership patterns within families (for example, joint ownership of the family's house) can affect estimated wealth concentration. Moreover, various assumptions must be made to infer family wealth from estimates of individual wealth holdings.

Another problem involves underreporting and non-filing for tax avoidance. Though the returns are subject to audit, the value of cash on hand, jewellery, housewares, and business assets are difficult to ascertain. Their value is typically understated in order to reduce the tax liability of the estate. Finally, *inter vivos* transfers, particularly in anticipation of death, can bias estimates of household wealth among the living. The reported concentration results for Britain are based on estate tax data and the individual unit of account, as are Smith's results for the US.

The second source is wealth tax return data. A few countries, such as Sweden and, recently, France, assess taxes not only on current income but also on the stock of household wealth. Though there is typically a threshold for paying wealth taxes, their coverage of the population can be considerably greater than that of estate tax returns. However, the measurement problems are similar to those of estate tax data. The filer has a great incentive to understate the value of his assets, or even not to report them, for tax avoidance. Moreover, the assets subject to tax do not cover the full range of household assets (for example, consumer durables are often excluded). In this case, the observational unit is the tax return unit, which does not necessarily correspond to the family unit.

The third source is the field survey. Its primary advantage is that it provides the interviewers with considerable discretion as to the information they may request of respondents. However, its major disadvantage is that information provided by the respondent is often inaccurate, and, in many cases, the information requested is not provided at all. Another problem is that because household wealth is extremely skewed, the upper tail is often considerably underrepresented in random samples. An alternative is to use stratified samples, based typically on income tax returns, which oversample the rich. However, studies indicate that response error and non-response rates are considerably higher among the wealthy than among the middle class.

The fourth type of wealth data is based on 'income capitalization' techniques, which are usually applied to income tax return data. In this procedure, certain income flows, such as dividends, rents, and interest, are converted into corresponding asset values based on the average asset yield. This source also suffers from a number of defects. First, only assets with a corresponding income flow are covered in this procedure. Thus, owner-occupied housing, consumer durables, and idle land cannot be directly captured. Also, in the US, state and local bonds cannot be estimated, because this source of interest income is exempt from federal income taxes. Second, the estimation procedure rests heavily on the assumption that asset yields are uncorrelated with asset levels. Any actual correlation between asset holdings and yields can produce biased estimates. Third, the observational unit is the tax return, which is not strictly comparable to the individual or family.

The fifth general source of data comes from various eclectic approaches. These involve combining two or more basic sources of data, as well as merging and matching of data sets. In the US, for example, tax return data from the Internal Revenue Service have been matched with US Census household survey data. Income capitalization has then been applied to the tax return data to obtain values of corresponding assets, and the Census data used to supply values for some of the missing assets (see the Wolff paper, for example). This approach has the advantage of combining the strengths of the basic data sources. However, the major disadvantage is that the joint distributions of non-common variables in the two data sources, imputed from statistical matches, are often unreliable.

6. Behavioural Models

Though not a central focus of the conference, issues about modelling household wealth accumulation were discussed in various contexts, particularly in relation to definitional and measurement concerns. Primary emphasis is placed on two opposing views of the wealth accumulation process. The first is the 'life-cycle model', originally developed by Modigliani and Brumberg (1954). In the basic version of this model, families save in order to smooth out consumption over their expected lifetime. Given a standard lifetime earnings pattern, with retirement occurring around age 65, families will accumulate wealth primarily for consumption during their retirement years. The result is the so-called 'hump-shaped' age profile of wealth, with wealth rising with age until the mid-60s and then declining with age. A vast literature has accumulated on this subject, which is beyond our scope to review here.[7] However, several chapters in this volume do present findings on the age–wealth profile. Radner and Vaughan find a hump-shaped pattern of mean wealth by age class for US families in 1979 and a significant decumulation of wealth after age 65. However, Greenwood finds mean wealth rising with age across all age classes in the US in 1973, and Wolff obtains a similar result for US households in 1969.[8] Another implication of the life-cycle model is that cross-sectional variation in disposable wealth should be largely due to age differences. Greenwood attempts one measure of the contribution of life-cycle factors to total wealth inequality, and finds that they account for very little of observed wealth inequality.

The second and alternative approach is the so-called 'Kaldorian' or class model. In the simple version of this model, two classes are posited: the capitalist class and the working class. It is assumed that all saving is done by the capitalist class, and their primary motive is to pass on their capital to succeeding generations. This model suggests very different determinants of wealth accumulation patterns and the cross-sectional size distribution of wealth than the life-cycle model. In particular, factors such as the relative price movements of assets, the rate of economic growth, the population growth rate, and the number of heirs per estate become the key variables in this analytical framework.[9] In this volume, Kessler and Masson suggest a decomposition of wealth inequality based on a 'neo-Kaldorian' model of wealth accumulation.

7. Inequality Indices

Though not a major theme of the conference, issues regarding the measurement of household wealth inequality also receive some attention in these chapters. Because many of the data used in wealth analysis are limited to the upper percentiles of the wealth distribution, the most common concentration measures are the shares of the top 1, 2 or 5 per cent of the wealth distribution. Where wealth data for representative samples are available, the most popular measure is the so-called 'Gini coefficient'. This is derived from a Lorenz curve, where the cumulative share of wealth held by the bottom n percentiles is plotted against the nth percentile (see the Greenwood paper for a diagram). The diagonal or 45° line represents perfect equality, since the cumulative share of wealth would exactly equal the cumulative share of households. The Gini coefficient measures the deviation of the Lorenz curve from the line of perfect equality. Gini coefficients, by construction, range from a low of zero to a high of unity. Gini coefficients for household wealth are typically of the order of 0.7 to 0.8. In comparison, those for income are typically in the neighbourhood of 0.4. Several attempts have also been made to adjust the Gini coefficient for sources of inequality related strictly to life-cycle factors (see the Greenwood paper, for example).

The remaining three sections of this chapter present an overview of the conference papers. The next section (Section II) summarizes the results of, three papers which investigate changes in wealth inequality over time in Great Britain, Sweden, and the United States. Section III focuses on recent cross-sectional analyses of household wealth distribution in the United States and France, with particular emphasis on the asset holdings of different demographic groups. Section IV considers other topics in estimating household wealth, including the imputation of public and private pension wealth, the replacement rate of retirement income, and the role of relative price changes on wealth concentration. The last section presents some concluding remarks.

II. The Decline in Wealth Inequality

The three chapters included in the first section of the volume highlight the decline in household wealth inequality in Western Europe and North America. The first of these, by Anthony Shorrocks, summarizes results of several previous studies of long-term trends in household wealth inequality in the United Kingdom.[10] The principal finding of his study is that there was a dramatic decline in the degree of household wealth inequality in the UK from 1923 to 1980. Based on a conventional definition of wealth, the share of the top 1 per cent of wealth holders fell from 61 per cent to 23 per cent; the share of the top 5 per cent declined from 82 to 43 per cent; and the share of the top 10 per cent dropped from 89 to 58 per cent.

The results reported in this chapter are based on estate duty data. Such information refers to individuals and is, as a result, sensitive to changes in ownership patterns within families. In particular, any tendency to share legal title to various household assets between husband and wife, such as the family home or automobile, will lead to a reduction in the share of wealth held by the richest individuals, even if there is no change in the distribution of family wealth. Shorrocks believes that part of the decline in the share of the top 1 per cent of wealth holders in Britain is attributable to this factor. In evidence, he cites the fact that the share of total wealth held by the top 10 per cent declined substantially less than that of the top 1 per cent. Indeed, the share of total wealth held by those in the top decile, but outside the top percentile, actually increased from 28 per cent in 1923 to 38 per cent in 1972.

Shorrocks presents two additional series on household wealth distribution, which use a wider notion of household wealth defined as conventional wealth plus rights to private and state pension plans. The shares of the top wealth holders are considerably lowered by the addition of retirement wealth, since the latter is more equally distributed than disposable wealth. In 1980, for example, the share of disposable wealth held by the top 1 per cent was 23 per cent, while the share of expanded wealth was only 12 per cent. Moreover, since pension entitlements have grown enormously since 1900, the inclusion of pension wealth in household wealth serves to strongly reinforce the downward trend observed for wealth inequality.

Another factor responsible for the equalizing trend in household wealth is the widespread ownership of homes and the rapid appreciation of house values. Shorrocks estimates that a home valued at £50,000, net of mortgage, would have placed the holder among the top 3 per cent of wealth holders in 1980. (Also, see the Harbury and Hitchens chapter for a more detailed analysis of relative asset price changes in the UK.)

Several problems with the estate data source and methodology are discussed by Shorrocks. First, the estate multiplier method is likely to lead to some bias in estimated wealth shares because of the positive correlation between wealth and life expectancy (wealthier individuals tend to live longer) within age–sex groups. Second, the value of household goods and small businesses are likely to be understated in estate data, since their value is considerably greater when in use than when put up for sale. Third, the values of life insurance policies are considerably greater in estates, since they are fully paid out, than comparable policies in the hands of the living. Fourth, except for life insurance policies, the total value of assets based on estate tax data falls far short of national balance sheet figures for the household sector.

Shorrocks also offers two interesting comments on observed age–wealth profile data. As noted in Section I, the life-cycle model would lead one to expect a hump-shaped wealth profile across age groups, with the peak occurring near the normal age of retirement. Shorrocks notes first that the age pattern of household wealth found in a cross-sectional profile for a single year may bear little relation to the age–wealth profile of a cohort of individuals over their lifetime. Indeed, if the economy is experiencing real growth in per capita income, the cross-sectional evidence is biased towards a hump-shaped profile, even when no actual cohort experiences such a pattern. Second, the inclusion of pension wealth in the household portfolio virtually guarantees a hump-shaped age profile. Almost by construction, pension wealth doubles the wealth of all individuals, on average, and triples the wealth of those in the 55–65 age cohort.

The second chapter in this section, by Roland Spånt, investigates time trends in wealth concentration in Sweden from 1920 through 1983. The analysis is confined to the distribution of disposable wealth. The data for the period from 1920 through 1975 are based on actual tax returns. The results for 1983 are computed from projections based on relative asset price movements from 1975 through 1983.

Tax return data are subject to error, like other sources of wealth data. The principal problem with tax return information is under-reporting due to tax evasion and legal tax exemptions. However, some assets, such as housing and stock shares, are extremely well covered, because of legal registration requirements in Sweden. Also, the deductibility of interest payments from taxable income makes it likely that the debt information is very reliable. On the other hand, bank accounts and bonds are not subject to similar tax controls, and it is likely that their amounts are considerably underreported.

In 1975, owner-occupied housing comprised close to 40 per cent of gross assets, and other real estate about a fourth. Bank deposits accounted for 14 per cent and stock shares 5 per cent of gross assets. However, household wealth in Sweden was not always dominated by real estate. Indeed, the relative holdings of different asset types have changed dramatically in Sweden. Between 1945 and 1975, the share of owner-occupied housing and secondary dwellings in household assets rose from 18 to 44 per cent. During this period, stock shares as a proportion of household assets declined from 12 to 6 per cent, while the value of farms and unincorporated businesses fell from 30 to 20 per cent. However, liabilities have remained almost proportional to total assets over this period.

As noted in the introduction, the major finding of this study is the dramatic reduction in wealth inequality in Sweden. Based on the years for which data are available, the decline appears to be a conti-nuous process between 1920 and 1975. Over the whole period, the share of the top percentile declined from 50 per cent to 21 per cent of total household wealth in tax value terms. In market price terms, the top 1 per cent held 17 per cent of total wealth in 1975. On the other hand, the share of the bottom 95 per cent increased from 23 to 56 per cent of total wealth. Moreover, the per cent of households that declared any taxable wealth increased from one-fifth in 1920 to three-fourths in 1975. Indeed, because of differential underreporting by asset type, the concentration of wealth is probably even more equal in 1975 than the official figures indicate. Still, wealth is considerably less equally distributed than income. Whereas the richest decile of income earners received 20 per cent of total disposable income in 1975, the top decile of wealth holders owned 55 per cent of total wealth.

Spånt estimates that the concentration of wealth in Sweden increased between 1975 and 1983. The 1983 results are based on asset price series from 1975 through 1983. The extrapolation assumes that the composition of asset holdings remained constant across wealth groups. During this period, real-estate prices tended, on average, to lag behind the inflation rate. The same was true of savings accounts, bonds, and other financial assets. Liabilities, which amounted to 30 per cent of total assets, were halved in real terms. However, stock share prices almost doubled in real terms over this period. Since stock shares are held by the very wealthy (the top percentile owned half of all stock shares in 1975), while real estate and financial assets are more evenly distributed, the net effect has been increased concentration of wealth. Spånt estimates that the share of the top percentile in market price terms increased from 17 per cent in 1975 to almost 20 per cent in 1983.

The third study in this section, by James Smith, investigates time trends in wealth concentration in the US from 1958 through 1981 based on estate tax data. The series from 1958 through 1976 is consistent with respect to the categorization of assets, the estate multiplier technique in use, and the aggregate balance sheet estimates. The 1981 results were prepared by the Internal Revenue Service (IRS) and are based on a somewhat different estate multiplier technique, which Smith feels tends to bias upward the shares of the top wealth groups.

Smith finds that the share of wealth held by richest 0.5 per cent and the richest 1 per cent of the population remained essentially unchanged between 1958 and 1972, with the share of the top percentile fluctuating between 27 and 31 per cent of total net worth. However, between 1972 and 1976, the share of the top half-percentile fell from 22 to 14 per cent and the share of the top percentile declined from 28 to 19 per cent. The main reason for the decline in concentration is the sharp drop in the value of corporate stock held by the top wealth holders. The total value of corporate stock owned by the richest 1 per cent fell from US$491 billion in 1972 to US$297 billion in 1976. Moreover, this decline is directly attributable to the steep decline in share prices, rather than a divestiture of stock holdings.

The 1981 estimates show an increased concentration of wealth. The share of the richest eight-tenths of 1 per cent was 20 per cent in 1981, while the share of the top percentile was 19 per cent in 1976. Smith believes that the IRS estimates for 1981 are biased upward by about 20 per cent and, if properly adjusted, would show no change in wealth concentration between 1976 and 1981. He surmises that the egalitarian trend of the 1970s will likely persist into the future.

III. Cross-Sectional Estimates of the Concentration of Household Wealth

The three chapters included in the second section of the book focus on cross-sectional estimates and analyses of the distribution of household wealth in the US and France. Moreover, in the Kessler–Masson chapter, measures of wealth concentration are presented for several other industrialized countries. In addition, the two American chapters also include analyses of the relation of household wealth to age, family size, and household income.

The first chapter, by Daniel Radner and Denton Vaughan, is based on the 1979 Income Survey Development Program (ISDP) file for the US. The chapter focuses on the relation between household wealth, the age of the household 'reference person' (the household member in whose name the home is owned or rented), and household income. Three concepts of wealth are used in the paper: (a) conventional net worth (NW); (b) conventional net worth less consumer durables and home equity (NWCH), a concept designed to measure assets with financial returns; and (c) financial assets less unsecured debt (FAD), a concept designed to emphasize liquidity. Radner and Vaughan first note that the ISDP file suffers from substantial underreporting, particularly in the upper tail, since the survey was designed primarily for low-income and middle-income families. This may bias some of the resulting analysis.

Radner and Vaughan find that both mean and median household net worth followed a hump-shaped profile with respect to age, rising with age from the youngest to the 55–64 age cohort and then declining monotonically with age cohort thereafter. The ratio of mean wealth by age cohort to overall mean wealth increased from 0.14 for the cohort under 25 years of age to 1.69 for the 55–64 age cohort and then fell to 1.04 for the age cohort 75 and over. Mean NWCH rose more sharply, from a ratio of 0.08 for the youngest age group to 1.87 at peak and then declined to 1.17. Finally, FAD increased even more steeply, from a ratio of 0.06 for the youngest to 2.27 at peak, but then fell to only 1.87 for the oldest age group.

Mean income also had a hump-shaped pattern with respect to age, though it increased less sharply with age and peaked in the 45–54 age cohort. As a result, the ratio of mean net worth to mean income by age cohort rose almost monotonically with age, from a low of 0.63 for the youngest age group to 5.89 for the oldest.

The composition of household wealth also varied by age cohort. Financial assets increased in importance with age, whereas business equity and consumer durables declined as a share of household wealth. Home equity remained relatively constant as a percentage of net worth across age groups.

Though income and net worth had a positive correlation across quintiles, there was still a considerable amount of dispersion in net worth within each of the income quintiles. In the bottom income quintile, 41 per cent of households were in the bottom net worth quintile, while only 7 per cent were in the top wealth quintile. In contrast, 45 per cent of the households in the top income quintile were also in the top wealth quintile, while only 5 per cent were in the bottom wealth quintile. Yet, no net worth quintile contained more than 45 per cent of the households in the corresponding income quintile.

In the last part of the chapter, Radner and Vaughan construct various measures of economic well-being based jointly on household income and wealth. They focus on the bottom part of the income distribution to determine whether such low-income households are also relatively deprived in terms of wealth. They find that 12.9 per cent of all households were in both the bottom income quintile (under US$7,325) and in the bottom two net worth quintiles (under US$15,609), while the corresponding figure for elderly households (age 65 or over) was 20.1 per cent. This percentage for elderly families exceeds the corresponding figures for each of the other age groups. The authors then adjust for size of household unit to obtain a better measure of economic well-being. Both income and wealth are adjusted using an equivalence scale based on US poverty thresholds. With this adjustment, the per cent of elderly families with both low income and low wealth fell from 20.1 to 15.4 per cent, because elderly households tended to have only one or two members. Yet, even so, the per cent of elderly households with low adjusted income and wealth still remained above that of each of the other age cohorts except for the very young.

The second chapter in this section, by Daphne Greenwood, investigates the distribution of household wealth in the US in 1973. The 1973 data are based on imputations derived from survey data, income tax returns, and estate tax returns. Income tax returns from the 1973 Individual Income Tax Model were first merged with observations from the 1973 Current Population Survey. From the income tax data, dividends were capitalized into the value of corporate stock and interest into the value of debt instrument assets. Reported property tax was used to obtain estimates of the value of real estate owned by the household. Special imputations from the Office of Tax Analysis yielded estimates of state and local bond values. Finally, based on a sample of 1972 estate tax returns, a linear regression was estimated of total net worth on the sum of corporate stock, financial assets, and real estate. The resulting regression coefficients on these three assets were then used to impute net worth to each family record in the larger matched file. Greenwood estimates an aggregate net wealth of US$2.6 trillion, compared to the national balance sheet total of US$3.5 trillion for the household sector in 1972. Greenwood's figures underestimate consumer durables, inventories, and real estate but are very close to the aggregate totals for corporate stock and interest-bearing assets.

The chapter focuses on the question of how much of the observed inequality in household wealth is attributable to differences in age and household size. The theoretical link between household wealth and age is due to the life-cycle model (see Section I above). On the basis of this, many have argued that a large proportion of overall inequality can be explained by differences in position in the life-cycle. Household size also exerts an effect on household wealth independent of age. In particular, single person households tend to have lower household wealth, on average, than larger households.

This could be due to less need to invest in housing and consumer durables than for larger families.

Greenwood finds that the top 1 per cent of households held 33 per cent of household wealth and the top 10 per cent 71 per cent in 1973. Moreover, the Gini coefficient for household wealth is 0.82. These results indicate a somewhat higher concentration of household wealth than those of Smith, who estimates a 28 per cent share of the top percentile in 1972. Also, Smith's results refer to individuals and are based on estate tax data, while Greenwood bases her results on the family unit.[11] However, in Lampman's estimates for the 1922–53 period, wealth concentration was uniformly lower for the family unit than for the individual unit.[12] Thus, it is unlikely that the difference in observational unit explains the higher concentration figures in the Greenwood data. A more likely possibility is that the underestimation of consumer durables and real estate biases downward her estimated shares for the lower and middle classes.

Greenwood then divides her sample into six age classes. She finds that mean wealth by age class increased with age and, in particular, rose between households 56 to 65 years of age and those over 65. This result is consistent with Wolff's findings but contrasts with that of Radner and Vaughan, who find wealth peaking for the 55–64 age group and declining with age thereafter.

Greenwood also finds that wealth inequality within age cohort is generally of the same magnitude as overall wealth inequality. Gini coefficients of household wealth by age class range from 0.75 to 0.89 and for three of the six age groups are higher than the overall Gini coefficient of 0.82.

In the next part of the chapter, Greenwood computes a so-called 'corrected Gini coefficient', where the line of perfect equality is adjusted for variations in wealth due to both age and family size (see the paper for details). She finds that the adjustment lowers the Gini coefficient by only 7 per cent, from 0.82 to 0.76. Greenwood concludes that age and family size explain relatively little of the total variation in household wealth. The major part of wealth inequality appears due to differences in income, saving rates, investment returns, and inheritances received among families.

The third chapter in this section, by Denis Kessler and André Masson, focuses on wealth distribution in France, though some comparative data are presented for other countries as well. The first part of their chapter presents a very interesting comparison of estimates of the size distribution of wealth in France based on different estimating techniques. Four different methods have been used over the last 10 years in France. The first, based on direct sample surveys, has been carried out for 1973, 1975, 1977, and 1980. Extreme underreporting is evident from these surveys. In the first two, reported survey wealth amounted to only half of the national balance sheet estimate of household wealth. In the latter two surveys, the declared value of corporate stock represented only 15 per cent of the total value held by households. Moreover, the relative degree of underreporting of household assets tends to be a positive function of the level of household wealth. This fact helps explain why household surveys tend to understate the concentration of household wealth.

The second method, the income capitalization technique, has been used on income tax data for 1975, and the third, the estate duty method, has been applied to probate records for 1977. However, because of legislation, a large number of inheritances are not recorded in the estate tax sample. The fourth source is from an annual wealth tax that was first imposed in 1981. This tax is levied on all taxpayers whose wealth exceeds 3 million francs, after a 2 million franc deduction for so-called 'professional assets'. Data are available for the first year of the tax, 1981. Underestimation is believed to be in the order of 15 to 20 per cent.

Despite the difference in sources and methods, the results on wealth inequality do not differ that greatly. The Gini coefficient based on household surveys is 0.71 for 1975 and 0.70 for 1980, while that based on income capitalization is 0.72 for 1975. The share of the top 10 per cent of households in 1975 is estimated to be 50 per cent based on sample survey data and 54 per cent based on income capitalization. From sample survey data, the share of the top 1 per cent of households in 1975 is estimated to be 13 per cent, while from estate tax data, the share of the top percentile in 1977 is estimated to fall between 13 and 19 per cent.[13] Finally, the top 0.5 per cent of households were estimated to hold between 9 and 13 per cent of total wealth in 1977 based on estate tax data, whereas the top 0.45 per cent of tax-paying units were estimated to own a minimum of 10 per cent of total wealth in 1981, on the basis of annual wealth tax data.

The chapter also includes comparative data on wealth concentration for eight industrialized countries. The share of total wealth of the top 1 per cent ranges, in descending order, from 32 per cent in the United Kingdom (1974), 28 per cent in Belgium (1969) and the Federal Republic of Germany (1973), 25 per cent in Denmark (1973) and the United States (1972), 20 per cent in Canada (1970), and 19 per cent in France (1977), to 16 per cent in Sweden (1975).

The final part of the chapter discusses the appropriate wealth concept and models underlying wealth accumulation. The authors propose an eclectic approach to modelling wealth behaviour, which they term 'neo-Kaldorian' and which involves class motives as well as life-cycle factors. They divide household assets into three groups, based on the motives for saving. The first group, which they call S-wealth, covers assets held for future consumption, liquidity, precautionary, and transaction purposes. They include residential housing, durable goods, life insurance, annuities, pension rights, cash, and checking and savings accounts. Low- and medium-income families will tend to hold largely, if not exclusively, S-wealth in their portfolio. The second form, which they call K-wealth, includes assets held mainly for their returns (both income flows and capital gains), as well as productive and professional assets. This form of wealth includes stocks and shares, bonds and other securities, investment in real estate, and business equity and is held largely by the upper income classes. The third form is human capital or H-wealth.

They argue that S-wealth accumulation will roughly follow the life-cycle model, and, in particular, have a hump-shaped pattern with respect to age. K-wealth, on the other hand, is held largely for economic and social power. Moreover, K-wealth is often transmitted between generations. As a result, K-wealth will tend to rise with age over the whole life span.

One implication is that K-wealth is likely to be considerably more highly concentrated than S-wealth, since the large majority of people will save for consumption needs, rather than for power. They find this to be the case, with the top 10 per cent of households holding 78 per cent of total K-wealth and only 45 per cent of total S-wealth. Moreover, they find that the share of total wealth held in the form of K-wealth rises sharply with wealth level, from 4 per cent for the lowest wealth decile to 66 per cent for the top decile. These results lend strong support to their argument that different segments of the population accumulate wealth for different motives.

IV. Other Topics in Estimating Household Wealth

The first two chapters in this section consider alternative ways of measuring retirement wealth as part of the household portfolio. The first of these, by Michael Wolfson, investigates the adequacy of retirement resources for the Canadian population. The analysis is carried out in terms of 'replacement rates', which measure the ratio of post-retirement to pre-retirement income. Both 'gross' (before-tax) and 'net' (after-tax) replacement rates are computed. The purpose of the study is to determine what proportion of families would experience a decline in net income after retirement (a replacement rate less than one) and what would be the degree of decline. Public pensions, private pensions, and income from (traditional) household wealth are included in the estimation of post-retirement income.

The results are based on a simulation model used to project various components of post-retirement income. Alternative assumptions are made with regard to each component of income to test the model's sensitivity. There are four principal components of the model. The first is the public pension system and other mandatory public programmes. The second is the private pension system, consisting of employer-sponsored pension plans. Pension coverage, vesting, and benefit levels are imputed to households based on a Monte Carlo simulation model. The third consists of household balance sheets based on the 1977 Statistics Canada Survey of Consumer Finances. Various assumptions are made about future yields on household assets and patterns of dissaving after retirement. The fourth is the income tax system, which is simulated to convert gross income into net income.

The first set of simulation results indicates that based solely on income from the public pension system, the net replacement rate for a (pre-retirement) median income family is approximately 60 per cent. Moreover, net replacement rates vary inversely with pre-retirement income, from a high of 98 per cent for the bottom decile to 30 per cent for the upper 5 per cent of the income distribution. A later set of results shows the net replacement rates that would arise strictly from personal wealth and private pension income.[14] Homeowners in the middle wealth deciles would experience net replacement rates that range from 30 to 40 per cent from private source alone, while renters in the same wealth deciles would face

replacement rates of the order of 10 to 20 per cent. Moreover, net
replacement rates from private sources vary directly with wealth
level. Among (pre-retirement) middle-income homeowners, net
replacement rates range from a low of 11 per cent for the lowest
wealth decile to 143 per cent for the top wealth decile.

Finally, combining the public pension system with private
sources, the results indicate that under the most likely assumptions
about future income flows, about half of all Canadian households
would experience no decline in their standard of living after retirement. On the other hand, 30 per cent would face net replacement
rates of 0.85 or less and 16 per cent rates of 0.75 or less. However,
the results turn out to be relatively sensitive to the simulation
assumptions, with the proportion of families experiencing net
replacement rates of unity or greater varying from 41 to 89 per cent.

The second of these chapters, by Edward Wolff, investigates the
effect of public and private pensions on the distribution of household wealth in the US in 1969. The chapter develops an augmented
concept of personal wealth, called household lifetime wealth
(HLW), defined as the present value of the discounted stream of
expected net income flows. This measure includes traditional or
disposable wealth, human capital, and the net value of pension and
social security income (that is, future benefits less future contributions). Different simulations are run for various assumed growth
rates of income and benefits to generate estimates of pension and
social security wealth as well as of human capital. The major
purpose of the chapter is to compare estimates of inequality
obtained from the broader lifetime measures with those of traditional wealth.

All estimates are based on the 1969 MESP data base. This data
set is formed from a statistical match between the 1970 Census
Public Use Sample and the 1969 Internal Revenue Service Tax
Model. Wealth imputations are made by a variety of techniques.
House value is directly available in the Census data. Consumer
durables and inventories are imputed using regression analysis.
Most financial assets are estimated by the income capitalization
method.

There are four major sets of results. First, social security wealth is
found to be more equally distributed than traditional household
wealth, but the two are about equal in the aggregate. The Gini
coefficient for traditional wealth is 0.73, whereas those for social

security wealth range from 0.43 to 0.55, depending on the assumptions used. Moreover, the addition of social security wealth to disposable wealth causes a marked reduction in measured wealth inequality. However, the degree of reduction depends rather strongly on the simulation assumptions, with the Gini coefficient for the sum of disposable wealth and social security wealth ranging from 0.49 to 0.61.

Second, pension wealth is found to be more unequally distributed than disposable wealth but much smaller in magnitude. Its inclusion in the household portfolio thus has a minimal effect on measured wealth inequality.

Third, human capital is found to dominate in magnitude all other components of household lifetime wealth. It was less equally distributed than social security wealth but more equally so than disposable wealth. The addition of human capital to disposable wealth causes the Gini coefficient to decline from 0.73 to 0.55. The further addition of social security wealth causes the Gini coefficient to fall to 0.50. Moreover, a decomposition of wealth by component indicates that the two dominant elements in the overall inequality of lifetime wealth are traditional wealth, because of its high degree of concentration, and human capital, because of its relative magnitude.

Fourth, social security wealth and human capital have different effects on total wealth inequality within age cohort than within the whole population. The distribution of conventional wealth was as unequal within age cohort as within the full population. The average Gini coefficient across age cohorts is 0.70, while its value for the whole sample is 0.73. Moreover, the Gini coefficient declines between the youngest age cohort (under 35 years of age) and the 35–44 age cohort from a value of 0.70 to 0.60, rises over the next two age cohorts (45–54 and 55–64), and peaks at a value of 0.81, and then falls to a value of 0.73 for the last (65 or over). In contrast, Greenwood finds that inequality declines with age from the youngest age cohort to the 56–65 cohort and then sharply increases among the elderly. Wolff also finds that inequality in household lifetime wealth increases across age cohorts, from a Gini coefficient value of 0.33 for the youngest age cohort to a value of 0.56 for the oldest, which is somewhat higher than the level of inequality for the full sample.

The difference in age patterns is due to the lessening importance of human capital in the household portfolio for the older cohorts. The reduction in measured wealth inequality from the addition of human capital to traditional wealth is quite pronounced for the youngest age cohort, with the Gini coefficient falling from 0.70 to 0.35. As human capital's share in total lifetime wealth diminishes with age, so does the decline in measured inequality. Social security wealth, on the other hand, increases in relative importance with age, and its effect on inequality is greater than that of human capital for the two oldest age cohorts. However, on net, the quantitative importance of social security wealth in overall inequality is smaller than that of human capital, which accounts for rising lifetime wealth inequality with age.

The last chapter in this volume, by C.D. Harbury and D.M.W.N. Hitchens, investigates the effect of changing relative asset prices on the size distribution of personal wealth in the United Kingdom. Their analysis covers the period from 1960 to 1980. Their figures, drawn from the same data sources as Shorrocks, show that the share of the top 1 per cent in the United Kingdom fell from 34 per cent in 1960 to 23 per cent in 1980. Their basic argument is that part of this change may be due to changes in relative prices over time, since the composition of wealth held by different wealth classes varies substantially and asset prices diverge over time. In regard to wealth composition, they find that in 1973 the top wealth class (£200,000 or more) held 23 per cent of their net wealth in the form of real estate, while the bottom wealth class (£5,000 or less) held 60 per cent. Moreover, 26 per cent of the net worth of the lowest wealth class took the form of life insurance policies, while the corresponding figure for the top wealth group was 2 per cent. In contrast, financial assets made up 54 per cent of the net worth of the top wealth class and only 2 per cent of the wealth of the lowest group.

Price movements differed considerably by asset class over the period from 1960 to 1980. The price of land rose by a factor of 13, that of dwellings by a factor of 10, while stock shares increased two and a half times, and the value of fixed interest securities actually fell by half. Thus, relative price movements seem to have strongly helped the middle class.

Their analysis involves regressions of the shares of the top wealth holders on relative price movements of different asset classes over the period from 1960 to 1980. Their general conclusion is that price effects appear to explain only a relatively small part of the decline in overall wealth inequality in Britain over the entire period. These results accord with those of similar studies on British wealth inequality. The authors, however, do find that relative price movements can be an important determinant of wealth concentration trends for shorter periods, particularly 1973 to 1980, when the stock market collapsed while housing prices rose rapidly.[15]

The second part of the chapter contains an analysis of the importance of relative price movements on inheritance patterns. Using a specially constructed data set matching estates of fathers with those of sons among top wealth holders in Britain, the authors are able to determine the initial value of bequests made to each son. Then, using a variety of price indices, the authors are able to project what the value of estates left by fathers would be worth a generation later as a proportion of their son's estate. They find that, after adjustment for relative price movements over time, inheritances are quite important in determining the son's relative wealth position. They estimate, for example, that 90 per cent of the fathers of sons who were top wealth holders in one generation were also in the top wealth class in the preceding generation. Their results, though tentative, suggest a fairly stable class structure in Great Britain.

V. Concluding Comments

The chapters included in this volume raise several provocative questions and point the way towards future research on the distribution of household wealth. First, what factors are responsible for the sharp decline in wealth inequality observed in Europe and the US? Are the causes the same in different countries? What role has government policy played in this development? Second, despite the dramatic reduction in wealth inequality, the concentration of household wealth is still very high today, particularly in comparison to income. Moreover, there appears to be a convergence among industrialized countries in the level of wealth inequality. Does this suggest some 'natural' law of development or some remarkable stability in class structure, or do these apparent similarities across countries mask different social forces? Moreover, attempts to account for the high degree of wealth inequality in these countries on the basis of life-cycle and other demographic factors have yielded very little. This suggests major modifications in formal models of household wealth accumulation to include more behavioural and institutional factors. Possible items are the distribution of entre-preneurial skills, bequest behaviour, government policy variables, and class-specific behaviour based on either different motives for saving or liquidity constraints on asset portfolios.

Third, more attention should be paid to the reconciliation of household wealth data from different sources, particularly those based on different units of observation. The Kessler–Masson chapter provides one illustration of such an effort. Moreover, eclectic approaches which involve combining different parts of the wealth distribution from sources where they are particularly well represented should be explored. Fourth, it is apparent that no single wealth concept can adequately meet all the purposes for which it is used. In regard to savings behaviour, is the appropriate concept conventional wealth or financial assets? In regard to welfare measurement, is current wealth or expected lifetime resources a better gauge? In wealth studies, it seems reasonable to report several wealth measures, which may reflect different motives for saving, different degrees of liquidity or substitutability, or different needs, as, for example, between current consumption and future consumption. In conclusion, we hope this volume provides some interesting insights about the distribution of household wealth and stimulates further research.

Endnotes

1. Actually, Soltow (1971 and 1975) argued that wealth concentration in the US may have been relatively constant from about the mid-1800s up until the Great Depression. From US Census data, he estimated that the top 1 per cent of all free males held 29 per cent of total wealth in 1860 and 27 per cent in 1870. Gallman (1969), on the basis of a smaller sample of representative communities from the 1860 and 1900 censuses, estimated that the share of the top 1 per cent was 24 per cent in 1860 and between 26 and 31 per cent in 1900. Lampman, using estate tax data, estimated that the top 1 per cent of individuals held 32 per cent of total wealth in 1922 and the top 1 per cent of families owned between 23 and 26 per cent of household wealth. Thus, the decline in wealth inequality was not nearly as dramatic in the US as it was in Europe. On the other hand, the US was a more egalitarian society than European nations in the nineteenth and early twentieth centuries.

2. See, in particular, the chapters by Shorrocks, Wolfson, and Wolff.

3. For a comparison of alternative wealth measures, see, in particular, the chapters by Shorrocks, Radner and Vaughan, Kessler and Masson, and Wolff.
4. Another possibility is a generational concept of the family. This might be appropriate for very rich families, whose motivation is to increase their wealth holdings over their lifetime in order to pass it on to succeeding generations.
5. See the chapters by Shorrocks, Smith, and Kessler and Masson for a comprehensive discussion of these issues. Also, see the Kessler and Masson chapter for a comparison of wealth concentration estimates from the various data sources.
6. In the UK, the threshold is considerably lower, so that the vast majority of estates are required to file tax returns.
7. See King (1983) for a recent review of this literature.
8. Lydall (1955), Smith (1975), Mirer (1979), and Menchik and David (1983) also found no significant reduction of wealth after retirement.
9. See, for example, Stiglitz (1969) and Vaughan (1979) for various formulations of this type of model.
10. It should be noted that the earlier data reported by Shorrocks, principally 1923 to 1965, refer to England and Wales only.
11. On the other hand, the results for corporate stock are quite comparable. Greenwood estimates that the top 1 per cent held 60 per cent of all corporate stock owned by households in 1973, while Smith calculates a 63 per cent share.
12. The 1922 figures are given in endnote 1. In 1953, the share of the top 1 per cent of individuals was 24.3 per cent, while the top 1 per cent of families were estimated to own between 18 and 22 per cent of household wealth (also, see Williamson and Lindert (1980)).
13. The top 1 per cent of individuals were estimated to hold 19 per cent of total wealth in 1977. The range for households is derived from extreme assumptions with regard to mating patterns among individual wealth holders.
14. With regard to home ownership, it is assumed that half the value of home equity is liquidated and used in a manner equivalent to the purchase of a fully indexed life insurance annuity.
15. Lampman (1962) examined a similar question for the US over the period from 1922 through 1956. He concluded that the decline in wealth concentration observed for the US over this period could be only partially explained by relative price movements and suggested that the decline in saving by the wealthy and greater bequest dispersion were probably more important factors.

References

Feldstein, M. 'Social Security, Induced Retirement, and Aggregate Capital Accumulation,' *Journal of Political Economy*, 82 (Sept/Oct 1974), 905–26.

Gallman, R.E. 'Trends in the Size Distribution of Wealth in the Nineteenth Century,' In: Soltow, L. ed. *Six Papers on the Size Distribution of Wealth and Income* (New York, 1969).

196988

King, M.A. 'The Economics of Savings.' National Bureau of Economic Research, Working Paper No. 1247 (1983).

Lampman, R. *The Share of Top Wealth-Holders in National Wealth, 1922–56* (Princeton, New Jersey, 1962).

Lydall, H. 'The Life Cycle in Income, Saving, and Asset Ownership,' *Econometrica*, 23 (April 1955), 131–50.

Menchik, P.L., David, M. 'Income Distribution, Lifetime Savings, and Bequests,' *American Economic Review*, 73 (Sept 1983), 672–90.

Mirer, T.W. 'The Wealth–Age Relationship among the Aged,' *American Economic Review*, 69 (June 1979), 435–43.

Modigliani, F., Brumberg, R. 'Utility Analysis and the Consumption Function: An Interpretation of Cross-Section Data.' In: Kurihara, K.K. ed. *Post-Keynesian Economics* (New Brunswick, New Jersey, 1954).

Smith, J.D. 'White Wealth and Black People: The Distribution of Wealth in Washington, DC, in 1967.' In Smith, J.D. ed. *The Personal Distribution of Income and Wealth* (New York, 1975).

Soltow, L. 'Economic Inequality in the United States from the Period from 1860 to 1970,' *Journal of Economic History*, 31 (Dec 1971), 822–39.

—— *Men and Wealth in the United States, 1850–1870* (New Haven, Connecticut, 1975).

Stiglitz, J.E. 'Distribution of Income and Wealth among Individuals,' *Econometrica*, 37 (July 1969), 382–97.

Vaughan, R.N. 'Class Behavior and the Distribution of Wealth,' *Review of Economic Studies*, 46 (July 1979), 447–65.

Williamson, J.G., Lindert, P.H. 'Long-Term Trends in American Wealth Inequality. In: Smith, J.D. ed. *Modeling the Distribution and Intergenerational Transmission of Wealth* (New York, 1980).

I TIME TRENDS IN HOUSEHOLD WEALTH DISTRIBUTION

2

UK Wealth Distribution: Current Evidence and Future Prospects

Anthony F. Shorrocks[1]

I. Introduction

Empirical research on wealth holdings in the United Kingdom has a long and distinguished history. Following Mallet's (1908) invention of the 'estate multiplier' method for deriving wealth estimates from estate data, a regular series of studies have sought to update the figures and improve the computational techniques. As a consequence, estimates of total UK personal wealth are available for over a century, and information on the share of wealth owned by the richest segments of the population has been provided for the majority of years since 1923.

Within the past couple of decades, a number of studies have had a significant impact both on the quality of the empirical evidence and on the assessment of that information. Three contributions stand out as being especially noteworthy: the work of Revell, particularly in connection with Personal Sector Balance Sheets, for which Revell (1967) is an early reference; a detailed examination of the methodology underlying the derivation of wealth distribution evidence from estate data, summarized in Atkinson and Harrison (1978); and research initiated by the Royal Commission on the Distribution of Income and Wealth (henceforth RCDIW: see, in particular, RCDIW (1975, 1977, 1979)) which has been continued by the Inland Revenue.[2] As a result of these developments, the United Kingdom might well claim to have the most reliable and comprehensive data on wealth distribution in the world. Any such claim, however, reflects more the paucity of information available for many other countries, than the inherent quality of the UK statistics. Wealth data are notoriously poor in comparison with data on most other economic variables of social importance, and in this respect the UK is no different from other countries. The construction and analysis of information on UK wealth holdings is still in need of further development, and there remain many opportunities for future research.

The aim of this chapter is to review the current state of knowledge regarding UK wealth distribution. As well as summarizing the principal empirical evidence and the interpretation placed on that evidence, a number of the most important conceptual and computational issues will be discussed. Attention is also paid to the questions that remain unresolved and to the direction in which future research might profitably proceed. Of necessity, such a brief survey can scarcely begin to do justice to the many detailed studies undertaken in the past. Those interested in pursuing the subject further will find many of the topics covered in the references cited in the bibliography.

The next section begins with a summary of the sources of data on UK wealth holdings. Section III considers the trend over time in the reported wealth shares owned by the richest groups of individuals and discusses the issues raised by these figures. This is followed by an examination of the estate multiplier method and of recent attempts to reconcile estate-based wealth estimates with independent valuations of aggregate holdings of specific assets. Other aspects of the pattern of wealth ownership, notably the relation between wealth and age and the composition of individual portfolios, are investigated in Section V. The chapter concludes with a few personal observations on the objectives of research into wealth ownership and the most challenging topics for future study.

II. Sources of Information on Wealth Holdings

There are three principal sources of information on wealth ownership: sample surveys of asset holdings; data collected as a byproduct of wealth taxes levied either on the current population (for example, annual wealth taxes) or on the estates of deceased persons (Estate Duty and Capital Transfer Tax in the UK); and the amounts of investment income recorded for income tax purposes. For the United Kingdom most empirical evidence on wealth distribution is derived from the number and value of estates by applying an appropriate 'mortality multiplier' to estimate the number of living individuals with a similar level of wealth. This estate multi-plier method effectively treats the estates of deceased persons as a sample of the wealth holdings of the existing population. It has the advantage of starting from estate assessments made by the Inland Revenue, which provide a good coverage of assets and consistent, if not always ideal, procedures for valuation. At the same time, since the wealth holdings of the living population are not observed directly, the reliability of the wealth estimates inevitably rests on the accuracy of the assumptions required to make the transition from the sample of estates to the wealth holdings of those still alive.

More direct estimates of the wealth distribution are not available for the UK, since we have never had either a wealth tax or a large-scale sample survey of wealth ownership that would generate the suitable data. A limited amount of information exists on the distri-bution of specific categories of wealth, mainly certain types of finan-cial assets and consumer durables (see, for example, RCDIW (1979), Chapter 6; Atkinson and Harrison (1978a), Section 6.3); but it does little more than supplement the evidence obtained from estates. Investment income figures provide another means of esti-mating wealth holdings, by applying an 'investment income multi-plier', computed from the rate of return on wealth, to the income data. This procedure implicitly assumes a high degree of homo-geneity across individuals with respect to both the portfolio compo-sition of asset holdings at a given level of total wealth, and the returns individuals obtain from a given type of asset. As a conse-quence it is generally regarded as less reliable than the estate multi-plier approach. It has been used on UK data (see, for example, Atkinson and Harrison (1978), Chapter 7), but is again seen as a check on the estate-based estimates, rather than an alternative source of accurate wealth statistics. For this reason, the remainder of this paper focuses on the estate-based estimates of UK wealth holdings, and on the procedures employed in the derivation of these figures.

III. The Concentration of Wealth Ownership

The questions first raised in connection with wealth distribution typically concern the degree of wealth inequality and its pattern over time. What proportion of total wealth is owned by the richest

Anthony F. Shorrocks

Table 2.1. *Shares in total wealth 1923–1980*

	England and Wales[a]			United Kingdom[b]		
	Top 1%	Top 5%	Top 10%	Top 1%	Top 5%	Top 10%
1923	61	82	89			
1924	60	82	88			
1925	61	82	88			
1926	57	80	87			
1927	60	81	88			
1928	57	80	87			
1929	56	79	86			
1930	58	79	87			
1936	54	77	86			
1938	55	77	85			
1950	47	74	—			
1951	46	74	—			
1952	43	70	—			
1953	44	71	—			
1954	45	72	—			
1955	45	71	—			
1956	45	71	—			
1957	43	69	—			
1958	41	68	—			
1959	41	68	—			
1960	34	60	72			
1961	37	61	72			
1962	31	55	67			
1964	35	59	71			
1965	33	58	72			
1966	31	56	69	33	56	69
1967	31	56	70	—	—	—
1968	34	58	72	—	—	—
1969	31	56	68	—	—	—
1970	30	54	69	—	—	—
1971	28	52	68	31	52	65
1972	32	56	70	—	—	—
1974	—	—	—	23	43	57
1975	—	—	—	24	44	58
1976	—	—	—	24	46	61
1977	—	—	—	23	44	58
1978	—	—	—	23	44	58
1979	—	—	—	24	45	59
1980	—	—	—	23	43	58

a. Atkinson and Harrison (1978).
b. 'Series C' Estimates, *Inland Revenue Statistics* 1980, 1982.

1 per cent or 10 per cent of the population? Is there a trend towards more or less inequality? Some response to these questions can be offered for the years since 1911, when the published estate data were first disaggregated by age. But attention is best confined to the period since 1923, when estates began to be separately reported for males and females.

Table 2.1 reproduces the series of top wealth shares constructed by Atkinson and Harrison (1978), together with subsequent calculations made by the Inland Revenue.[3] Taking average values for each decade, the figures show that the share of wealth owned by the top 1 per cent of wealth holders fell from 59 per cent in the 1920s to 33 per cent in the 1960s and 26 per cent in the 1970s. Corresponding estimates for the share of the top 5 per cent of wealth holders indicates a drop from 81 per cent to 57 per cent and then 48 per cent over the same period, while the share of the top decile decreased from 88 per cent in the 1920s to 70 per cent in the 1960s and 62 per cent in the 1970s. This evidence suggests a substantial downward trend in wealth concentration this century, particularly noticeable at the very top of the distribution.

This naive interpretation of the wealth share series can, however, be challenged on a variety of grounds. One reason for circumspection concerns the reliability of the reported figures: do they accurately measure the quantities they purport to represent? Since the figures are only estimates of wealth shares based on the estate multiplier method, they inevitably suffer from any shortcomings in either the raw estate data or the estimation procedure. The Atkinson and Harrison calculations for the years up to 1972 were made on a consistent basis, and may therefore claim to be broadly comparable. But there were many significant changes to estate tax legislation during this period, particularly with regard to the treatment of life insurance policies, settled property, discretionary trusts, and gifts *inter vivos* (see Atkinson and Harrison (1978a), Section 2.3), as well as regular revisions of the tax threshold. The sampling procedures and reporting practices employed by the Inland Revenue were also amended on several occasions. These changes have all had an impact on the wealth statistics, for the most part improving their quality, while at the same time raising questions concerning their comparability over the years. The Inland Revenue figures in Table 2.1, which provide the bulk of the evidence since 1970, were computed in a slightly different way to those of Atkinson and Harrison, and incorporate a number of adjustments that may account for some of the apparent decline in wealth concentration since 1970. This period has also seen major changes in estate taxation associated with the substitution of Capital Transfer Tax for Estate Duty. As well as these issues of comparability over time, the estate multiplier method itself poses several fundamental problems which will be discussed in the next section.

Questions concerning such factors as the appropriate economic unit and wealth definition provide other reasons for exercising caution when drawing conclusions from the evidence of Table 2.1. Although these aspects may be regarded as conceptual, rather than computational, in nature, they ultimately have a major impact on the way the data should be interpreted. Consider, for instance, the distinction between the individual and the family (or household) as the basic economic unit. Information derived from estates refers to individuals, and may therefore be influenced by changes in the pattern of ownership within families. In particular any tendency in modern times to spread the legal title to assets among family members (for example, joint ownership of housing) is likely to reduce the shares recorded for the richest individuals even if the distribution of family wealth remains unchanged. To take a simple case, if a couple in the 1920s owned sixty times the mean per capita wealth and all assets were held by the husband, they would appear in the wealth statistics as one member of the top 1 per cent of wealth holders and one person with no assets. If an equivalent modern couple divide their wealth evenly, so both hold title to thirty times mean per capita wealth and belong to the top 1 per cent of wealth holders, the share of the very richest individuals would show a reduction while the share of the moderately rich would increase (since the previously penniless wife displaces the marginal top percentile member into the next group, thus raising the average wealth of this group). This pattern of movements in wealth shares is qualitatively consistent with the evidence for Britain. For example, between 1923 and 1972 the share of the top percentile of wealth holders declined by 29 per cent, but the share of the top decile fell by only 19 per cent. The proportion of total wealth owned by those in the top decile, but outside the top percentile, therefore rose by 10 per cent, from 28 per cent in 1923 to 38 per cent in 1972.

Such evidence lends credence to speculation that intra-family changes in the pattern of asset ownership could account for much of the movement in wealth shares.[4] Assuming that the wealth of families, rather than individuals, is the more relevant variable for social policy, this line of reasoning suggests that the observed decline in wealth concentration is exaggerated, and possibly completely spurious. The quantitative impact of intra-family changes in the pattern of asset ownership is, however, difficult to assess in the context of UK wealth statistics, so the significance of this factor for the trend in wealth concentration remains an open question.[5]

The increase in life expectancy this century may also have influenced the observed wealth distribution series for two distinct, but related, reasons. First, the increasing proportion of the elderly, whose wealth is typically higher than average, will tend to raise the number of richer individuals and hence the wealth shares of the top wealth groups. Secondly, increased longevity means that inheritances will usually be received later in life, at an age when accumulated lifetime savings are close to their peak. This will have increased wealth inequality between age groups, thus reinforcing the effect due to the change in age composition to produce a tendency towards greater wealth inequality.[6] The longevity factor is therefore likely to have worked in the opposite direction to the pattern of asset ownership within families. The basic issue here is again conceptual, but one which relates to the accounting horizon rather than the economic unit. If the current wealth of the population is the objective of social interest, no adjustment to the wealth share figures is needed in respect of changes in life expectancy. If, on the other hand, some notion of average or lifetime wealth is regarded as more appropriate, increased longevity will distort the relationship between 'true' wealth concentration and the wealth shares reported in Table 2.1.

The definition of the wealth concept raises a rather different set of issues that affect both the wealth shares observed at a particular date, and the trend over time. Broadly speaking the wealth concept underlying the UK estate-based figures consists of those assets over which individuals have the right of disposal. Many economists have sought to extend this concept to cover entitlements to pensions and annuities, which provide a future stream of income in much the same way as bank deposits and other kinds of assets, but cannot normally be sold. The Inland Revenue has responded to these suggestions by producing 'Series D' wealth distribution figures that

Table 2.2. *Shares in total wealth (including pension rights), United Kingdom, 1971–1980*

	Estimates including entitlements to occupational pensions (Series D)			Estimates including entitlements to occupational and state pensions (Series E)		
	Top 1%	Top 5%	Top 10%	Top 1%	Top 5%	Top 10%
1971	27	46	59	21	37	49
1974	19	38	52	15	31	43
1975	20	38	52	13	27	37
1976	21	40	53	14	27	37
1977	19	38	51	12	25	35
1978	19	39	52	13	25	36
1979	20	38	51	13	27	37
1980	19	37	50	12	25	35

Source: *Inland Revenue Statistics* 1980, 1982.

include rights to occupational pension schemes, and 'Series E' estimates that also include rights to state pensions. These are reproduced in Table 2.2. The top wealth shares are lower than the corresponding 'marketable wealth' values of Table 2.1, as would be expected from adding in large amounts of a form of wealth that is more equally distributed than marketable assets. Furthermore, since pension entitlements have grown enormously this century, the inclusion of pension rights would reinforce the downward trend in top wealth shares noted in Table 2.1, if a suitable series could be constructed for the whole period. On these grounds, the figures recorded in Table 2.1 may be viewed as an underestimate of the 'true' decline in wealth inequality.

While the argument in favour of including pension rights in the wealth definition focuses on the observation that a future stream of pension income is often a substitute for investment income, the underlying issues are more fundamental, since they concern the precise criteria which determine whether or not any specific item should be viewed as a component of wealth. The current move towards a more comprehensive definition of wealth seems to accept that wealth is best regarded as a stock of potential future consumption or as an indicator of future access to economic resources. But on these criteria it becomes difficult to resist the claim that human capital and even social capital (measured, say, by the net worth of the public sector) should also be included. Any such move in this direction would almost certainly have another major impact on the wealth shares estimates, if the appropriate adjustments could be made to the UK figures.

The conception of wealth as a stock of potential future consumption has undoubted attractions. But it can also be objected to on the grounds that it gives little weight to the other characteristics normally associated with wealth, for example, insurance against future mishaps (the precautionary aspect), the greater freedom to plan ahead (for instance, by circumventing capital market constraints that would otherwise bind), and the control over other people's lives inherent in the landlord–tenant or employer–employee relationship (the power aspect). These considerations suggest that there may be a role for a narrower than conventional definition of wealth, as well as a wider one.[7] It would almost certainly exclude consumer durables from the wealth definition, and also perhaps owner-occupied housing.

The suggestion that owner-occupied housing might be excluded in a 'narrow wealth' concept has some arguments in its favour, and rather interesting consequences for the trend in UK wealth inequality. The special features of housing—its relative indivisibility, the high transaction costs, and the lack of close substitutes—set it apart from most other assets. Furthermore, in an environment like the UK, in which rented accommodation is either expensive or inaccessible to many people, the behaviour of individuals towards the equity in their own houses seems to be qualitatively different from the treatment of other assets. Even applying the 'potential future consumption' conception of wealth suggests that the market value of homes exceeds the valuation placed on them by their owner occupiers, since housing wealth is not usually seen as a source of finance for goods and services other than accommodation.

The exclusion of owner-occupied housing from the concept of wealth would have significant implications for the assessment of the wealth series in Table 2.1, since a major feature of the post-war period has been the rise in house prices. Real estate has shown a significantly higher rate of return than all other major asset categories, and now accounts for more than half net personal wealth. This appreciation in house values has been sufficient to catapult the owners of fairly modest dwellings into the top echelons of the wealth distributions: in 1980, for instance, a home valued at £50,000 (net of mortgage) would have been sufficient to place its (single) owner within the top 3 per cent of wealth holders. The relatively wide-spread ownership of housing combined with the high real level of capital appreciation has undoubtedly had a major equalizing influence on the observed wealth shares. If owner-occupied housing was excluded from wealth, or if the increase in its value could be excluded on the grounds that it is locked into the asset and seldom realized by its owners, then the post-war trend in wealth inequality would look somewhat different. The precise impact is again difficult to judge. The limited amount of available information (RCDIW (1979), Chapter 5) suggests that the real increase in house prices of 71 per cent over the period 1960–76 accounted for around three-quarters of the change in the share of wealth held by the top 1 per cent and 5 per cent of wealth holders, but this evidence refers to the appreciation of all dwellings, as opposed to just owner-occupied houses.[8]

Thus, whilst the wealth distribution statistics for the UK this century first appear to point towards a substantial degree of equalization, closer inspection reveals a number of factors that have a major influence on the way these statistics are interpreted. Caution is clearly the watchword when it comes to drawing conclusions from wealth distribution data.

IV. The Estate Multiplier Method

The estate multiplier method of deriving UK wealth statistics from estate data is discussed at length in a number of recent publications including *Inland Revenue Statistics* (RCDIW (1975)), and Atkinson and Harrison (1978, 1978a). The procedure is based on the assumption that estates can be treated as a sample of the wealth holdings of the living population. It is not, of course, a random sample, since mortality depends on age, sex, and a variety of other factors. But, employing the standard techniques for stratified sampling, this can be taken into account by scaling up the estate observations by 'mortality multipliers', defined as the reciprocal of the corresponding mortality rate, to obtain an estimate of the overall wealth distribution among living persons. However, there are problems associated with the estate multiplier method which ultimately influence both the reliability and usefulness of the estimates. These problems can be grouped into three broad categories relating to the sampling process, the population coverage, and the valuation of wealth.

One type of sampling difficulty results from the low mortality rate of the young which, together with their lower than average level of wealth, means that few estates are recorded in the high wealth ranges. This causes the usual problems associated with small sample sizes. But their significance is enhanced by the large mortality multiplier applied to young age groups. The appropriate solution (employed to some extent by the Inland Revenue) is to smooth out the fluctuations in the annual number of observations by averaging over several years.

A second source of difficulty is the correlation between mortality and wealth likely to occur within age–sex groups. If this correlation is neglected, the wealth distribution estimates will be biased, because the wrong multiplier is being applied at some wealth levels. The precise relationship between mortality and wealth is complex, and unfortunately cannot be directly observed. However, the evidence provided by occupational and social class mortality rates suggests an inverse relationship. Wealth estimates for the UK make use of these social class mortality data, but the adjustment is not entirely satisfactory, since social class is an inadequate proxy for wealth.[9]

The issue of population coverage primarily concerns those persons excluded from the estate data because probate was not required on their estates.[10] For the most part, these are low wealth holders owning only certain types of assets. Approximately half the population falls into this category. Early Inland Revenue estimates (now called 'Series A') disregarded both these 'missing persons' and their wealth in computing the shares of top wealth holders. Marginally better are the 'Series B' estimates, which count the adult missing persons in the population, but assume they have zero wealth. The more recent 'Series C' computations, reported in Table 2.1, make an allowance for the wealth held by the excluded persons, but much of the published data and analysis still refer to the unsatisfactory Series A and Series B estimates.[11]

The valuation of wealth holdings involves two kinds of problems:

those concerned with the assets excluded from estates, and those relating to the valuation attached to specific assets. As already noted, UK estate data provide a comprehensive coverage of material assets,[12] but are not ideally suited for broader definitions of wealth that encompass pension rights and/or human capital. To include these extra asset categories would not be a serious problem if a satisfactory mechanism for imputing values could be devised. But estate data record almost no personal information about the individuals appearing in the sample, other than their age and sex. Consequently it is impossible to match estates to pension entitlements and human capital with any degree of confidence. The construction of narrower wealth concepts, excluding owner-occupied housing for example, presents less of a problem; but even here it would be necessary to have access to more detailed data than those published regularly by the Inland Revenue.

Regarding the valuation of particular assets, a basic conceptual distinction needs to be made between the 'sell up' or 'realizable' value, and the assessment appropriate if the asset is a 'going concern'. The estate figures tend to reflect realizable values, with conservative judgements applied in cases of doubt. This leads to very low assessments for certain items, most notably household goods. However, the general rule of using 'sell up' values is not applied in the case of life insurance policies, which have the unique characteristic of contributing more to the wealth of those who have died, than of those still alive. Life policies appear in the estate data at their maturity values, which often exceed their value in the hands of the living by a large margin. Simple application of the estate multiplier method imputes these maturity values to the living population, and consequently exaggerates the importance of this asset, particularly among the younger age groups. This has seriously distorted certain features of wealth distribution (see, for example, Astin (1975); Shorrocks (1981)), although its impact on the wealth shares computed for the aggregate population is fairly modest.

The above discussion suggests that the concepts and valuation applied to estate assessments may not always coincide with those most appropriate to the calculations of the wealth holdings of living persons. In the past it has been difficult to identify and quantify the degree of divergence in a way that allows the wealth data to be improved. However, major advances have been achieved in recent years, following the construction of Personal Sector Balance Sheets.

These were pioneered by Revell (1967), who provided estimates of the aggregate personal holdings of various assets for the years 1957–61. Subsequent figures for 1966–7, compiled by the Central Statistical Office (CSO) for the Royal Commission, were published in *Economic Trends* (CSO (1978)) and a number of Royal Commission reports. Revell, Atkinson and Harrison, the Royal Commission, and the CSO have all made comparisons between balance sheet figures and corresponding estate multiplier totals, and there have been several attempts to reconcile the differences that arise (see, for example, RCDIW (1979), Appendices C and D). These in turn have influenced the 'Series C' estimates of wealth shares, which are consistent with the asset totals recorded in the balance sheets.

Attempts to reconcile the estate multiplier and balance sheet figures provide valuable insights into the quantitative significance of many of the problems described earlier. Table 2.3 summarizes the calculations of Dunn and Hoffman for 1975.[13] The overall discrepancy between the net wealth figures of £190 billions and £284 billions is substantial in itself; but it becomes even more marked when one takes into account the excessively high life-insurance component in the estate figures of column 1, resulting from the maturity valuation of all life policies. This exaggerated valuation produces the largest single item in the reconciliation exercise. A number of the other larger items in the table reflect alternative acceptable concepts or definitions underlying the two sets of estimates, rather than any clear deficiency in the estate-based values. On the whole, however, the balance sheet procedures and figures will tend to be preferred to the unadjusted estate multiplier totals, so the 'Series C' wealth share estimates are particularly welcome additions to the published wealth statistics.

V. Other Evidence on Wealth Distribution

Wealth information is valuable for a variety of purposes other than simply computing the figures for wealth inequality. It is relevant to many aspects of consumer behaviour, including consumption demand, portfolio choice, and intertemporal savings decisions. It also plays a role in policy issues linked to the impact of taxes and income maintenance programmes. A number of these topics have

Table 2.3. *Reconciliation of estate multiplier and balance sheet estimates for 1975 (£ billions)*

	Wealth of individuals identified by estate multiplier method	Adjustment due to				Unexplained residual	Balance sheet total household wealth
		Limitations of present estate multiplier method and data quality	Differences in asset coverage	Differences in method of valuation	Excluded wealth		
Dwellings	82	18.5			16	8.5	125
Other real estate and trade assets	14	0.5			2	9.5	26
Consumer durables	7	1.0		27	2		37
Savings Deposits	35	6.5			7	8.5	57
Government Bonds	3				1	2.0	6
Company Shares	18	4.0			5		27
Life Policies	29	2.5	18	-37.5	6		18
Pension Rights	0		14				14
Other Assets	22	2.5				-12.5	12
Total Assets	210	35.5	32	-10.5	39	16	322
Debts	20	2.5			8	4.5	37
Net Wealth	190	33	32	-10.5	31	-10.5	284

Source: Dunn and Hoffman (1978).

been explored using wealth statistics for the UK, but the nature of the available evidence places a severe constraint on the questions that can be addressed, primarily because the estate procedure generates little information about wealth holders other than their wealth, age, and sex. This situation compares very unfavourably with the volume of detail typically provided in a sample survey.

One issue that has received a good deal of attention is the relationship between wealth holdings and age. This is seen as being relevant to an appraisal of the life-cycle saving hypothesis, which leads us to anticipate an inverse U-shaped age–wealth profile reflecting accumulation during the working period followed by dissaving in retirement (see Atkinson (1971)). The precise pattern observed empirically in the UK, and the conclusions that may be drawn for the life-cycle hypothesis, are somewhat ambiguous. Revell (1962) produced figures for 1957–8 which appear broadly consistent with the expected 'hump' feature. But other evidence on the cross-section age–wealth relationship indicates a rather different pattern, suggesting either a continual rise in wealth over the lifetime (see, for example, Atkinson (1971); Shorrocks (1975); Atkinson and Harrison (1978), p. 253), or else a relatively flat profile with net saving occurring well into old age (Shorrocks (1981)). However, a number of considerations need to be taken into account before judgement is passed.

One complication, emphasized in Shorrocks (1975), is that the age–wealth profile observed in a single year may bear little resemblance to that corresponding to a cohort of individuals over their lifetime. If the economy is experiencing real growth, the cross-section evidence is biased towards observing a hump pattern, even when no such feature applies to any of the constituent age cohorts. A second factor concerns the maturity valuation of life insurance policies discussed in the previous section. The inappropriate assignment of maturity values has a greater impact at young ages, and consequently flattens out the age–wealth profile. The significance of this distortion is examined in Shorrocks (1981). When life policies are valued in a more satisfactory way, the hump feature tends to disappear, and the predicted peak is replaced by no more than a minor dip in the profile. A more recent study by Dunn and Hoffman (1983) makes similar corrections to life policy values, along with many other adjustments. The results indicate an age–wealth profile for all adults similar to that of Shorrocks (1981), but the pattern is different when the population is disaggregated by sex and marital status. The figures for males alone suggest something more in line with a hump pattern, although the peak is earlier than anticipated (around age 45) and there remains an unexplained rise in wealth after retirement.[14]

Another important consideration is the exclusion of pension rights in the traditional wealth statistics. The existence of pension income certainly needs to be recognized in any serious attempt to evaluate the age–wealth relationship predicted by the life-cycle savings hypothesis. But this can be done in two different ways. The pension stream can be incorporated into the theoretical life-cycle model, in which case the 'hump' prediction for marketable assets is still likely to apply, so the conventional evidence remains a relevant test of the theory. Alternatively, the capitalized value of pension income can be added into the wealth figures. The problem with the latter option is that the pension wealth values are so large, and the hump pattern so prominent, that it completely dominates whatever is happening to holdings of marketable wealth. In essence, a hump pattern is more or less guaranteed once pension wealth is included, so empirical evidence on the age–wealth profile loses much of its interest. This is evident from the figures reported in Dunn and Hoffman (1983) which show that pension wealth raises the average wealth of all individuals by a factor of two, and of those aged 55–65 by a factor of almost three. The regular hump pattern apparent in their marketable plus pension wealth figures for all adults, with the peak at the 'right' age, may at first sight be regarded as impressive support for the life-cycle savings theory. But on further reflection we may well conclude that these refinements to the data have merely completed a circular argument.

Another topic of interest is the composition of wealth: the significance of particular assets in the typical portfolio of different persons. The available information is again constrained by the limitations of estate-based data, which means that individuals can only be classified into age, sex, and wealth categories. Nevertheless there is still much useful material that can be extracted. Variations in portfolio patterns by age and sex were discussed in Revell (1962), and a limited amount of empirical evidence has subsequently been published regularly in *Inland Revenue Statistics*. Shorrocks (1982) provides a more systematic analysis based on disaggregated estate data, and attempts to identify the influence of age and wealth level as determinants of portfolio composition. The results suggest that a minimum of five types of assets need to be distinguished when examining wealth holdings. These are liquid financial assets with known returns; liquid financial assets with risky returns; equity in private businesses; illiquid personal wealth; and dwellings. Such a five-way classification system would seem an appropriate basis for exploring a number of questions concerning the impact of changes in asset prices, the determinants of asset choice, the degree of substitutability between assets, and so on. The observed portfolio patterns bear little resemblance to the usual predictions of portfolio choice models, so empirical evidence on this issue may well provide the stimulus for a more realistic analysis of portfolio selection behaviour.

VI. Concluding Remarks

The ingenuity and effort devoted to the study of UK wealth holdings in recent years has had a major impact on the quality of basic wealth statistics. One has only to compare the figures for 1980, as represented by, say the Inland Revenue 'Series C' estimates of wealth shares, with those available a decade earlier, to appreciate the significance of the improvements that have occurred. As a consequence of these developments it is possible to argue that there is little scope for further refinement to either the estate multiplier procedure or the accuracy of the UK wealth statistics conventionally reported.

However the process of investigation and improvement has also led us to question the relevance of much of the empirical evidence that is the focus of public debate. A variety of fundamental questions crucially affect the interpretation placed on the wealth figures, and have to be resolved, or at least taken into account, before conclusions can be drawn with any degree of confidence. Some of these questions are well documented in the literature: for example, the relationship between the wealth distribution over individuals and that across households; the items that should be included in the definition of wealth; and the procedures to be followed when valuing assets. Others, such as the significance of changes in longevity, have been mentioned in the course of this chapter. These questions invariably raise issues of a conceptual, as

Anthony F. Shorrocks

well as computational, nature, and typically have not been settled in a satisfactory manner. Too often the proposed 'solutions' (including those outlined in this paper) take the form of piecemeal responses to the immediate problem. Rarely do they appear to be based on any underlying set of consistent criteria.

To my mind the basic problem lies in the relatively little attention given to the objectives of research into wealth holdings. We are inclined to collect, report, and analyse wealth data without a clear idea of why this information is of interest or how it should be used. This lack of clear-cut objectives tends to raise doubts concerning the relevance of many of the wealth calculations. But more importantly, perhaps, it undermines the basis on which the conceptual issues and choices might hope to be settled. Consider, for instance, the figures for the share of wealth owned by the rich, so frequently examined and discussed. Reasons for interest in these data are seldom mentioned at all. When reasons are offered, they are invariably vague, appealing to the need to have data that reflect social inequalities or economic power, or that might be used, in conjunction with information on incomes, to assess differences in the command over resources. Such arguments provide little assistance when it comes to evaluating the significance of wealth share evidence, and even less help in discriminating between alternative wealth concepts, economic units, and so on.

If wealth research is to progress in the future, the need for clearly stated aims and a coherent research framework will, I believe, become even more apparent. These needs may be satisfied in a variety of different ways. But as a first step it will be useful to explicitly recognize the benefits associated with wealth holdings: the future consumption possibilities; the ability to circumvent financial constraints; the power and influence often associated with sizeable wealth holdings; the advantages transmitted to future generations; and so on. The motives for wealth holding can then be linked to individual and household welfare via a model that captures the consumption, saving, investment, and bequest decisions of individuals. Once completed, this modelling exercise will supply the framework for a detailed empirical examination of the accumulation and asset choice behaviour of individuals, as well as their response to other economic and institutional factors. It will also enable the relevance of wealth statistics to be judged with more

confidence, and provide a basis for settling the outstanding conceptual issues.

Endnotes

1. University of Essex. I should like to thank Alan Harrison, Michael O'Higgins, and an anonymous reviewer for comments on an earlier version of the chapter. Needless to say, they are not responsible for any errors, nor for my personal assessment of the weaknesses of current wealth data and research.

2. But not for much longer, perhaps. There is a prospect that the work on wealth holdings undertaken by the Inland Revenue may be curtailed or even disconti-nued altogether.

3. For earlier estimates of wealth shares see Clay (1925), Daniels and Campion (1936), Campion (1939), Barna (1945), Langley (1950; 1951; 1954), Cartter (1953), Lydall and Tipping (1961), and Revell (1968), together with RCDIW (1975) and various issues of *Inland Revenue Statistics*.

4. See, for example, Atkinson (1972, pp. 21-4), Horsman (1975), and Atkinson and Harrison (1978), Section 9.3.

5. The discussion contained in RCDIW (1975) and Atkinson and Harrison (1978, Section 9.3) suggests that the transition from an individual to a family unit would reduce the observed wealth share of the top 1 per cent in any given year by no more than 5 percentage points. The impact of a change in the basic economic unit on the *trend* in wealth shares is, however, too uncertain for any estimates to be given. The proportion of total wealth held by females has been regarded as a proxy for intra-family variations in asset ownership and, some-what surprisingly, this proportion appears to have changed little over the period 1923-72 (Atkinson and Harrison (1978), p. 249). But a number of other factors need to be taken into account such as changes in male longevity and in the timing of capital transfers to children. The investment income method might seem a more promising approach to the problem of determining the distribution of family wealth since the tax unit is normally a married couple or unattached individual. But it is unlikely that this approach will ever generate data of the quality necessary to examine wealth trends with confidence.

6. The impact of similar demographic changes on UK income inequality has been examined by several authors: see, for example, Semple (1975), Dinwiddy and Reed (1977), and Mookherjee and Shorrocks (1982). I am unaware of any similar study performed for wealth inequality, although Harrison (1979, p. 35) considers the age structure to be an important consideration when comparing wealth distributions across countries.

7. Some evidence on wealth shares constructed for narrower wealth concepts is given in RCDIW (1977), Chapter 4.

8. Atkinson and Harrison (1978, Chapter 9; 1979) also provide evidence on the significance of owner-occupied dwellings. They regress the logarithm of the wealth share of the top 1 per cent against a number of variables including 'popular wealth', defined as the value of owner-occupied houses and consumer durables expressed as a proportion of all other wealth. Their results indicate

that a rise in this ratio of 10 percentage points might reduce the share of the top 1 per cent by a (relatively modest) half a percentage point.

9. For a detailed appraisal of mortality multipliers see Atkinson and Harrison (1975) or (1978), Chapter 3.

10. It is also closely allied to the distinction between individuals and households discussed in the previous section.

11. Dunn and Hoffman (1983) is a recent exception. Among other things they compare wealth shares calculated under the assumptions of Series A, B, and C, thus providing some indication of the quantitative significance of the problems related to the excluded population.

12. There are a variety of circumstances in which certain items of wealth are excluded from estate values. Significant among these are assets settled on a surviving spouse, and part of the wealth held under discretionary trusts. For more details see Atkinson and Harrison (1978a), Section 3.2.2.

13. For background details see Dunn and Hoffman (1978a). A similar reconciliation of the 1977 data is contained in Dunn and Hoffman (1983).

14. Shorrocks (1975) offers an explanation for both of these features. The early peak can occur because cross-section, rather than cohort, profiles are being observed in a period of real growth; while the wealth of the elderly can *appear* to rise because the higher mortality of the less wealthy raises the average holdings of the surviving cohort members. The increase in the average wealth of retired persons with age would have been more evident in the Dunn and Hoffman study had they provided separate figures for those over 85 (which is feasible with estate information).

15. This is not to say that no justification for interest in wealth data has ever been given: see, for example, Atkinson (1972), especially Chapter 5. Rather that the reasons do not provide a coherent framework to answer questions concerning, for instance, the appropriate concept of wealth.

References

Astin, J.A. 'The Distribution of Wealth and the Relevance of Age,' *Statistical News*, 28 (1975), 28.1–28.8.

Atkinson, A.B. 'The Distribution of Wealth and the Individual Lifecycle,' *Oxford Economic Papers*, 23 (1971), 239–54.

—— *Unequal Shares* (London, 1972).

—— *Social Justice and Public Policy* (Wheatsheaf Books, 1983).

Atkinson, A.B., Harrison, A.J. 'Mortality Multipliers and the Estate Duty Method,' *Oxford Bulletin of Economics and Statistics*, 37 (1975), 13–28.

—— *Distribution of Personal Wealth in Britain* (Cambridge, 1978).

—— 'Wealth,' In: Maunder, W.F. ed. *Review of United Kingdom Statistical Sources*, vol. VI (Oxford, 1978a).

—— 'The Analysis of Trends Over Time in the Distribution of Personal Wealth in Britain,' *Annales de l'INSEE*, 33–34 (1979). Reprinted in Atkinson, A.B. ed. *Wealth, Income and Inequality*, Second edn (Oxford,

1980), and in Atkinson (1983).

Barna, T. *Redistribution of Income 1937* (Oxford, 1945).

Board of Inland Revenue *Inland Revenue Statistics* (London, various years).

Campion, H. *Public and Private Property in Great Britain* (Oxford, 1939).

Cartter, A.M. 'A New Method of Relating British Capital Ownership and Estate Duty Liability to Income Groups,' *Economica*, 20 (1953), 247–58.

Central Statistical Office 'Personal Sector Balance Sheets,' *Economic Trends*, 291 (1978). Reprinted in CSO, *Studies in Official Statistics No. 35* (London, 1978).

Clay, H. 'The Distribution of Capital in England and Wales,' *Transactions of Manchester Statistical Society* (1925).

Daniels, G.W., Campion, H. *The Distribution of National Capital* (Manchester, 1936).

Dinwiddy, R., Reed, D. *The Effects of Certain Social and Demographic Changes on Income Distribution*, Background paper No. 3 to the Royal Commission on the Distribution of Income and Wealth (London, 1977).

Dunn, A.T., Hoffman, P.D.R.B. 'The Distribution of Personal Wealth,' *Economic Trends*, 301 (1978), 101–18.

—— 'Current Developments in Inland Revenue Estimates of Personal Wealth.' In: Central Statistical Office, *Studies in Official Statistics No. 35* (London, 1978a).

—— 'Distribution of Wealth in the United Kingdom: Effect of Including Pension Rights and Analysis by Age Group,' *Review of Income and Wealth*, 29 (1983), 243–82.

Harrison, A.J. *The Distribution of Wealth in Ten Countries*, Background paper No. 7 to the Royal Commission on the Distribution of Income and Wealth (London, 1979).

Horsman, E.G. 'The Avoidance of Estate Duty by Gifts Inter Vivos: Some Quantitative Evidence,' *Economic Journal*, 85 (1975), 516–30.

Langley, K.M. 'The Distribution of Capital in Private Hands in 1936–1938 and 1946–1947' (Article in two parts), *Bulletin of the Oxford University Institute of Statistics*, 12 (1950), 339–57, and 13 (1951), 33–54.

—— 'The Distribution of Private Capital, 1950–1951,' *Bulletin of the Oxford University Institute of Statistics*, 16 (1954), 1–13.

Lydall, H.F., Tipping, O.G. 'The Distribution of Personal Wealth in Britain,' *Bulletin of the Oxford University Institute of Statistics*, 23 (1961), 83–104.

Mallet, B. 'A Method of Estimating Capital Wealth from the Estate Duty Statistics,' *Journal of the Royal Statistical Society*, 71 (1908), 65–84.

Mookherjee, D., Shorrocks, A.F. 'A Decomposition Analysis of the Trend in UK Income Inequality,' *Economic Journal*, 92 (1982), 886–902.

Revell, J.R.S. 'Assets and Age,' *Bulletin of the Oxford University Institute of Statistics*, 24 (1962), 363–78.

—— *The Wealth of the Nation* (Cambridge, 1967).

—— 'Changes in the Social Distribution of Property in Britain During the Twentieth Century,' *Third International Conference of Economic History, Munich, 1965* (Paris, 1968).

Royal Commission on the Distribution of Income and Wealth *Initial Report on the Standing Reference* (London, 1975).

—— *Report No. 5, Third Report on the Standing Reference* (London, 1977).

—— *Report No. 7, Fourth Report on the Standing Reference* (London, 1979).

Semple, M. 'The Effect of Changes in Household Composition on the Distribution of Income 1961-73,' *Economic Trends*, 266 (1975), 99-105.

Shorrocks, A.F. 'The Age Wealth Relationship: A Cross Section and Cohort Analysis,' *Review of Economics and Statistics*, 57 (1975), 155-63.

—— 'Life Insurance and Asset Holdings in the United Kingdom.' In: Currie, D., Peel, D., Peters, W. eds. *Microeconomic Analysis* (London, 1981).

—— 'The Portfolio Composition of Asset Holdings in the United Kingdom,' *Economic Journal*, 92 (1982), 268-84.

3

Wealth Distribution in Sweden: 1920–1983

Roland Spånt

This chapter concerns the development of the distribution of wealth in Sweden during the period from 1920 to 1983. It has two sections. In the first section, the period 1920–75 is analysed. Some characteristic features of the distribution in 1975 are also presented. The second section of this paper deals with developments since 1975.[1]

The aim of this chapter has been to provide some idea of how wealth is distributed in Sweden and how its distribution has developed over time. The study concentrates on assets owned directly by households and does not deal with those that are owned indirectly via the public sector, companies, and so on.[2] There is no generally accepted definition of wealth that can incorporate all the aspects that are relevant for economic policy. The choice open to researchers and producers of statistics is restricted, moreover, by the supply of relevant data. At the same time, the choice of concept has a major bearing on the degree of inequality in the distribution studied.

This report is confined in principle to assets that can be converted into cash, so that in practice it deals with taxable assets and ignores pension rights and human capital. The emphasis here is on assets in terms of liquidity and convertibility. No consideration is paid to the power or influence they may confer.

Results for the 1920–75 period are based on actual microdata samples of household wealth. The 1983 results are based on a forecasting technique applied to the 1975 data. Forecasting involves a number of special problems. Is it at all possible to forecast the distribution of wealth? Do we know enough concerning its distribution and the determinants of that distribution to come up with real forecasts as opposed to trend projections or conjectures?

In my opinion, the answer to this question varies from one country to another and from one period to another. In Sweden, an even distribution of wealth and incomes is a priority target of official policy, on a level with full employment, stability of prices, and rapid economic growth. We greatly need, therefore, to be able to detect changes in the distribution of wealth relatively quickly, whereas with traditional methods, absolutely dependable research findings may not become available until perhaps 5 years after a change in the distribution of wealth has taken place.

This is particularly serious if, during a particular period, drastic changes occur in factors having a major bearing on the distribution of wealth, especially if there is cause to suspect the inflection of a long-term trend. I believe the years between 1975 and 1983 to have been exactly such a period, with much slower economic growth, extra rapid inflation, and steeply climbing share prices. During this period the impact of prices on the distribution of wealth in Sweden was far greater than for any other 8-year period during the post-war era. At the same time the quantitative effects of saving on the distribution of wealth in Sweden are probably small, annual financial household saving amounting to less than 1 per cent of available income.

The wealth distribution forecast for 1975–83 presented here, which is based on price effects, is of couse subject to marginal uncertainties, and in future, therefore, the determinants of wealth distribution should be analysed in greater depth, especially as regards the importance of relative price movements for the reduction of inequality between 1920 and 1975.

I. The 1920–1975 Period

Our basic data source consists of a sample of about 5,000 families selected at random to represent the wealth position of 'ordinary' households plus about 3,000 households with more than 200,000 kronor in taxed wealth. The latter group comprised all households in Sweden with more than 10 million kronor in net wealth, half of those with 5–10 million, one in five of those with between 2 and 5 millions, and so on. The combined total of 8,000 households had submitted about 17,000 tax returns, from which in principle all data on wealth were extracted and processed. It is this material, reflecting the wealth position at the turn of 1975, that constitutes our primary base. The data from the tax returns have been corrected, however, in the light of available statistics on the relationship between the market prices and tax values of property.[3] Certain estimates have also been made concerning the effects of tax evasion and other forms of underdeclaration.

Our base material enables us to describe both the composition of assets owned by households at the end of 1975 and the inequality in the distribution of this wealth. These estimates have been carried out both at tax values and after converting property values to market prices. Our results for 1975 are compared with available results from earlier Swedish studies for the years 1970, 1966, 1958, 1951, 1945, 1935, 1930, and 1920. In this way we are able to describe changes in the structure of household assets in the period 1945-75 as well as how the inequality in wealth distribution has developed in the period 1920-75. The results from 1975 are also used for a forecast of the development of the distribution of wealth 1975-83.

The tax value of the assets declared by Swedish households at the end of 1975 totalled about 350 billion kronor and liabilities about 150 billions, so that taxed net wealth amounted to almost 200 billions. If the tax values for property are replaced by estimated market prices, gross wealth rises to over 500 billion kronor and net wealth to around 350 billions. All these amounts refer to the declared assets.

A major problem with tax return data is the extent of under-reporting and avoidance through evasion and legal tax exemptions. Many of the assets and liabilities included in the data are extremely reliable. This is presumably true for owner-occupied houses, summer houses, apartment houses, and farms. In these cases the tax authorities have access to control data, an estate file, which makes it nearly impossible for an estate owner to avoid registration. We can therefore conclude that almost 100 per cent of these types of assets are included in the survey and have been included in earlier surveys. Another sector which should be covered extremely well is the ownership of company shares. The control of received dividends should be of the same magnitude as that of estates. The pure self-interest of the households makes it plausible that all debts are also extremely well covered. (Paid interest are according to Swedish tax laws fully deductible from taxable income and the marginal tax rates comparatively high.)

The statistical deficiencies are primarily connected with assets on bank accounts, and with bonds and owner-occupied apartments.

The tax control is much weaker or non-existent for these types of assets. The incentives for controls are weak because of tax reliefs in the treatment of low interest income. About 30 per cent of the total value on bank accounts belonging to households is neither included in the wealth study nor distributed among households. This figure is based on estimates of household balance sheets and has been relatively stable over time.

If all forms of underdeclaration are included, too, gross assets lie in the region of 570 billion kronor and net wealth 420 billion. In this case, however, the margins of uncertainty amount to several tens of billions in either direction. One may observe that premium bonds, bank deposits, and so on are assets which are held by normal or 'poor' households.

Total assets are dominated by a few types, namely real estate, bank assets, shares, cars and boats, claims, stocks and reserve stocks, bonds, and what are termed other inventories. Taken together these items accounted for almost 97 per cent of total wealth. By far the most important of them was real estate—owner-occupied houses, farms, secondary dwellings, and apartment houses—which accounted for about two-thirds of gross wealth at market prices. The other items' shares of gross assets at market prices were about 14 per cent for bank deposits (excluding underdeclaration), 5–6 per cent for shares, 3 per cent for claims, 1–2 per cent for bonds, 3 per cent for cars, and so on, and about 2 per cent each for other inventories, stocks, and other assets. Owner-occupied houses alone made up around 40 per cent of gross assets.

It is shown in Tables 3.1 through 3.5 that some of these shares

Table 3.1. *Residential property as a percentage of household gross assets at market prices 1935–1975*

Year	Owner-occupied houses	Secondary dwellings	Apartment houses	Total (%)
1935				31.0
1945	17.5		17.2	34.7
1951	20.3		16.8	37.1
1958	24.0	2.9	8.4	35.3
1966	29.3	11.1		40.4
1970	46.0		6.3	52.3
1975	39.2	5.1	4.1	48.5

Table 3.2.   *Agriculture and unincorporated business as a percentage of household gross assets at market prices, 1935–1975*

Year	Farm property	Unincorporated business	Farm stocks and inventories	Unincorporated business stocks and inventories	Total (%)
1935	21.0				27.0
1945	18.5	1.6	5.6	2.4	28.1
1951	19.5	1.5	4.0	4.2	29.2
1958					34.0
1966	16.9	1.4	2.8	1.9	23.0
1970	12.5	0.6	3.5		16.6
1975	17.6		3.2		20.8

have undergone dramatic changes since 1945. Those which have diminished most markedly in importance are apartment houses, farms and unincorporated businesses claims, and shares. In the case of apartment houses, the share of gross assets at market prices has fallen by three-fourths, from 17 per cent at the end of the war to only 4.5 per cent 30 years later. Assets in farms and unincorporated business combined decreased from almost 30 per cent in 1945 to around 20 per cent, though part of this decline may reflect the transformation of much personal business into limited companies.

Table 3.3.   *Bonds, claims, bank deposits, and children's wealth as a percentage of household gross assets, 1945–1975[a]*

Year	Bonds		Claims	Bank deposits	Children's wealth
	Total	Premium bonds			
1935			6.3	15.5	
1945	2.9	1.6	5.7	14.1	0.3
1951	1.4	0.7	6.5	12.6	0.5
1958	1.0		3.6	16.9	
1966	1.1		4.5	17.0	0.5
1970			4.7	17.4	0.7
1975	1.4	0.7	3.5	13.9	0.5

a. Based on declared amounts at market prices.

Table 3.4. *Shares and bonds as a percentage of household gross assets, 1935–1975*[a]

Year	Shares			Shares and bonds	Shares and participatory rights
	Total	Listed	Others		
1935	(13.5)				
1945	12.0			14.9	
1951	10.2	5.9	(4.3)	11.6	
1958	(8.0)			(9.0)	(9.5)
1966					9.2
1970	8.6			8.6	
1975	5.4	3.8	1.6	6.8	6.7

a. Based on declared amounts at market prices.

Table 3.5. *Liabilities as a percentage of household gross assets 1935–1975 and types of liability as a percentage of total indebtedness*[a]

Year	Total liability	Type of liability				
		Mortgage debt	Other loan debt	Commercial debts	Tax debts	Other debts
1935	(30)					
1945	28.0					
1951	30.4	62.9	18.5	8.0	2.6	8.0
1958	25.9					
1966	25.6	67.1	19.7	4.9	3.1	5.2
1970	29.5					
1975	29.8	69.3	5.5	2.7	1.9	20.6

a. Based on declared amounts at market prices.

Declared shareholdings also decreased, from about 12 to about 5.5 per cent of total wealth. This development may have been exaggerated, however, because the market value of unlisted companies is greatly underestimated. In the case of listed shares alone, their percentage of total wealth fell from 6 to 4 during these 30 years.

Extremely rapid growth is shown by owner-occupied houses and secondary dwellings, from a combined share of about 17 per cent to about 45 per cent, that is, almost a threefold increase. This is probably the most important change to have occurred during the period and perhaps since the turn of the century.

There are other assets whose share was largely constant during this period, in contrast to the major changes in gross wealth and in the assets enumerated above. These comprise bank deposits, bonds, and assets declared as children's wealth. Liabilities, too, have been strikingly stable as a share of gross assets.

Table 3.1 shows that in 1945 owner-occupied houses and secondary dwellings accounted between them for 17.5 per cent of household's total declared assets at market prices, while in 1975 owner-occupied houses alone made up 39.2 per cent. Table 3.2 shows unincorporated business value as a per cent of total assets. In the 1975 property assessment, farm property made up 90.7 per cent and business property 9.3 per cent of the total of this group. At market prices the farm share was probably higher (above 93 per cent). Note that in Table 2, 1945, 1951, and 1966 compare best with 1975. The figures for 1935 have been derived from those for 1945. The 1970 data are not comparable with other years in certain respects: business property is no doubt greatly underestimated.

The international comparison shows that in 1975 the composition of household assets in Sweden was fairly typical of Western Europe. In all the West European countries studied, dwellings of various kinds amounted between them to roughly half of gross wealth. In the US, on the other hand, dwellings had a much smaller share. Company shares are somewhat more important for household wealth in Sweden than in Denmark, the Federal Republic of Germany, and France; on the other hand, their contribution in Sweden was lower than in the UK and definitely lower than in the US. The relative value of unincorporated non-farm business was definitely lower in Sweden than in the other countries, perhaps partly because small business tends to be incorporated in Sweden and also because the intangible assets of personal business are not reflected in the tax statistics.

Another noteworthy phenomenon is the substantially higher average debt/asset ratio for Swedish and Danish households compared with households in the other countries.

1. Inequality in the 1920–1975 Period

The data on the distribution of wealth in 1975 pointed, not unexpectedly, to large differences between households in this

Table 3.6.   *Distribution of wealth in 1975: percentage declared by most wealthy 0.1–20.0 per cent of households*[a]

Most wealthy fraction of households (%)	Percentage of total household wealth			
	At taxed values		At market prices	
	Net	Gross	Net	Gross
0.1	8	7	6	6
0.2	10	9.5	8	8.5
0.5	15	14	12.5	13
1.0	20.5	18.5	17	17
2.0	28	25.5	24	24
5.0	44	38	38	37
10.0	60	52	54	52
20.0	80	71	75	71

a. The most wealthy 0.1 per cent of all households accordingly owned 8 per cent of total household net wealth in 1975 in terms of taxed values and 6 per cent at market prices; the corresponding figures for gross assets, i.e. disregarding liabilities, are 7 per cent at taxed values and 6 per cent at market prices.

respect. The distribution at market prices was consistently somewhat more uniform than at tax values. (See Table 3.6.) The international comparison naturally involves a greater element of uncertainty but it does suggest that the distribution of wealth in Sweden and Denmark was more uniform than in the Federal Republic of Germany, the UK, and the US. This comparison concerns the very richest households' share of total net wealth, that is, the relationship between the position of these households and all the rest. The material did not permit us to compare the position of the intermediate groups and those at the bottom of the wealth pyramid.

Although the distribution of wealth in 1975 can be described as highly unequal compared, say, with the distribution of income or consumption, our historical analysis shows that the distribution of taxed net wealth became very much more uniform in the period 1920–75. This has been a continuous process, so that the distribution in each year studied (1920, 1930, 1935, 1945, 1951, 1966, 1970, and 1975) was more uniform than it had been earlier (see Tables 3.7 and 3.8 and Figures 3.1 and 3.2).

Table 3.7. *Evolution of wealth distribution 1920–1975: Share (per cent) of total taxed net worth owned by the richest 0.01, 0.03, 0.1, 0.2, 0.5 and 1.0 per cent of households*[a]

Year	Richest households (per cent of all households)					
	0.01	0.03	0.1	0.2	0.5	1.0
1920	9	15	24	31	40	50
1930		13	21	28	37	47
1935	6.5	11	18	23	33	42
1945		9	15	20	29	38
1951		7	12	17	25	33
1966	3.6	5.5	9	12	18	24
1970	3.3	5	8.5	11	17	23
1975	3.0	4.7	8	10	15	21
1975 at market prices	2.2	3.7	6	8	12.5	17
Taxed net wealth in 1975 exceeded (1000s of SEK)	6,500	3,200	1,500	1,000	600	450
No. of households in 1975	410	1,230	4,100	8,200	20,500	41,000

a. The table shows, for instance, that in 1920 the richest ten thousandth (0.01 per cent) of all households owned 9 per cent of total household declared net wealth. In 1975 the 410 households whose taxed net wealth exceeded 6.5 million SEK (the richest 0.01 per cent) owned 3.0 per cent of total household declared net wealth.

This development has chiefly taken the form of considerably slower growth, compared with other households, for the wealth of the richest 2 per cent. Their share of declared total net wealth has accordingly fallen very markedly, from about 60 per cent in 1920 to 28 per cent in 1975. The households which have increased their share of total wealth are chiefly the 'poorest' 95 per cent, from about 23 per cent of *registered* net wealth in 1920 to 56 per cent in 1975.

These figures refer to wealth at tax values. It seems that the same tendencies apply to wealth at market prices or if allowance could be made for underdeclaration. The trend towards greater equality would probably have been still stronger if the measure of wealth had been extended to include claims on private and public pension funds and so on.

Table 3.8. *Evolution of wealth distribution 1920–1975: Share (per cent) of total taxed net wealth owned by the richest 1, 2, 5, 10, and 20 per cent of households*[a]

Year	Richest households (per cent of all households)				
	1	2	5	10	20
1920	50	60	77	91	100
1930	47	58	74	88	98
1935	42	53	70	84	97
1945	38	48	66	82	96
1951	33	43	60	76	92
1966	24	32	48	64	82
1970	23	31	46	62	84
1975	21	28	44	60	80
1975 at market prices	17	24	38	54	75
Taxed net wealth in 1975 exceeded (1000s of SEK)	450	320	200	130	80
No. of households in 1975	41,000	82,000	205,000	410,000	820,000

a. The table shows, for instance, that in 1920 the richest percentile of households owned 50 per cent of total household declared net wealth, while the richest decile owned 91 per cent. In 1975 the 41,000 households whose taxed net wealth exceeded 450,000 SEK (the richest percentile) owned 21 per cent of total household declared net wealth.

Another typical feature of development is the marked increase in the proportion of households that declare some form of wealth. This rose from one-fifth in 1920 to three-fourths in 1975. The true number of wealth holders today, however, is probably still higher, between 90 and 100 per cent.

We have already noted that the distribution of wealth was still very unequal in 1975 and a description of this inequality is naturally of particular interest. The richest percentile of households owned about 17 per cent of total net wealth, the richest 5 per cent owned 38 per cent, and the richest decile about 55 per cent. In other words, the richest percentile owned seventeen times the wealth they would have held if all wealth had been distributed uniformly among all households. The concentration of wealth was still more marked at the very top of the hierarchy, where 800 households owned about

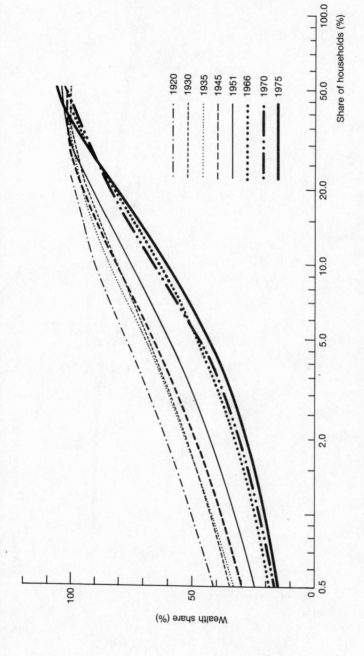

Fig. 3.1   *Development of wealth distribution 1920–1975 in the interval 0.5–100 per cent of households (taxed value)*

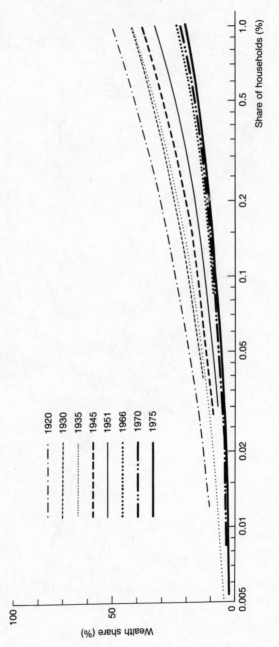

Fig. 3.2   *Development of wealth distribution 1920–1975 in the interval 0.005–1.0 per cent of households (taxed value)*

3 per cent of the total, or 150 times more than they would have done if the distribution had been completely uniform. If allowance is made for underdeclaration, the distribution is probably somewhat more equal than these figures indicate. That is because under-declaration is strong for bank deposits, premium bonds, and so on—assets predominantly held by lower deciles of households. The tax data are much more reliable for real estates, shares, and so on—assets held by 'rich' households. But the distribution of wealth is still more unequal than other economically relevant distributions: whereas the richest decile of households owned around 55 per cent of total wealth, the top decile of income earners received only about 20 per cent of total household disposable income.

Certain types of assets, moreover, were still more unequally distributed than total net wealth. Some of the distributions concerned are presented in Table 3.9. The chief items here are apartment houses and shares. Only 72,000 households (1.8 per cent of all households in Sweden) declared assets in apartment houses and 5,000 of them (0.1 per cent of all households) owned 60 per cent of all apartment houses. In the case of shares, holdings were declared by 455,000 households, of which 334,000 declared listed shares, units in investment funds, and so on, 13,000 foreign shares, 54,000 shares in the 15,000 medium-sized companies, and 123,000 other shares. This means that 11 per cent of all households declared some form of shareholding, 8 per cent declared listed shares, 1.3 per cent shares in one or several of the medium-sized companies, 0.3 per cent in foreign companies, and 3 per cent in other companies. Many households owned more than one type of share.

The distribution of shareholding is also very unequal among the households that own shares. One-fifth of the households with listed shares had holdings below 1,000 kronor and one-half had less than 10,000 kronor. This half of the owners held only 2.5 per cent of the total owned by households. At the same time, the 5,500 largest owners held four-tenths of the total. The 11,000 largest owners of listed shares, less than 0.3 per cent of the 4 million households in Sweden, held half the stock of listed shares.

The holdings of listed shares declared by households totalled 19.3 billion kronor, which is less than half of the total value of listed shares in 1975.

Table 3.9. *Composition of gross wealth, by size of net wealth in 1975 (per cent)*

Taxed net wealth (1000s of SEK)	Real property	Bank assets	Shares	Claims	Bonds	Cars and boats	Other inventories	Stocks	Other assets	Total assets[a]
Above 5,000	25.2	9.5	39.2	17.7	3.5	0.2	0.8	1.4	2.6	100.0
2,000–5,000	33.2	8.9	31.2	14.6	2.7	0.4	0.8	5.1	2.7	100.0
1,000–2,000	35.9	9.3	30.3	12.9	2.9	0.5	1.9	2.7	3.5	100.0
500–1,000	40.5	13.8	19.8	10.6	2.4	0.7	3.4	3.9	4.9	100.0
300–500	41.1	20.4	12.7	7.7	2.9	1.0	4.0	6.1	4.0	100.0
200–300	46.3	22.8	8.4	6.0	2.8	2.0	4.5	3.8	3.4	100.0
100–200	53.7	24.1	3.8	3.6	2.4	3.3	2.7	3.3	3.3	100.0
50–100	53.0	27.1	3.6	2.5	1.8	5.8	1.7	1.5	3.2	100.0
10–50	54.6	22.1	1.4	1.7	1.1	12.2	2.7	1.3	3.0	100.0
0–10	52.5	11.5	3.4	0.7	0.9	23.4	6.4	0.5	0.8	100.0
0										
–50–0	72.4	7.1	1.1	1.1	0.8	10.0	2.6	1.9	3.1	100.0
Below –50	72.8	5.0	2.2	7.2	1.5	4.2	4.4	0.5	2.3	100.0
Total	51.0	19.8	7.9	5.1	2.0	5.2	2.8	2.7	3.3	100.0

a. Total may not sum to 100 per cent due to rounding errors.

II. The 1975–1983 Period

The past 8 years in Sweden have differed in a number of essential respects from the rest of the post-war era. In the political arena, Sweden acquied its first non-socialist government for 40 years in September 1976. A succession of non-socialist governments then ruled Sweden for 6 of the 8 years, until September 1982.

Economically these 8 years were by far the worst period in Swedish post-war history, with gross national product (GNP) rising on average by less than 1 per cent annually. Inflation, on the other hand, was unprecedentedly high, with consumer prices rising by almost 9.5 per cent annually. There are many different reasons for this high rate of inflation. They include, for example, the rise in oil prices during 1979 and 1980, and several devaluations of the Swedish krona which Swedish governments found themselves obliged to undertake between 1976 and 1982.

Record inflation has had extensive distributive effects, especially through its erosion of the value of bank savings and its effects on the real value of household debts.

During this period, real-estate prices tended on average to lag behind the inflation rate. Inflation for the period between December 1975 and December 1983 is forecast at about 104 per cent. During the same period, according to the available statistics, the prices of agricultural property rose by 53 per cent, those of weekend cottages by 100 per cent, those of tenement buildings by 88 per cent, and those of detached houses by 80 per cent.[4] One possible reason for the failure of these real assets to keep up with inflation may be that a great deal of the latter was 'imported' from other countries, partly as a result of the devaluations of the Swedish krona. In certain respects, Sweden as a nation grew poorer. Perhaps a better explanation, however, can be found in the jerky development of real-estate prices. The prices of agricultural property, especially those with timber resources, had risen very steeply during the great forestry boom just before 1975. The prices of detached houses and weekend cottages had for a long time kept well ahead of inflation, owing to excess demand and short supply. The somewhat slower movement of prices during the period 1975–83 as a whole may have constituted a technical recoil from an overheated situation.

Although GNP virtually stagnated between 1975 and 1983, we

have good reason to suspect that a distinct change may have taken place in the distribution of wealth. If we take as our starting point the situation prevailing at the New Year 1976, the following can be said to have happened, in *real* terms, by the New Year 1984. The real value of bank savings, bonds, receivables, and so on, declined by more than 50 per cent. Financial assets of this kind constituted almost 20 per cent of declared assets in 1975. (To this figure must be added a large volume of undeclared banking assets.) Thus inflation eliminated one-tenth of real household wealth.

Liabilities, comprising about 30 per cent of gross assets, were also halved in real terms.

In the real-estate sector, the real value of weekend cottages remained unaltered on the whole, while single-family housing properties declined in real terms by 16 per cent, agricultural properties by 28 per cent, and tenement properties by 11 per cent.

There is, however, one type of asset which definitely kept ahead of inflation during this period, and that is shares. Share prices have risen slowly during the early and mid-1970s, and the real value of shares declined. The curve took an upward turn, however, in 1980, and as a result of special tax concessions for shareholders, the general upturn on world stock markets, and the steep rise in company profits following the 1981 and 1982 devaluations, share prices have risen so fast that today, at the end of 1983, they are four times what they were at the end of 1975. Allowing for inflation, this means that real share prices have doubled.

In the actual fact the rising share prices have been so steep as to offset the real losses sustained on real property. Shareholdings are by tradition very unevenly distributed throughout the population, and this means that the rise in share prices has probably had far-reaching distributive effects. Half of all shares in 1975 were owned by the wealthiest 1 per cent of households.

During the 1975–83 period the real value of real estate of various kinds has declined by a total of between 12 and 25 per cent, while bank savings and liabilities have been halved (see Table 3.10). By contrast, the real value of shares has more than doubled. When attempting to determine the distributive effects of these developments, one can employ either a real or a nominal approach; in both cases the result will be the same. For present purposes, we have applied a nominal approach, and changes are therefore stated in current prices. The nominal value of certain household assets and

Table 3.10. *Percentage rise in prices by wealth component, 1975–1983*

	Nominal value December 1975	Percentage price rise	Nominal value December 1983
Banking assets, etc.	100	0	100
Agricultural properties	85	53	130
Tenement properties	21	88	40
Weekend cottages	26	101	53
Single-family housing properties	200	80	360
Shares	28	306	112
Liabilities	150	0	150

liabilities in 1975 developed as follows during the period ending December 1983 (SEK billions).[5]

There are naturally any number of reasons for the structure and distribution of household wealth having changed over the past 8-year period. These include, for example, inheritance, the purchase and sale of various assets, emigration and immigration, new saving, and the contracting of new loans. It will be a long time before we are able to evaluate fully the detailed development of the actual distribution of wealth during this inflationary period. The changes in the prices of shares and real assets as stated above, however, are so substantial that their effects on wealth merit investigation in themselves. Let us therefore see whether these changes in value influenced the inequality of the distribution of wealth.

To this end we have taken as our starting point the distribution of wealth in 1975, with assets valued at market prices (net wealth at market prices) and we have projected this distribution in accordance with the changes undergone by the prices of real estate and shares. In an inflationary economy of the kind which existed in Sweden between 1975 and 1983, certain very distinct distributive effects are to be expected. Bank savers are adversely affected, as are households which have invested a large proportion of their wealth in bonds and receivables. Households with debts are at an advantage, especially those which have borrowed in order to purchase real estate or real assets of other kinds.

In several studies during the past few years, I have presented the effects of inflation on distribution of income in Sweden. The combination of high inflation, high marginal taxation rates, and low nominal rates of interest has had very far-reaching redistributive effects. Generally speaking, persons in high income brackets and the 'upper' social classes have been greatly benefited, while persons in low income brackets, pensioners, and the 'lower' classes have been disfavoured. This result applied to the distribution of income.

The distribution of wealth may have been differently affected. Generally speaking, we may expect heavily indebted households to benefit whatever their wealth status, while inflation has mainly benefited households which are so heavily in debt that their registered net wealth remains negative in spite of extensive real-estate holdings. Our findings confirm this hypothesis.

There is also reason to suppose that the disfavoured groups are located in the broad intermediate band of households with modest assets, in which bank saving has by tradition played an important part. Our calculations also confirm this hypothesis.

The main problem which we have analysed, however, is whether the very wealthiest households have been favoured or disfavoured by the changes in value occurring between 1975 and 1983. Estimates are shown in Table 3.11. Considering the inertia normally characterizing the distribution of wealth, the changes estimated here are remarkably large. It is the wealthiest 0.2 per cent of households that have gained by the changes of value occurring since 1975. These figures correspond to a net wealth of some SEK 70 billion held this year by the households concerned, which number about 8,000. SEK 14 billion of this amount can be ascribed to the wealthiest households benefiting by the structure of value changes

Table 3.11. *The share of wealth held by the top percentiles, 1975 and 1983*

Most wealthy fraction of households (per cent)	Percentage of total net household wealth at market prices	
	1975	1983
0.1	6	8
0.2	8	10
0.5	12.5	14.5
1.0	17	19.5
2.0	24	26

between 1975 and 1983. One of the main reasons is the movement of share prices, shareholding being heavily concentrated within the very wealthiest households.

Considering the very great distributive effects which changes in the values of shares and real estate have probably had over the past 8 years, one cannot help asking: can other factors influencing the distribution of wealth have offset these price effects, or has the trend been reversal, so that the distribution of wealth in Sweden, after nearly 60 years of almost uninterrupted progrss towards less inequality, has now become more unequal again? Let us consider some effects which can influence the result: the emigration of wealthy Swedes, inheritance, saving, and a change in the structure of wealth. It is a well-known fact that a number of wealthy Swedes leave Sweden every year, mostly emigrating to countries with lower rates of income and wealth taxation. This can be said to mean that the Swedish economy generates greater inequalities of income and wealth than the statistics reveal. This emigration, however, is of relatively modest proportions; to offset the price effects calculated above, about 30 or 40 per cent of the wealthiest 8,200 households in 1975 would have had to emigrate since then. Emigration, therefore, cannot offset the effects of prices. Nor is there any real likelihood of inheritance assuming such proportions; when allowance is made for succession tax, inheritance mainly implies a redistribution of wealth within the same stratum. Household saving in Sweden is very low by international standards, annual financial household saving corresponding to just over 1 per cent of gross assets. This makes it hard to imagine that such saving can have substantially influenced the distribution of wealth.

Personally, on the other hand, I believe that changes in the structure of assets may have played a more important part. New investments in first and second homes, which in Sweden are mainly financed by loans, may to some extent have influenced the structure of wealth. This is particularly the case with purchases during the 1970s. These effects are, however, probably limited in relation to the combined wealth of all households.

One interesting phenomenon which has been observed in several studies is that the direct household share of Stock Exchange value has gradually fallen from 45 per cent in 1975 to about 25 per cent in 1983. At the same time a number of tax-sheltered mutual funds have come into being which are characterized by a relatively widespread ownership and now control about 6 per cent of Stock Exchange value. Many households selling off portions of their shareholdings have probably missed out on the rise in share prices over the past 3 years. We do not know at present how extensive these sales have been or what effects they have had on the distribution of wealth.[6]

Swedish business journals state that a number of very large private fortunes have been created in Sweden within a short space of time. Some of these can probably be put down to the rise in share prices and real-estate prices, but most of these fortunes have probably been generated in personally owned limited companies concerned with productive enterprise or through the systematic utilization of the effects of inflation on liabilities. According to one estimate published in the journal *Affärsvärlden*, sixty-seven Swedish finance families in 1983 between them controlled gross assets totalling at least SEK 100 million. Altogether these families controlled between SEK 30 and 40 billion. Some of these assets are owned by expatriate Swedes, a large proportion of them are mortgaged, and some have been invested in public shares and are therefore included in our previous calculations. Allowing for these items, however, there still remains net wealth totalling at least SEK 5 or 10 billion, most of which was generated after 1975 and is therefore not included in the material for that year. If this amount is added to the assets of the wealthiest households, the inequality of the distribution of wealth in 1983 will be seen to be greater still.

III. Conclusion

During the period 1920–75 the distribution of wealth in Sweden became very much more equal. The most wealthy 1 per cent of all households owned 50 per cent of total household declared net wealth compared to 21 per cent in 1975. This long trend towards less inequality now seems to be broken and the richest groups' share of total wealth was probably higher in 1983 than in 1975. The brake in the earlier trend was caused by exceptionally high rates of inflation and a stock market boom.

Endnotes

1. The original study was undertaken for the Swedish Commission on Wage-Earners and Capital Formation. Detailed results for the 1920–75 period are published in Spånt (1979). An English summary appears in Spånt (1980) and Spånt (1981b). A special report on shareholding is also available from Spånt (1981a).
2. See Spånt (1975) for treatments of more inclusive measures of household wealth.
3. This correction is based on statistics compiled by the National Central Bureau of Statistics. The relation between market prices and taxed values is calculated on all representative purchases (not purchases by relatives) of agricultural real estates, owner-occupied houses, secondary dwellings, apartment houses, and so on. In 1975 the market prices of owner-occupied houses were 73 per cent higher than the taxed values. The corresponding figure was 150 per cent for agricultural real estate, 101 per cent for secondary dwellings, and 45 per cent for apartments houses.
4. Statistics of real property prices cover the period up to and including 1982. Prices in 1983 have been assumed to follow the general rate of inflation.
5. Households have assets of many different kinds besides those mentioned here. Some of these assets too have risen in nominal value during the period under consideration. For calculation purposes, however, these have been equated with financial assets.
6. To neutralize the effects of price changes on the distribution of wealth altogether, however, the wealthiest households would have had to have sold more than half their shares before the rise in prices which took place in 1980 and then retained the proceeds as cash or bank assets. Sales of this magnitude have not occurred.

References

Spånt, R. 'Förmögenhetsfördelningen i Sverige,' Mimeo. (Stockholm, 1975).
—— *Den Svenska Förmögenhets Fördelningens Utveckling* (Stockholm, 1979).
—— 'Wealth Distribution and its Development in Sweden—With an International Comparison,' Mimeo. (Stockholm, 1980).
—— 'Hushållens Aktieägande i Sverige,' Mimeo, (Stockholm, 1981a).
—— 'The Development of the Distribution of Wealth in Sweden,' *Review of Income and Wealth*, 27 (March 1981b), 65–74.

4

Recent Trends in the Distribution of Wealth in the US: Data, Research Problems, and Prospects

James D. Smith

I. Introduction

No matter whose research one examines, the distribution of personal wealth emerges as an incomplete pattern, the interpretation of which is more a vindication of Gestalt psychology than of economic empiricism. Thus, the *general* shape of the distribution of wealth and, indeed, the joint distribution of wealth with other variables, have been known for some time, but because our methodologies have been too crude and too narrow, we have failed to advance much beyond our understanding of 20 years ago. In part the narrowness of methodology by which individual researchers measure wealth holding is a product of the higher cost of eclectic approaches. Perhaps even more important is the uneasiness with which researchers approach new methods; old methods, used over and over, like an old sweater, baggy and thin at the elbows, are a ready source of solace. My intent is to do two things: present a few new data and be critical of our tendencies to cling too tightly to our old ways.

I will begin with a time series of wealth concentration estimates for the United States which span about two decades. The estimates were all produced using the estate multiplier method and have been otherwise carried out to maximize consistency. In the second part of the chapter I comment briefly on the strengths and weaknesses of basic methodological alternatives one has available for measuring wealth holdings, namely estate multiplier, income capitalization, and field surveys. The third part of the chapter deals with the use of emerging eclectic approaches and, finally, I suggest an approach for significantly improving our measurement of wealth.

II. Current Trends in the Concentration of US Wealth

Table 4.1 is a time series of the concentration of US wealth in the hands of the richest 1 per cent and 0.5 per cent of the US population for selected years from 1958 through 1981. The series from 1958 through 1976 is internally consistent with respect to the categorization of assests and the application of the estate multiplier technique as it has evolved in the author's application of it over the last 10 years.[1] It is also consistent in that estimates of wealth holding by the two affluent groups are compared to national balance sheet estimates for each year prepared by Richard and Nancy Ruggles (1981).[2] In Table 4.2 the time series is extended by a preliminary estimate of the concentration of wealth in 1981. The 1981 estimate differs in several respects from the estimates for 1958 through 1976. The estate multiplier application, performed by Marvin Shcwartz of the Internal Revenue Service and reported in Schwartz (1983), used procedures which are similar but different in certain technical respects from those of the author.[3] Because I have not received machine-readable microdata from the Internal Revenue Service (IRS) for the 1981 estate tax returns, it was impossible to produce figures for the top 1 per cent or 0.5 per cent of the population as we have done for the time series in Table 4.1. Schwartz's tabulations, available to us in hard copy, were limited to persons with $300,000 or more and $500,000 or more in gross assets in 1981. Using IRS procedures, Schwartz estimated there were 1.8 million persons in the United States with gross assets of $500,000 or more in 1981—this would account for about 0.8 per cent of the US population in that year, and it is his tabulation of assets for the $500,000 plus population that is compared to national balance sheet estimates in Table 4.2. The last point for which national balance sheet data are available from the Ruggles is end-of-year 1980. The balance sheet data shown in Table 4.1 are the Ruggles' data averaged by pairs of years so that they represent mid-year values for each year for which an estate multiplier estimate is shown. For the Schwartz numbers in Table 4.2, the end-of-year 1980 Ruggles' values were extrapolated to mid-year 1981. This 6-month extrapolation is unlikely to seriously differ from the values the Ruggles ultimately estimate.

When one looks at the time series of total assets or net worth in Table 4.1, the first five observations suggest that wealth

James D. Smith

Table 4.1. The shares of personal wealth owned by the richest 0.5 per cent and richest 1 per cent of the US population, 1958–1976 (amounts in billions of dollars)

Asset	1958 Value held by richest 100.0%	0.5%	1.0%	1958 Share held by richest 0.5%	1.0%	1962 Value held by richest 100.0%	0.5%	1.0%	1962 Share held by richest 0.5%	1.0%
Real estate	620.9	62.5	93.9	10.1	15.1	755.7	79.6	117.8	10.5	15.6
Corporate stock	289.4	175.9	199.2	60.8	68.8	423.6	227.3	264.4	53.7	62.4
Bonds	83.6	31.3	36.0	37.4	43.1	95.2	33.2	38.4	34.9	40.3
Cash	220.8	22.5	32.8	10.2	14.9	284.7	28.9	42.5	10.2	14.9
Debt instruments	46.7	12.5	16.3	26.8	34.9	59.2	16.5	21.8	27.9	36.8
Life insurance (CSV)	70.1	7.5	11.3	10.7	16.1	84.0	7.1	10.7	8.5	12.7
Miscellaneous and trusts	341.8	45.6	52.8	13.3	15.4	387.6	NA	NA	—	—
Trusts	31.2	25.8	27.9	82.7	89.4	46.4	NA	NA	—	—
Miscellaneous	310.6	19.8	24.9	6.4	8.0	341.2	39.8	52.7	11.7	15.4
Total assets	1642.1	332.0	414.4	20.2	25.2	2043.6	432.4	548.3	21.2	26.8
Liabilities	227.6	29.2	38.3	12.8	16.8	314.4	47.8	61.0	15.2	19.4
Net worth	1414.5	302.8	376.1	21.4	26.6	1729.2	384.6	487.3	22.2	28.2
Number of persons (millions)		0.87	1.74				0.93	1.87		

Table 4.1 (*cont*):

Asset	1965 Value held by richest			1965 Share held by richest		1969 Value held by richest			1969 Share held by richest	
	100.0%	0.5%	1.0%	0.5%	1.0%	100.0%	0.5%	1.0%	0.5%	1.0%
Real estate	886.3	94.4	135.8	10.7	15.3	1172.5	117.0	170.7	10.0	14.6
Corporate stock	541.4	317.2	364.9	58.6	67.4	731.3	366.3	423.3	50.1	57.9
Bonds	100.2	57.5	63.2	57.4	63.1	141.2	63.7	71.5	45.1	50.6
Cash	376.2	43.7	62.7	11.6	16.7	505.6	48.1	71.2	9.5	14.1
Debt instruments	68.6	19.8	25.4	28.9	37.0	88.9	21.9	29.6	24.6	33.3
Life insurance (CSV)	97.8	6.5	10.9	6.6	11.1	119.7	8.4	13.8	7.0	11.5
Miscellaneous and trusts	447.8	85.3	101.8	19.0	22.7	606.0	107.0	133.2	17.7	22.0
Trusts	59.9	49.0 ⎫	52.7	81.8	88.0	73.6	60.0	64.5	81.5	87.0
Miscellaneous	387.9	36.3	49.1	9.4	12.7	532.4	47.0	68.7	8.8	12.9
Total assets	2458.4	575.4	712.7	23.4	29.0	3291.6	672.4	848.8	20.4	25.8
Liabilities	416.6	57.0	73.1	13.7	17.5	559.9	75.8	100.5	13.5	17.9
Net worth	2041.8	518.4	639.6	25.4	31.3	2731.7	596.7	748.1	21.8	27.4
Number of persons (millions)		0.97	1.94				1.01	2.03		

Table 4.1 (*cont*):

| | 1972 | | | | | 1976 | | | | |
| | Value held by richest | | | Share held by richest | | Value held by richest | | | Share held by richest | |
Asset	100.0%	0.5%	1.0%	0.5%	1.0%	100.0%	0.5%	1.0%	0.5%	1.0%
Real estate	1501.9	150.9	225.0	10.0	15.0	2435.1	209.0	305.7	8.6	12.6
Corporate stock	784.1	429.3	491.7	54.8	62.7	647.5	248.2	297.8	38.3	46.0
Bonds	159.1	82.5	94.8	51.9	59.6	249.7	64.1	74.4	25.7	29.8
Cash	683.4	63.6	101.2	9.3	14.8	1023.5	68.5	111.8	6.7	10.9
Debt instruments	90.6	30.3	40.8	33.4	45.0	121.5	33.1	44.8	27.2	36.9
Life insurance (CSV)	141.8	6.2	10.0	4.4	7.1	178.9	7.8	12.7	4.4	7.1
Miscellaneous and trusts	752.7	139.8	172.7	18.6	22.9	1084.3	161.7	200.6	14.9	18.5
Trusts	93.1	80.3	89.4	86.3	96.0	97.2	NA	NA	—	—
Miscellaneous	659.6	59.5	83.3	9.0	12.6	987.1	NA	NA	—	—
Total assets	4020.5	822.4	1046.9	20.5	26.0	5643.3	776.9	1032.1	13.8	18.3
Liabilities	719.5	100.7	131.0	14.0	18.2	1047.2	117.0	148.4	11.2	14.2
Net worth	3301.0	721.7	915.9	21.9	27.7	4596.1	659.6	883.2	14.4	19.2
Number of persons (millions)		1.04	2.09				1.08	2.15		

Estate Multiplier Estimates

a. Richness is measured in terms of gross assets. Net worth is preferred to gross assets as a classifier, but the microdata for 1958 which would have permitted such an arrangement were destroyed by the IRS. The microdata for 1962, 1965, and 1969, and 1972 and 1976, were therefore ordered by gross assets to produce estimates consistent with those for 1958.

b. Real estate is shown as its market value without deduction of mortgages, liens, or other encumbrances. In 1953 and 1958 only real estate located in the US is included. In 1962 the value of real estate located outside the US was brought into the estimate by a change in the law which made foreign real estate subject to estate taxes. The amount of such real estate is, however, seriously underrepresented because the law took effect late in 1962. Only estates for decedents who died after 16 October 1962 and who had acquired foreign real estate (except by gift or inheritance) after February 1962 were required to report it on estate tax returns. In 1965 and 1969 foreign real estate was included along with other real estate.

Included in real estate are land and structures for personal and business use. All other business assets are included in the 'miscellaneous' category. Real estate held in trust is included here to the extent of the trust interest. A relatively small proportion of trust assets are in real estate, but the absolute value of all trust assets is adjusted here for reasons explained elsewhere (see n. g).

c. Corporate stock includes all common and preferred issues. The value of shares in domestic or foreign firms whether traded or closely held are included. Also included are the value of certificates and shares of building and loan and savings loan associations, Federal Land Bank stock, and the value of other instruments representing an equity interest in an enterprise. Accrued dividends are also included. Stock held in trust is also included, but the absolute value is understated.

d. Cash includes balances in checking and savings accounts, currency on hand or in safety deposit boxes, cash balances with stock brokers, and postal savings accounts. Cash in trust is also included (see n. g).

e. Liabilities includes all legal obligations except loans on life insurance policies.

f. Life insurance (cash surrender value) is the amount individuals could expect to receive were they to surrender their policies to the carriers. It takes account of policy loans, accrued dividends, and unearned premiums. Life insurance proceeds reported on estate tax returns are adjusted to reflect the cash surrender value on the date of death because that would be the asset value to living persons whom decedents represent. The adjustment is based on data supplied to us by the Institute of Life Insurance. The adjustment is:
ln(CSV/Proceed) = −5.4458 + 0.0669(Age).

g. 'Miscellaneous' includes such items as consumer durables, personal effects, business assets (excluding real estate), mineral rights, tax sale certificates, judgements, lifetime transfers, and growing crops if not included in the value of real estate.

Trusts represent the actuarial value of reversionary and remainder interests in trusts. This actuarial value is substantially less than the total market value of assets held in trusts.

The separate value of trusts could be estimated directly only for 1965. For other years indirect estimates were made.

National Balance Sheet Estimates

Assets and liabilities are derived from Richard and Nancy D. Ruggles' 'Integrated Economic Accounts for the United States 1947–1980', Working Paper No. 841 from the Institution for Social and Policy Studies at Yale University, 1981 and *Survey of Current Business*, May 1982.

Some rearrangement and some adjustments in the numbers reported by the Ruggles are necessary to align the aggregates with the concepts and classification of wealth used by the Internal Revenue Service in organizing and releasing informations from federal estate tax returns. Households' assets are from Ruggles' Table 2.40. Non-corporate, non-farm assets are from Ruggles' Table 2.22, and farm assets are from Ruggles' Table 2.23. Since Table 2.23 includes corporate and non-corporate farms, asset components are adjusted by the proportion of farm equity held by households, Table 2.40, to net worth of 'corporate and non-corporate' farms, Table 2.23. Farm liabilities are also adjusted by this proportion. All balance sheet items have been adjusted to mid-year estimates b averaging pairs of end-of-year values.

Trusts' asset shown is 54.3 per cent of household's estates and trust reported by the Ruggles. This adjustment is made to provide a direct comparison with trust interest reported in estate tax returns, because for estate tax purposes, one's interest in a trust is the actuarial value of that interest as reflected in a set of tables provided by the IRS for calculating contingency values.

The nature of the IRS tables is that if one took all the beneficiaries of a trust, the sum of their actuarial value would be less than the value of the trust. Analysis using the 1965 estate tax file, the only microdata file in existence which has trust assets separate from other assets, indicate that the actuarial value of trust assets included in the estate tax return will average 54.3 per cent of the value of trusts were the value of a beneficiary's proportionate share of the total trust reported. This analysis will be reported in a forthcoming article in the *Review of Income and Wealth*.

The 1981 estimates of assets are increased by one-half of the percentage increase in total household assets which occurred between the end of 1979 and 1980. Similarly, 1980 liabilities are increased by one-half of the percentage increase from the end of 1979 to 1980 of total household liabilities.

Table 4.2.   *Share of personal wealth held by richest 0.8 per cent of population, 1981 (amounts in billions of dollars)*[a]

Asset	Value held by all persons	Value held by richest 0.8 per cent	Per cent held by richest 0.8 per cent
Real estate	4540.3	592.7	0.13
Corporate stock	1172.1	483.7	0.41
Bonds	391.0	117.7	0.30
Cash	1756.2	167.4	0.10
Debt instruments	228.7	74.5	0.33
Life insurance (CSV)	267.6	23.4	0.09
Miscellaneous and trust	1803.2	495.0	0.27
Total assets	9997.4	1954.5	0.20
Liabilities	1885.5	293.9	0.16
Net worth	8101.9	1660.6	0.20

a. Information for richest 0.8 per cent of population are from Schwartz (1983). National balance sheet figures for all persons are for mid-year 1981 and are derived from Ruggles and Ruggles by extrapolation. The same procedure for distributing trust and farm assets as used in Table 4.1 apply here. Estimate of the asset holding of the richest 0.8 per cent of the population are from Schwartz. See notes at the end of Table 4.1.

concentrated in the hands of the richest 1 per cent or 0.5 per cent of the population remains essentially unchanged. In 1976, however, the time series shows a marked drop in the share of total personal wealth held by these two groups. Indeed, both groups lost about one-quarter of their share in total personal wealth from 1972 to 1976. Was the decline real? Was society becoming markedly more egalitarian? The answers to both questions appear to be Yes. A logical follow-up question is, Will it last? The answer is, Maybe. Let us turn to the basis for these answers.

If one looks at the portfolios of these two rich groups in 1972 and 1976, one finds that with two significant exceptions the total dollar value of assets in their portfolios increased in the interval between the two observations. Of the two exceptions, one is particularly striking, however. In 1972 (mid-year) the richest 0.5 per cent of the population owned $429 billion in corporate stock. In 1976 (mid-year) the corporate stock in the portfolio of this group amounted to $248 billion, a decline of $178 billion. Similarly, the richest 1 per cent of the population held $491 billion in corporate stock in 1972 and only $297 billion in 1976, a decline of $194 billion. There were also declines in bond holdings, but on a much smaller scale. Were the rich abandoning Wall Street or was Wall Street abandoning the rich. Probably some of both, but much more of the latter than the former. Consulting the integrated Accounts, cumulative revaluation of corporate stock held by households over the years 1973, 1974, and 1975 was − $197 billion. One can hardly argue that these two most affluent groups were selling off corporate stock to other households because if that were the case, one could find significant increases in the dollar value of other items in their portfolios. A more reasonable conjecture is that the wealthy sold off some shares at lower market values, but they suffered substantial portfolio losses as the market declined and these losses account for the smaller share of the total personal net worth and total assets they held in 1976. Thus, the decline in concentration was real and the society more egalitarian. Table 4.2 sheds some light on the question of the permanency of the redistribution.

Keep in mind that Table 4.2 is the wealth holding and portfolio composition for the richest eight-tenths of 1 per cent of the population in mid-year 1981 as estimated by Marvin Schwartz of the Internal Revenue Service. Thus, we are talking about a group of affluent wealth holders which does not line up with either of the two groups in Table 4.1, being a little bit larger than the smaller one and a little bit smaller than our larger one. We would thus expect that the concentration of wealth in the hands of this group of wealth holders in any year would fall somewhere between the shares reported for the two groups in Table 4.1 if the procedures for estimating their wealth were identical. However, the procedures used by the Internal Revenue Service tend to produce somewhat higher estimates than those used for Table 4.1. On the basis of past comparison between the IRS procedures and our own, it is believed their procedures would result in estimates about 20 per cent higher than those shown in Table 4.1. The IRS results in Table 4.2 are not inconsistent with the 1976 estimates in Table 4.1 and certainly do not suggest that we have moved away from the relatively egalitarian estimate for 1976. When one looks at the holding of corporate stock in the new IRS estimates, the share held by the richest 0.8 per cent is also consistent with the 1976 estimate. This is interesting because cumulative revaluation from the end of 1976 to the end of 1980 amounted to $386.6 billion. The value of corporate stock held by households was more than 50 per cent greater at the end of 1980 than it was at the end of 1976. Why then did not the share of the richest 1 per cent, and 0.5 per cent of wealth holders return to its earlier levels? When we receive the microdata for the 1981 estimates, we will, of course, make direct comparisons using the procedures employed for Table 4.1, but there is nothing in the IRS published data to suggest that the 1976 estimates are a transitory deviation in the long-term trend. For the time being the best guess is that the reduction in the share of wealth held by those in the 1 per cent and 0.5 per cent groups will persist.

In Figure 4.1 the share held by the richest 0.5 per cent of the population is plotted from 1922 to 1976 and then tentatively extended to include the Schwartz estimate for the richest of 0.8 per cent in 1981. This provides a longer term perspective which also corroborates the conjecture of declining wealth concentration at the very top of the wealth pyramid. This perspective supports the notion that there are long-term dynamics at work which are acting to reduce the share of the crème-de-la-crème of wealth holders. Cross-sectional observations showing large declines in concentration, such as for 1976, may be the synergistic impact of short-term market adjustments and changes in social structure. When figures become available for 1983 we may well see that the concentration of wealth has increased in the face of the sustained and sharp increase in corporate equity prices in the preceding 18 months.

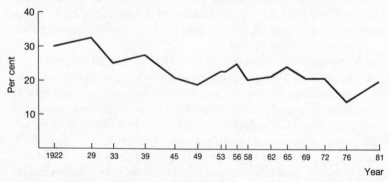

Fig. 4.1 *Share of net assets owned by 0.5 per cent of the US population 1922 to 1981*[a]

a. Point for 1981 is share owned by richest 0.8 per cent of population.
It was estimated from Schwartz (1983), Fig. G, p. 7.

III. The Basic Estimation Approaches

In this section we comment briefly on the advantages and disadvantages of the three direct wealth estimation techniques: the estate multiplier, income capitalization, and field surveys. None of these methods is adequate for estimating the total distribution of wealth. Each has some advantages and some disadvantages.

1. The Estate Multiplier Approach

This approach will in principal produce relatively precise estimates of the distribution of wealth among individuals. It has generally been used for estimating wealth holding of persons in the upper tail of the distribution, but can under certain circumstances provide estimates of the entire distribution. Furthermore, it is relatively inexpensive to apply if one treats machine-readable data from estate tax returns as a free good, produced as a by-product of the operation of the tax system. Its precision is due to the fact that completing tax returns is a non-voluntary exercise of citizenship scrutinized by the state.[3] As with other estimation procedures, there are a number of problems which are quite well known to practitioners. For instance, there is a marked tendency for non-filing by estates only moderately above the filing threshold. One would expect that the number of returns filed would be a monotonically decreasing function of size of estate. One finds in IRS data that starting at the filing level, the number of returns filed first increases with estate size and then decreases, a most unlikely representation of the distribution of estates.[4]

It also probably understates the value of cash and other bearer instruments as well as jewellery, housewares, works of art, and similar assets which can be distributed informally among heirs. It also is likely to understate business assets and real estate which are not traded in active merkets and whose value is determined for tax purposes by appraisal or estimation. The heirs are, in general, motivated to provide the lowest plausible appraisal or estimation.

The estate multiplier method can be applied to the entire population of decedents, not just those sufficiently affluent to file a federal estate tax return. Such an application requires a dual-frame sample and systematic access to probate records and/or death tax records at the state and local level.[5] (More on this in the next section.)

Although the estate multiplier method produces relatively precise results and could be applied so as to capture the entire distribution, the results are most suited to analytical issues related to national saving and capital formation, not to welfare, because it does not associate wealth holding with family units.

It is also the case that the estate multiplier method relies on mortality rates to weight the estate tax return data. There remain important questions about the degree to which social class differentials in mortality rates are captured by the traditionally used adjustments.

2. *Income Capitalization*

Income capitalization methods can be applied inexpensively to income tax return data to estimate the value of certain assets whose yields are reported.[6] The method suffers a number of important problems, however. First, the asset holding unit is a tax return, not necessarily representative of a family nor of an individual. It is useful only in estimating the value of assets which have explicit yields which are reported on tax returns. Thus, consumer durables, residential structures, and idle land are not directly captured. Similarly, state and local bonds cannot be estimated because their yields are not reported on tax returns. Furthermore, the appropriate capitalization rate across income recipients is not well understood and although a mean rate of return is perfectly adequate for estimating aggregates, even small differentials in yields which are correlated with level of asset holdings will result in distributions which may deviate substantially from the real distribution.

3. *Field Surveys*

One perceived advantage of field surveys is that they provide researchers with substantial discretion about the information they request of respondents. Unfortunately, what is requested of respondents and what is supplied are often quite different. The issue of asking people about their wealth has deep historical roots. Questions on asset holdings were asked in the 1860 Census (see, for example, Soltow (1975)). The Survey Research Center has over the years done a number of field surveys in which some information on asset holding and debt has been collected (see Katona and Lansing

(1964) or Barlow et al. (1966), for example). Indeed, an effort is currently under way to collect information on selected assets and pension rights. In general, the Center has resisted serious studies which would result in detailed estimates of the distribution of wealth, particularly in the upper tail.

The most serious attempt to measure the distribution of wealth by survey research techniques was carried out by the Census Bureau for the Board of Governors of the Federal Reserve System (see Projector and Weiss (1966)). Even with several years of methodological work preceding the survey, measurement errors and sample biases precluded satisfactory measurements of the upper tail of the distribution. It has long been clear to sampling statisticians in applied research that measuring high variance characteristics in rare populations with single-frame, area probability samples is prohibitively expensive. This is exactly the problem faced in measurements in the upper tail of the distribution of wealth. Five or 6 per cent of the population holds between 35 and 45 per cent of private net worth and 90 to 100 per cent of some financial assets. The richest of these 5 or 6 per cent of the asset holders hold close to 1,000 times the amount of net worth held by their less prosperous but affluent peers. The obvious strategy is to use multi-frame samples.

In the case of income and wealth measurements, federal income tax returns used as list frames have been coupled with area probability frames to construct samples. Although this is a technically appropriate strategy, it may create delicate situations for tax administrators. For instance, a *Washington Post* editorial earlier this year attacked the Internal Revenue Service for providing names from tax records to the Survey Research Center. This helped preclude delivery of additional sample names and the survey, which had run into very high non-response rates for persons whose names had been provided by the IRS, ended up with unacceptable sample sizes in the upper tail.

Unfortunately, sampling frames are not the only problem which render sample surveys inadequate for measuring a complete wealth distribution. Greater problems are posed by non-response bias and response error.[7] When careful methodological studies are carried out simultaneously with field measurements, it becomes abundantly clear that non-response (both interview non-response and item non-response) increase with economic status. Doormen,

gatekeepers, and telephone answering services prevent interviewers from making physical or phone contact with high income
and high wealth respondents. There is every reason to believe that
these barriers will become even more widespread with advances in
consumer electronics which already provide a variety of inexpensive means of filtering phone calls and making uninvited visits to
grounds and structures difficult.

IV. Eclectic Approaches to Measuring Wealth Holders

By eclectic approach, I mean combining two or more or the three
basic approaches as well as merging and matching data sets. Work
of this kind was carried out by Martin David over two decades ago.
In the Wisconsin Asset and Income Study (WAIS) he matched
income and property tax records with social security earning
records and information collected through personal interviews (see,
David et al. (1974)). The matching was done using a variety of
identifiers, including social security numbers. Scheuren combined
Current Population Survey, Social Security, and income tax return
data using Social Security number (see Kilss and Scheuren (1978)
and Kilss et al. (1978)). There have also been matches of estate tax
returns with the last income tax returns filed by decedents and by
heirs of the decedents (see Steuerle (1982)). Smith (1975) combined
tax returns, death certificates, and social security earning information for residents of Washington DC. It appears that some
Scandinavian countries will soon use administrative record
matches in lieu of interviews to conduct censuses.

Richard and Nancy Ruggles (1974) pursued statistical matching
of data sets in the 1960s. Basically, this approach attributes to
records of one data set one or more variables from records of
another data set on the basis of some variables common to both data
sets. Although the approach has some obvious uses, it requires
caution in interpreting the relationship which will appear to exist
between the non-common variables in the two records. For
instance, if age and sex of individuals are available in one record
and age and labour income are available in another record, matching on age is no assurance that sex and labour income are meaning-
fully related in the resultant data set. Indeed, it is likely that some
systematic bias will be introduced into the perceived sex–labour

income relationship. Ben Okner (1972) statistically matched tax returns and survey schedules in the 1970s.

Greenwood (Chapter 6) and Wolff (1980) have both been imaginative users of synthetic data sets for estimating household wealth. They have been cautious in interpreting the joint distributions which result from their data sets. There will be a continuing need for wealth estimates that emerge from statistical matching operations. The procedure, however, is better applied to concerns with the distribution of welfare, rather than for measurements which will support subsequent analytical studies of the dynamics of wealth accumulation or economic growth. Just as those of us who have used basic approaches will agree they are limited, I think the producers and users of synthetic data sets will agree that their methods represent a second-best solution to the problem of unavailable data bases which relate income, wealth, and other variables. Although better solutions are expensive and require the cooperation of organizations which see little incentive for cooperating, if we are to make significant progress in understanding distributed and behavioural issues related to wealth at the household level, systematic planning and subsequent cooperation by researchers in and out of government will be necessary.[8]

1. A Suggested Eclectic Approach for Better Wealth Estimates

Finally, let me outline a rather simple eclectic approach for improving the quality of information we have on the size distribution of household wealth, and, for that matter, probably the quality of balance sheet data. The approach requires considerable advance planning, but would be a relatively inexpensive way of significantly increasing our knowledge of wealth and associated variables at the household level. The method requires an ability to draw a stratified sample of decedents by size of decedent's estate and other characteristics such as age, ethnicity, residential location, and marital status. This ability is provided by the combined use of the Uniform Death Certificate and federal estate tax return. Death certificates can be thought of as a census of decedents over a period of time, such as a year. Using the basic estate multiplier approach, information on death certificates permits one to infer certain characteristics of the living population. A death certificate does not, however, contain information on decedents' wealth. For each decedent for whom a federal estate tax return is filed, however, there exists a death certificate. It is, therefore, possible to ascribe to each death certificate for which an estate tax return exists the value of gross assets. Once this is done a statistician is in a position to design a stratified sample of death certificates using the demographic information contained on the death certificate and gross assets ascribed from the estate tax return. All those death certificates for which federal estate tax returns were not filed would be ascribed a gross asset value of 'less than the estate tax filing threshold'. Legislation now provides for this threshold to increase from its current (1983) level of $275,000 to $325,000 in 1984, to $500,000 in 1986, and $600,000 in 1987 and after. Once a sample is selected, exact matching can be used to bring into the data base detailed information from federal estate and income tax returns and from social security earnings records. Not only would it be possible to bring in information from income tax returns recently filed by the decedent, but also information for the income tax returns filed by the heirs of the decedents. Matching estate and income tax returns is not a new departure (see Steuerle (1982)). We, of course, at this point would have detailed asset information only for the decedents who filed federal estate tax returns. Detailed asset information for the rest of the sample would require information from death tax returns and probate records at the state or county level. This poses some problems, but moving from death certificates to probate and death tax returns is not new (see French (1966) or McGowan (1972)). The sample of the lower asset group could be relatively small—10,000 might well suffice.

Finally, stratified sub-samples of the full sample could be selected for personal interviews of decedents' survivors. This too has been done. Sussman et al. (1970) report interviewing survivors of decedents about the assets of decedents and about survivors' use of inheritances, and their personal relations with the decedents.

Endnotes

1. The author's use of the method and the refinements which evolved have benefited from a long association with the work of Raymond Goldsmith and Nancy and Richard Ruggles with respect to national balance sheets. Robert Lampman contributed significantly to the conceptualization of certain procedures. Guy

Orcutt and Steve Franklin contributed to a number of statistical insights.
2. The Ruggles' data are modified slightly to suit the uses here. See notes to Table 4.1 for further details.
3. Estimates in the United States have generally been made with pre-audited returns. Such applications understate the value of assets held by the living population sufficiently affluent to file returns by between 5 and 20 per cent. The exact amount by which returns understate assets is not clear but conversations with knowledgeable persons suggest that the understatement is in the range indicated.
4. For a discussion of the non-filing problem, see Smith et al. (1977).
5. For examples of local area wealth estimates, using the estate multiplier technique, see French (1966), McGowan (1972), and Smith (1975).
6. See, for example, Yaple (1936) and Stewart (1939). More sophisticated uses of income capitalization in conjunction with other tools have been undertaken by Greenwood (1973).
7. In the Survey of Financial Characteristics of Consumers, which used an income tax return list frame for the upper tail, non-response rates were 60 per cent for the richest stratum. See Projector and Weiss (1966).
8. It is not the intent of this chapter to address the issue of how advanced planning and cooperation might be achieved, but it is clear that neither the incentive structures facing academically based researchers nor those in government are such that they will come together 'as though moved by an invisible hand'.

References

Barlow, R., Brazer, H., Morgan, J. *The Economic Behavior of the Affluent* (Washington, DC, 1966).

David, M., Gates, W., Miller, R. *Linkage and Retrieval of Microeconomic Data* (Lexington, Massachusetts, 1974).

French, R. 'An Estate-Multiplier Estimate of the Personal Wealth of Oklahoma Residents, 1960.' Ph.D. dissertation, University of Oklahoma (1966).

Greenwood, D. 'An Estimation of US Family Wealth and its Distribution from Microdata, 1973', *Review of Income and Wealth*, 29 (March 1983).

Katona, G., Lansing, J. 'The Wealth of the Wealthy', *Review of Economics and Statistics*, 46 (Feb 1964).

Kilss, B., Scheuren, F.J. 'The 1973 CPS-IRS-SSA Exact Match Study', *Social Security Bulletin*, 41 (Oct 1978).

Kilss, B., Scheuren, F.J., Aziz, F., DelBene, L. 'The 1973 CPS-IRS-SSA Exact Match Study: Past, Present and Future'. In: Social Security Administration, *Policy Analysis With Social Security Research Files*, proceedings of workshop held in Williamsburg, Virginia, Report No. 52 (March 1978).

McGowan, D.A. 'The Measurement of Personal Wealth in Centre

County, Pennsylvania.' Ph.D. dissertation, Pennsylvania State University (1972).

Okner, B. 'Constructing a New Data Base From Existing Microdata Sets: The 1966 MERGE File', *Annals of Economic and Social Measurement*, 1 (July 1972).

Projector, D.S., Weiss, G.S. *Survey of Financial Characteristics of Consumers* (Federal Reserve Board, Washington, DC, 1966).

Ruggles, R., Ruggles, N. 'A Strategy for Matching and Merging Microdata Sets', *Annals of Economic and Social Measurement*, 3 (April 1974).

Ruggles, R., Ruggles, N. 'Integrated Economic Accounts of the United States: 1957–1980', Institution for Social and Policy Studies Working Paper No. 841 (1981).

Schwartz, M. 'Trends in Personal Wealth, 1976–1981', *Statistics of Income Bulletin*, 3, (Summer 1983).

Smith, J.D. 'White Wealth and Black People: The Distribution of Wealth in Washington, DC'. In: Smith, J.D. ed. *The Personal Distribution of Income and Wealth, Studies in Income and Wealth*, vol. 39 (New York, 1975).

Smith, J.D., Franklin, S.D., Orcutt, G.H. 'The Intergenerational Transmission of Wealth: A Simulation Experiment', In: Juster, F.T. ed. *The Distribution of Economic Well Being, Studies in Income and Wealth*, vol. 41 (New York, 1977).

Soltow, L. 'The Wealth, Income and Social Class of Men in Large Northern Cities of the United States in 1860'. In: Smith, J.D. ed. *The Personal Distribution of Income and Wealth, Studies in Income and Wealth*, vol. 39 (New York, 1975).

Steuerle, E.C. 'The Relationship Between Realized Income and Wealth', OTA Paper No. 50, US Department of Treasury (Dec 1982).

Stewart, C. 'Income Capitalization as a Method of Estimating the Distribution of Wealth by Size Groups', *Studies in Income and Wealth*, vol. III (New York, 1939).

Sussman, M., Cates, J., and Smith, D., *The Family and Inheritance* (New York, 1970).

Wolff, E.N. 'Estimates of the 1969 Size Distribution of Household Wealth in the US From a Synthetic Data Dase'. In: Smith, J.D. ed. *Modeling the Distribution and Intergenerational Transmission of Wealth, Studies in Income and Wealth*, vol. 46 (Chicago, 1980).

Yaple, M. 'The Burden of Direct Taxes as Paid by Income Classes', *American Economic Review*, 26 (Dec 1936).

II RECENT ESTIMATES OF THE CONCENTRATION OF HOUSEHOLD WEALTH

5

Wealth, Income, and the Economic Status of Aged Households

Daniel B. Radner and Denton R. Vaughan[1]

I. Introduction

This chapter examines the economic well-being of age groups in the US using data on both income and wealth. The emphasis is on aged households. Although income will be discussed, we will focus more on wealth in order to exploit relatively current data on wealth that have become available recently.

Annual money income before taxes is the most frequently used measure of economic well-being in the US. Estimates usually are obtained from household surveys, and the family unit or household ordinarily is used as the unit of analysis. Of course, annual money income before taxes is far from an ideal measure of economic well-being. An important exclusion is non-cash income, from both government and private sources, which is a significant source of economic resources for most groups of the population. Also, by using pre-tax income, the resources available to the unit can be distorted. In addition, an annual time period is not the most appropriate time period for many purposes. Lifetime income is often more appropriate for studies of inequality, while sub-annual income is more appropriate for examining short-run economic well-being.

Measures of economic well-being that are confined to income omit the wealth of the unit, although income from assets ordinarily is included in income. A relatively new data base, the 1979 Income Survey Development Program (ISDP) file, allows us to examine both income and wealth.

Several different methods of combining income and wealth have been used by researchers. Perhaps the best-known method converts the stock of wealth into a flow and adds that flow to the flow of income. In that method, wealth is converted into an annuity for the expected remaining life of the unit (for example Murray (1964), Weisbrod and Hansen (1968), Taussig (1973), Wolfson (1979)).[2] Moon (1977) has applied this method to the aged. A variant of the simple annuity approach has also been used; in that method the estimated annuity allows the unit to reach the same utility level as its optimal consumption path, rather than the highest constant consumption path (Nordhaus (1973), Irvine (1980), Beach (1981)).

Comparing different age groups using the annuity approach has been criticized on the grounds that the method does not take into account the likelihood that the income of young units will increase and that those units will ordinarily be able to increase their wealth as they age (Projector and Weiss (1969)). Some researchers have tried to take this into account essentially by estimating future earnings (Nordhaus (1973), Taussig (1973), Irvine (1980)). For limited purposes, some researchers have taken a simpler approach to combining income and wealth and summed current income and liquid assets (David (1959), Steuerle and McClung (1977)) or income and net worth (Steuerle and McClung (1977)).

In this chapter we take a different simple approach to considering both income and wealth. We utilize income and wealth primarily as a two-dimensional classification. Our approach does not implicitly spread the wealth out over the expected lifetime of the unit, as the annuity method does, but is concerned with a much shorter time horizon. For example, what resources do units have to withstand emergencies, to deal with unexpected expenses or loss of income? In examining this aspect of the problem, the liquidity of the assets held is very important, although even illiquid assets can often be borrowed against. In most cases we examine net worth, but more liquid concepts of wealth will also be examined.

In this chapter we are not directly interested in the question of what happens to overall measures of inequality if (the annuity value of) wealth is added to the income measure. Instead, we are more interested in the question of the short-term 'adequacy' of the economic resources of population groups.

Average amounts (for example of income or wealth) have often been used in analyses of the economic well-being of different groups. However, averages are not adequate to examine questions about the economic well-being of groups, especially for aged groups, which are of particular interest to us. Those groups contain units in very different economic situations. Thus, it is important to look behind the averages to the distributions of both income and wealth. Our two-dimensional classification facilitates the examination of distributions. Because we have a particular interest in the aged population, it will be useful to separate the population into age (of household reference person) groups, since wealth patterns would be expected to be different for different age groups.

All estimates shown in this chapter are on a household basis. For convenience we assume that the income and wealth of the household are resources for all members of the household and only for members of the household. Thus, relatives of persons in the household who do not live in the household (for example, parents or children) are assumed to have no claim on the resources of the household. In some cases we take into account the number of persons in the household when we examine the economic resources of the household.

Section II briefly describes the wealth data used and presents definitions of important concepts used in the chapter. In Section III summary data on net worth by age of household reference person are presented to provide an overview of the wealth holdings of the population. In Section IV the distribution of age groups among wealth and income quintiles and the joint distribution of income and wealth are examined. Section V discusses households with low income and low wealth, by age group. Adjustments are also made for size of household. Section VI contains a summary and conclusions.

II. Data and Definitions Used

1. Data

The ISDP was an interagency effort involving the Bureau of the Census and headed by the Department of Health and Human Services. The Program was established to develop and test a new household survey design for producing more accurate and, from a public sector point of view, more useful measures of the economic resources of the population of the US. Several field tests were carried out in the course of 1977–80. The 1979 panel, the largest of these, was essentially a pilot survey conducted as a final test prior to implementing a full-scale operational effort in the early 1980s (see Ycas and Lininger (1981) for a more detailed overview of the ISDP).

The sample for the 1979 panel was nationally representative and consisted of approximately 7,500 participating households.[3] The information obtained in the panel included labour force activity, income, assets, debts and detailed socioeconomic characteristics. The panel was multi-wave in design with an initial interview followed by four up-date interviews conducted at 3-month intervals over the course of a year. A final round-up interview was conducted in the second quarter of 1980. The data used in this paper are primarily from the fifth wave, which contained most of the data on wealth; interviewing for that wave was carried out in January, February, and March 1980. Despite the nature of the survey content and the level of respondent effort required, cooperation was quite good by general standards. Slightly more than 90 per cent of eligible households agreed to be interviewed for the first wave. By the completion of the sixth wave, participation had only dropped an additional six or seven points (to about 7,000 households).

The income data suffer from the underreporting which is common to household surveys. However, overall the ISDP data appear to be better than the income data in the Current Population Survey (especially in regard to transfer income), although much more analysis of the data is needed (Vaughan, et al. (1983), Vaughan (1983)).

There are known to be problems with the wealth data. While there is some evidence of marked increases in the identification of asset ownership compared to earlier estimates (Vaughan et al. (1983), Vaughan (1983)), unfortunately item non-response on asset values (for assets other than owner-occupied housing and vehicles) was quite high. Item non-response rates on those asset values ranged from a low of about 20 per cent for sample persons with savings and credit union accounts to a high of about 65–75 per cent for persons owning stocks and mutual fund shares (66 per cent) and non-active business interests (77 per cent). Thus, very substantial proportions of the final asset value aggregates stem from values assigned on the basis of 'hot deck' imputation.[4]

The post-imputation estimates of net worth and of most asset types presented here suffer from substantial underreporting. Financial assets appear to show the highest percentage of underreporting. However, a comparison of survey aggregates by type of asset to independent benchmarks suggests results that are similar to the 1962 Survey of Financial Characteristics of Consumers (SFCC) (Projector and Weiss (1966), Pearl et al. (1982)).

One characteristic of the ISDP wealth data is that the extreme upper tail of the net worth distribution shows a far lower share of net worth than other sources of wealth data show; the ISDP file does not contain any extremely large holdings of wealth. This 'absence' of the extreme upper tail is at least partly the result of the nature of this survey; the emphasis was on obtaining data for low- and middle-income units. Thus, it was expected that the upper tail would not be measured well. Non-response problems undoubtedly are an important factor, and coding and top-coding restrictions might also be important.[5]

Despite the very real problems with item non-response and underreporting, there are indications that the post-imputation estimates from this file are not unreasonable. Changes in portfolio shares over the 1962–79 period, as implied by a comparison of the ISDP and SFCC results, seem plausible (a decline in the importance of stocks and mutual fund shares and an increase in the importance of interest-bearing assets and of real assets) (Pearl et al. (1982)). Preliminary tabulations of net worth components and total wealth by household income, age, and other demographic variables (Radner (1981), Pearl and Frankel (1981)), appear to be quite sensible on the whole.

Taking these early results into account, and realizing that alternative sources of wealth information are also plagued by severe limitations in terms of completeness or availability of ancillary variables of interest, or can only be generalized to the US household population with some difficulty, we feel that further and more detailed exploration of the ISDP wealth data is warranted.

2. *Terms and Concepts*

In general the demographic concepts we use are the same as or similar to those employed by the Bureau of the Census in its Annual Demographic Supplement to the Current Population Survey. The data presented in the paper pertain to the civilian non-institutional population living in the fifty states and the District of Columbia at the dates of interview. All estimates are on a household basis. The household reference person (householder) is the person (or one of the persons) in whose name the home is owned or rented. Age classifications are based on the age of the householder at his or her most recent birthday.

Income is defined on a before-tax basis and is presented at annualized rates, that is, as the measured 3-month value times four. All money income received by household members during the 3 months preceding the month of interview is covered, including one-time or lump sum payments such as life insurance proceeds, gifts, or other irregular money income.[6] While capital gains are not expressly covered in the 3-month income concept, some capital gains may have been reported under lump sum payments. Bank withdrawals and money borrowed are excluded. Conceptually, all other sources of money income are included.

Net worth consists of all assets less all debts covered by the survey.[7] In our terminology net worth is defined to be wealth minus unsecured debt.[8] With the exception of home and vehicle equity, all net worth components were valued as of 31 December 1979. Home and vehicle equities, which are collected in wave two, were valued as of mid-1979. Both assets and debts are described more fully below.

Wealth is defined as the value of all assets covered by the survey, as described below, less any debts secured by those assets. Several items sometimes included in wealth are excluded. The most important exclusions are social security and private pension wealth (including equity in annuities). Also excluded are trusts, the value of royalties, and the equity value of life insurance. Wealth is the sum of the following items:

Home equity. The difference between the market value of owner-occupied housing, as estimated by the respondent, and the amount of any outstanding mortgages on the residence. Equity in other residential property, such as vacation homes, was measured separately and is included under the category 'other assets'.

Durable goods. The equity in vehicles owned by all household members plus the market value of household durables (furniture, television sets, stereos, appliances, and so forth).

Business equity. The value of owner-operated farm or non-farm businesses or professional practices net of debts secured by the business.

Liquid financial assets. This term includes cash on hand, amounts held in checking accounts, amounts held in savings and credit union passbook accounts, and the value of US savings bonds.

Non-liquid financial assets. The value of bonds (other than US savings bonds), certificates of deposit, personal loans, and mortgage debt owed to household members, and the market value of publicly traded stocks and mutual fund shares, net of associated secured debt.

Other assets. The market value of real assets other than own home (farm property other than an own farm business, and residential property including houses, apartments and condominiums, commercial or industrial property, and undeveloped land) less associated mortgages or other debts, the equity in farm and non-farm business interests when the household member was not actively engaged in the management and operation of the business, and the equity in assets not specified elsewhere.

In general, unsecured debt is any debt owed by members of the household as of the survey reference date that is not secured by the assets included in the concept of wealth. Specifically, unsecured debt includes instalment debt (store or credit card bills), and non-instalment debt (personal loans obtained through a financial institution, unpaid medical bills, and money owed to private individuals), and educational loans. Debt not classified elsewhere is also included here.

III. Summary Data on Net Worth

In this section data on net worth by age of reference person are summarized, including mean and median amounts, size distributions, and the composition of net worth.[9] Some data on income are also presented. Nine age classes are used in most tables in this paper: six summary classes that include all ages, and three detailed age classes within the age 65 and over summary class. The detail within the aged group is very important, not only because that group is of particular interest to us, but also because substantial differences in the distribution of economic well-being exist between the younger aged households and the older aged households.

When analysing the economic well-being of different age groups it is important to note that the composition by type of household differs greatly among age groups. Compared to non-aged households, aged households tend to be smaller and to have female householders more often. This is particularly true for households in the 75 and over age group. More than one-third of all aged households are females in one-person households, compared to one-tenth of non-aged households. These differences should be kept in mind when the income and wealth data for age groups are examined. Adjustments for size of household are made in some of the estimates shown later in this paper.

Mean and median amounts of income and net worth by age of reference person are shown in Table 5.1.[10] Mean household income (3-month income annualized) ranges from a low of $11,050 for the 75 and over age group to a high of $28,400 for the 45–54 group, showing the familiar pattern of relatively low means for the young and old age groups. Median incomes show a similar pattern, although the amounts are lower. Relative mean incomes (the mean for the group divided by the overall mean) range from 0.52 for the 75 and over age group to 1.34 for the 45–54 group (Table 5.2). Age groups under 35 and 65 and over have relative means of less than 1.00. Because the distribution of income is more skewed for aged than for non-aged households, relative medians (not shown) are below relative means for the aged groups. For example, the relative median is 0.52 and the relative mean is 0.61 for the 65 and over group.

Mean net worth ranges from a low of $8,880 for the under 25 group to a high of $105,740 for the 55–64 group. (It is important to note that these estimates are almost certainly understated, and to a greater extent than the income estimates.) In terms of relative means, the range is from 0.14 to 1.69. The pattern is low relative means in the under 35 groups followed by gradually increasing then decreasing relative means. Median net worth ranges from $3,450 to $51,440; of course, because of the skewness of the distributions, the median is far below the mean in every age group.

All age groups 55 and over show relative means for net worth that exceed their relative means for income; age groups under 55 show

Table 5.1. *Mean and median income and net worth, by age of householder, 1979*

Age of house- holder	Sample cases	Weighted number of households (thousands)	Annualized income ($)[a]		Net worth ($)[a]	
			Mean	Median	Mean	Median
All ages	6,922	82,211	21,260	16,500	62,430	25,770
Under 25	621	6,613	14,150	12,860	8,880	3,450
25–34	1,441	19,272	20,160	18,000	24,520	12,110
35–44	1,089	14,014	25,390	20,430	64,950	29,820
45–54	1,049	12,975	28,400	24,180	79,120	39,180
55–64	1,155	12,722	25,500	19,330	105,740	51,440
65 and over	1,567	16,614	13,070	8,630	79,380	38,720
65–9	489	5,570	15,560	9,750	90,040	47,300
70–4	411	4,818	12,790	9,040	85,480	45,440
75 and over	667	6,226	11,050	7,460	65,130	28,410

a. Dollar amounts are rounded to the nearest $10.

Table 5.2. *Relative mean values, by age of householder, 1979*

Age of householder	Income	Net worth	Net worth —consumer durables —home equity	Financial assets —debt
All ages	1.00	1.00	1.00	1.00
Under 25	0.67	0.14	0.08	0.06
25–34	0.95	0.39	0.23	0.06
35–44	1.19	1.04	1.00	0.63
45–54	1.34	1.27	1.29	0.98
55–64	1.20	1.69	1.87	2.27
65 and over	0.61	1.27	1.37	1.82
65–9	0.73	1.44	1.50	1.95
70–4	0.60	1.37	1.48	1.60
75 and over	0.52	1.04	1.17	1.87

the opposite situation. Another way of looking at the relationship between income and net worth is to examine the ratio of mean net worth to mean income. ·Those ratios range from 0.63 for the youngest age group to 6.68 for the 70–4 group, compared to the overall estimate of 2.94. Thus, not surprisingly, when mean amounts are used, the older age groups have far more net worth relative to income than the younger age groups.

Of course, there are large differences in economic well-being within age groups that cannot be shown using mean and median amounts. The size distribution of net worth within age groups is shown in Table 5.3. The principal point that we want to make in this table is that substantial dispersion is present in all age groups. For example, except for the youngest age group, in each age group the modal size class and the classes above and below that class contain less than 53 per cent of the households in the age group. Thus, in each of those age groups at least 47 per cent of the households are two or more classes away from the modal class in net worth.

Table 5.4 shows the percentage composition of net worth for each age group. Home equity is a relatively constant percentage of net worth across age groups. However, the mean amounts (which can be approximated using Tables 5.1 and 5.4) show large differences, ranging from $2,680 (under 25) to $31,450 (age 55–64). Financial assets are relatively low in importance for the younger groups and relatively important for the older groups. The differences are more pronounced using mean amounts, with the mean for the 55–64 group seventeen times the mean for the under 25 group. For the age groups under 35, financial assets are split about evenly between what we call liquid and non-liquid assets. For the age groups 35 and over, non-liquid assets are relatively more important, constituting about 75 per cent of the total.

Business equity shows a steady decline in importance in the older age groups, and the mean amounts also decline. Other assets are a relatively constant percentage of net worth except for the under 25 group. The 70–4 group shows a relatively high percentage, but that difference could result from a few sample cases with large amounts. Durable goods are quite important for the youngest age groups, but that importance declines rapidly with age; mean amounts peak in the 55–64 group, then decline as age increases. Unsecured debt is important only for the youngest age groups, although the mean

Table 5.3. *Percentage distribution by size of net worth within age groups, 1979*

Size of net worth ($)	Age of householder									
	Total	Under 25	25-34	35-44	45-54	55-64	65 and over	65-9	70-4	75 and over
Total	100.0	100.0	100.0	100.0	100.0	100.0	100.0	100.0	100.0	100.0
Negative	5.2	10.7	9.9	4.6	4.4	2.5	1.0	1.6	0.3	1.0
0	0.3	0.0	0.0	0.3	0.2	0.6	0.5	—	1.4	0.1
1-999	6.4	19.0	6.9	4.6	3.9	4.5	5.7	5.3	4.5	7.0
1,000-4,999	13.2	29.7	18.6	13.0	8.9	6.9	8.6	7.0	9.3	9.3
5,000-9,999	8.5	17.3	11.4	9.1	5.6	3.8	7.1	4.4	6.4	10.0
10,000-19,999	11.3	9.8	16.9	8.5	7.9	9.7	11.8	9.4	8.8	16.2
20,000-29,999	8.7	5.9	10.3	9.8	9.5	6.5	8.0	7.8	9.1	7.3
30,000-49,999	13.9	5.2	12.7	14.1	17.7	14.8	15.1	18.3	13.3	13.6
50,000-99,999	15.4	1.8	8.3	17.4	18.3	22.2	19.8	18.3	21.9	19.5
100,000-199,999	10.0	0.2	3.8	11.5	15.1	14.8	12.2	15.7	12.6	8.7
200,000-499,999	5.6	0.3	1.2	5.3	6.3	10.3	8.7	10.6	11.3	5.0
500,000 +	1.5	—	—	1.9	2.2	3.5	1.6	1.6	1.0	2.1

— No cases

Table 5.4. Percentage composition of net worth for age groups, 1979

Age of householder

	Total	Under 25	25–34	35–44	45–54	55–64	65 and over	65–9	70–4	75 and over
Net worth	100	100	100	100	100	100	100	100	100	100
Wealth	103	113	111	105	103	102	101	101	100	101
Home equity	33	30	40	34	34	30	32	33	32	30
Financial assets	27	23	15	20	22	34	35	34	29	44
Liquid	7	12	7	5	6	8	10	10	9	12
Non-Liquid	20	11	8	14	16	26	25	24	20	32
Business equity	13	16	14	20	16	11	7	9	7	5
Other assets	18	6	14	19	21	17	18	16	24	13
Durable goods	12	37	28	13	10	9	9	10	8	8
Unsecured debt	3	13	11	5	3	2	1	1	0	1

amount is highest for the 35–44 group.

We have seen in Table 5.4 that the composition of net worth differs among age groups. We will now examine the relative positions of different age groups using relative means of three alternative definitions of wealth. Net worth (NW) is the most comprehensive concept of wealth that is available in our data. Net worth minus consumer durables and home equity (NWCH) is a comprehensive definition that excludes two major asset types that primarily produce service flows, rather than financial returns. Financial assets minus unsecured debt (FAD) is a limited definition that emphasizes liquidity.

In Table 5.2 we see that the relative mean of each group age 65 and over rises as we move from NW to NWCH to FAD (that is from most comprehensive to least comprehensive definition). In most cases, the age groups under 55 show declines. Not only do the relative means for aged groups increase, but those relative means are greater than 1.00 for each definition. We will return to these differences later.

IV. The Distribution of Households Among Wealth and Income Quintiles

In this section the distribution of households among wealth and income quintiles and the joint distribution of wealth and income are shown. Table 5.5 shows the distribution of households of different ages among income quintiles and net worth quintiles. The income and net worth quintiles shown in this table are defined over all households. Before discussing the distributions in the table it is useful to mention the amounts of income and net worth represented by some of the quintiles. The bottom income quintile consists of households with $7,324 or less in annualized money income before tax, while the top quintile consists of households with $30,897 or more. The bottom net worth quintile consists of households with $3,143 or less, the second quintile consists of households with $3,144 to $15,608, and the top net worth quintile consists of households with $86,680 or more. The two bottom quintiles of net worth contain amounts that are quite low—for example, those amounts are all below median annualized household income ($16,500).

The top panel of Table 5.5 shows the distribution of households

Table 5.5.　*Percentage distribution of households among net worth and income quintiles, 1979*

	Age of Householder									
Quintiles	All ages	Under 25	25–34	35–44	45–54	55–64	65 and over	65–9	70–4	75 and over
Net worth										
1	20	47	29	18	14	12	12	11	11	13
2	20	36	28	19	14	11	18	12	16	24
3	20	12	25	20	21	17	19	19	18	21
4	20	5	13	22	24	28	24	26	21	24
5	20	1	6	22	27	32	27	32	34	18
Total	100	100	100	100	100	100	100	100	100	100
Income										
1	20	27	12	13	13	17	40	32	39	48
2	20	25	21	16	12	16	30	30	34	28
3	20	26	24	21	18	19	14	15	12	14
4	20	18	29	21	23	21	7	10	5	4
5	20	4	14	29	35	26	9	12	10	6
Total	100	100	100	100	100	100	100	100	100	100

in each age group among net worth quintiles. We see that the under 35 age groups tend to be concentrated in the lower net worth quintiles, the 35–44 age group is fairly evenly spread among the quintiles, and the 45 and over age groups tend to be more concentrated in the upper quintiles. Within the aged group, the 65–74 groups are concentrated in the upper quintiles, while the 75 and over age group is spread fairly evenly among the quintiles. Thirty per cent of the 65 and over group is in the bottom two quintiles. Of course, these patterns are consistent with the differences in size distributions shown in Table 5.3. It is apparent here also that there is a great deal of dispersion in amounts within each age group.

The bottom panel of Table 5.5 shows the distribution of households among income quintiles. The age groups under 55 in general show more households in the upper income quintiles than in the upper net worth quintiles and fewer in the lower income quintiles than in the lower net worth quintiles. For example, the 35–44 group shows 29 per cent in the top income quintile, but only 22 per cent in the top net worth quintile; that group shows only 13 per cent in the bottom income quintile, but 18 per cent in the bottom net worth quintile. Thus, as we saw earlier (Table 5.2), the households under 55 have relatively more income than net worth. The households 55 and over show the opposite pattern; this opposite pattern also holds for the detailed aged groups. For example, for the 75 and over group, 6 per cent were in the top income quintile, but 18 per cent were in the top net worth quintile.

We will now turn to the joint distribution of income and net worth by examining, for each income quintile, the distribution of households among net worth quintiles (Table 5.6). We see the familiar positive correlation between income and net worth. For example, in the bottom income quintile, 40.5 per cent (8.1/20.0) of the households are in the bottom net worth quintile, while only 6.5 per cent (1.3/20.0) are in the top net worth quintile. In contrast, in the top income quintile only 4.5 per cent are in the bottom net worth quintile, while 44.5 per cent are in the top net worth quintile. This general pattern of positive correlation between income and net worth holds within each of the age groups also (Radner and Vaughan (1984)).

Despite the correlation between income and net worth, there is still a substantial amount of dispersion of net worth within income groups. For example, no net worth quintile contains more than

Table 5.6.   *Percentage joint distribution of households among net worth and income quintiles, 1979*

Income quintiles	Net worth quintiles					
	1	2	3	4	5	Total
1	8.1	4.8	3.5	2.2	1.3	20.0
2	5.5	4.5	3.5	3.5	2.9	20.0
3	3.6	4.9	5.0	3.5	3.1	20.0
4	2.0	4.5	4.6	5.1	3.8	20.0
5	0.9	1.2	3.4	5.6	8.9	20.0
Total	20.0	20.0	20.0	20.0	20.0	100.0

44.5 per cent of the households in the income quintile. In the three middle income quintiles, each net worth quintile contains at least 10 per cent of the households in the income quintile.

V. Households with Relatively Low Income and Relatively Low Wealth

We will now look at the two-dimensional classification of income and net worth and examine the proportion of households in each age group at the bottom of the income–net worth distribution. The percentage of households with low income and low wealth for each age group is shown for three different definitions of low wealth in Table 5.7. These definitions are: (a) the bottom 40 per cent of the distribution of net worth (NW); (b) the bottom 60 per cent of the distribution of net worth minus consumer durables and home equity (NWCH); and (c) the bottom 60 per cent of the distribution of financial assets minus unsecured debt (FAD). Although large percentages of these distributions are included in the 'low' group, the distributions are so skewed that in general the groups are confined to small amounts of wealth (Table 5.8). In all cases, the definition of low income is the bottom 20 per cent of the income distribution.

Using NW, for all ages, 12.9 per cent of all households are in the lower group defined above. For the youngest group, 23.4 per cent are in the lower group, while for the 25–64 groups only 9.3 to 10.2 per cent are in that group. For aged households, 20.1 per cent are in

Table 5.7. *Percent of households in each age group in the specified income–wealth percentiles, 1979*

Income–wealth percentiles	Age of householder									
	All ages	Under 25	25–34	35–44	45–54	55–64	65 and over	65–9	70–4	75 and over
Unadjusted for household size										
Income 1–20% and:										
Net worth 1–40%	12.9	23.4	9.7	9.9	9.3	10.2	20.1	14.7	18.4	26.0
Net worth—consumer durables—home equity 1–60%	16.1	24.9	11.0	11.2	11.1	12.9	28.9	21.1	32.3	33.3
Financial assets—debt 1–60%	15.4	25.9	11.5	10.9	11.3	12.2	25.3	20.8	26.8	28.1
Adjusted for household size										
Income 1–20% and:										
Net worth 1–40%	12.8	20.8	12.2	12.7	9.6	9.3	15.4	11.3	14.9	19.4
Net worth—consumer durables—home equity 1–60%	16.3	20.6	13.8	13.8	13.3	12.4	25.0	17.4	27.5	29.9
Financial assets—debt 1–60%	16.3	21.8	14.5	16.0	13.8	12.4	20.7	17.2	20.5	23.8

Table 5.8. *Upper bounds for income and wealth amounts, 1979 (amounts in US$)*

Household size	Annualized Income 1–20%	Net worth 1–40%	Net worth–consumer durables–home equity 1–60%	Financial assets–debt 1–60%
Unadjusted for household size	7,324	15,608	5,267	2,214
Adjusted for household size				
1 Person				
aged	5,047	9,875	3,722	1,449
non-aged	5,480	10,723	4,042	1,574
2 Persons				
aged	6,369	12,462	4,697	1,829
non-aged	7,075	13,844	5,218	2,032
3 Persons	8,392	16,420	6,189	2,410
4 Persons	10,752	21,038	7,930	3,088
5 Persons	12,732	24,913	9,390	3,657
6 Persons	14,381	28,138	10,606	4,130
7 Persons or more	17,817	34,861	13,140	5,117

the lower group, ranging from 14.7 per cent for the 65–69 group to 26.0 per cent for the 75 and over group. Thus more than one-fourth of the 75 and over group had annual income of less than $7,325 and net worth of less than $15,609 (Table 5.8).

Using NWCH, 16.1 per cent of all households are in the lower group. Again, the percentages for the youngest group (24.9) and the aged group (28.9) are relatively high, with the age groups between showing much lower percentages (11.0 to 12.9). One-third of the 75 and over group is in the lower group.

Using FAD produces results that are generally between the results for the other two definitions. Looking at all households, 15.4 per cent are in the lower group. The percentages for the youngest group (25.9) and the aged group (25.3) are about the same, with the age groups between again showing much lower percentages (10.9 to

12.2). The 75 and over group shows 28.1 per cent in the lower group.

Thus, all three definitions show the same pattern by age: high percentages in the youngest (under age 25) and oldest (65 and over) groups, with fairly constant relatively low percentages in the age groups between. All three detailed aged groups show percentages above the percentages for each age group in the 25–64 range, using all three definitions.[11]

In order to facilitate comparisons among the three definitions of wealth, standardized percentages of households with low income and low wealth (all ages = 1.00) are shown in Table 5.9. The relative positions of the 25–64 age groups show little change when the definition is altered. The under 25 group has its highest value using the net worth definition (the only definition that includes home equity and consumer durables) and lowest using NWCH. For the 65 and over group, the percentage is lowest for NW and highest for NWCH. Two of the three detailed aged groups deviate from the pattern for the 65 and over group. For the 65–9 group the percentage is highest for FAD, while for the 75 and over group the percentage is lowest for FAD.

1. Adjustment for Size of Household

When the distribution of income is examined as an indicator of the distribution of economic well-being, researchers often adjust that distribution for differences in size of unit. In this chapter we will adjust income and wealth for size of unit using an equivalence scale based on the US poverty lines. The amounts were divided by the scale values to obtain the adjusted amounts.[12] We make no claim that this is obviously the best scale to use, but only that it is a familiar scale that can be used to see whether this adjustment makes a substantial difference.[13] It is appropriate to adjust wealth as well as income because here we are viewing wealth primarily as a resource for consumption in the short run, and that resource is being viewed as spread over the persons in the household. Looking at the distribution of net worth, these adjustments produce relative improvements for households age 65 and over, with the 35–54 group showing a relative decline (Radner and Vaughan (1984)). The change in the income distribution is substantial, with aged households moving up and households in the 35–54 groups moving down.

Table 5.9. *Relative percentage of households in each age group in the specified income–wealth percentiles, 1979*

Income–wealth percentiles	Age of householder									
	All ages	Under 25	25–34	35–44	45–54	55–64	65 and over	65–9	70–4	75 and over
Unadjusted for household size										
Income 1–20% and:										
Net worth 1–40%	1.00	1.81	0.75	0.77	0.72	0.79	1.56	1.14	1.43	2.02
Net worth—consumer durables—home equity 1–60%	1.00	1.55	0.68	0.70	0.69	0.80	1.80	1.31	2.01	2.07
Financial assets—debt 1–60%	1.00	1.68	0.75	0.71	0.73	0.79	1.64	1.35	1.74	1.82
Adjusted for household size										
Income 1–20% and:										
Net worth 1–40%	1.00	1.62	0.95	0.99	0.75	0.73	1.20	0.88	1.16	1.52
Net worth—consumer durables—home equity 1–60%	1.00	1.26	0.85	0.85	0.82	0.76	1.53	1.07	1.69	1.83
Financial assets—debt 1–60%	1.00	1.34	0.89	0.98	0:85	0.76	1.27	1.06	1.26	1.46

Looking at the two-dimensional classification of adjusted income and adjusted net worth, and using the bottom income quintile and the bottom two net worth quintiles as the lower group, for all ages we find 12.8 per cent in that group (Table 5.7). This shows no significant change from the unadjusted data. For the youngest group, 20.8 per cent are in the lower group (a small decline), while the 25–64 groups show 9.3 to 12.7 per cent (generally a small increase). For aged households, 15.4 per cent are in that group (down from 20.1); the range is from 11.3 per cent (65–9) to 19.4 per cent (75 and over).[14] In general, the gap between aged and non-aged has been reduced, but not eliminated.

Using NWCH and FAD, the same pattern of changes occurs as for NW. The under 25 and aged groups show declines in their percentages, while the 25–54 groups show increases; the 55–64 group shows little change. The relative percentages for these definitions show the same basic patterns as before adjustment (Table 5.9). Despite the shifts, the percentage for the 65 and over group still exceeds the percentage for each other age group over age 24, for all three definitions of wealth, both before and after adjustment for household size.

The cutoff points that were used to define low wealth, of course, were arbitrary. The sensitivity of the results to those definitions for aged households with low income is examined in Table 5.10. That table shows a classification based on the ratio of size of wealth to the income cutoff point for the bottom 20 per cent of the income distribution, after adjustment for household size (Table 5.8, column 1). The three definitions of wealth are shown. Thus, we see that 15 per cent of aged households have income in the bottom quintile and net worth that is less than double the income cutoff. This table can be related to Table 5.7 in a simple way; for net worth, the bottom 40 per cent consists roughly of households with a ratio below 2.00. For NWCH, the bottom 60 per cent consists roughly of households below 0.75, and for FAD, the bottom 60 per cent consists roughly of households below 0.25.

Looking at net worth, we can see that the results are not very sensitive to the cutoff point chosen. For example, for households age 65 and over, using a cutoff that is only half the original cutoff (1.00) only excludes 3 per cent of the households in the age group. This would leave the aged percentage above the percentages for the 45–64 age groups, even when those age groups use the original

Daniel B. Radner and Denton R. Vaughan

Table 5.10. *Percentage of households in the specified income and wealth ranges, after adjustment for household size, 1979*

Ratio of wealth to income cutoff amount	Age of householder			
	65 and over	65–9	70–4	75 and over
	Net worth			
Income 1–20%	32	23	34	39
and ratio[a]				
less than 0.50	9	7	9	10
less than 1.00	12	9	13	14
less than 2.00	15	11	15	19
less than 3.00	19	13	17	25
	Net worth–consumer durables–home equity			
and ratio[a]				
less than 0.25	19	16	19	22
less than 0.50	22	17	25	25
less than 0.75	25	17	28	30
less than 1.00	26	18	28	31
	Financial assets–debt			
and ratio[a]				
negative or zero	7	6	11	5
less than 0.25	20	17	20	23
less than 0.50	24	18	27	27
less than 1.00	27	19	30	32

a. Ratio of the household's amount of wealth to the household's bottom quintile income cutoff.

cutoff (12 per cent compared to 9 or 10 per cent). Raising the cutoff by 50 per cent (to 3.00) also does not have a large impact.

NWCH and FAD also show little sensitivity to changes in the cutoff point. The percentages for these two definitions (for the same ratio) are very similar. This similarity results from the fact that aged households with income in the bottom 20 per cent do not have much wealth in business and other assets (the differences between NWCH and FAD). The amounts of NW are higher than the

NWCH and FAD amounts, so that the NW percentages are lower than the NWCH and FAD percentages for the same ratio.

In a very crude way, Table 5.10 can also be used to examine the length of time wealth could be used to replace the cutoff amount of income for households in the bottom income quintile.[15] For example, for the 65 and over group, 19 per cent of households had income in the bottom quintile and net worth that would replace the cutoff income for less than 3 years, while for 15 per cent it would replace cutoff income for less than 2 years. Turning to the more liquid definitions of wealth, 24 per cent of the 65 and over group had income in the bottom quintile and FAD that would cover the cutoff income for less than 6 months; the corresponding percentage was 22 for NWCH. Comparing these percentages to the 32 per cent of aged households with income in the bottom 20 per cent, we see that three-fourths of aged households in that income group had FAD that would cover the cutoff income for less than 6 months. It should be noted that these comparisons would show somewhat higher ratios (longer coverage times) if the household's income rather than the quintile income cutoff amount had been used as the standard. We did not think that actual income amounts should be used as the standard because some of these amounts were extremely low; a floor on the amounts was needed, and the quintile cutoff amount was chosen.

VI. Summary and Conclusions

Annual money income before taxes is the measure ordinarily used to assess the economic well-being of the US population. One of the deficiencies of that measure, at least for some purposes, is the omission of wealth. In this paper we summarize the patterns of household wealth holding for age of householder groups shown in the 1979 Income Survey Development Program file. Our emphasis on age groups results from the substantial differences in wealth between the age groups, as well as our particular interest in the economic well-being of aged units.

Our overview of wealth holding patterns shows increasing mean net worth as age increases up to the 55–64 age group, then a decline (Table 5.1). All age groups show substantial dispersion in amounts of net worth within the age group (Table 5.3). Patterns of the composition of wealth also differ among age groups, with older households holding a higher percentage of their net worth in financial assets than younger households do (Table 5.4). When less comprehensive definitions of wealth (e.g. financial assets minus debt) are used, the mean for aged households increases relative to the means for other age groups (Table 5.2).

When households are distributed among overall quintiles by size of net worth, the under 35 age groups tend to be concentrated in the lower quintiles, and the 45 and over age groups tend to be more concentrated in the upper quintiles (Table 5.5). When the distribution among income quintiles is examined, the age groups under 55 in general show more households in the upper income quintiles than in the upper net worth quintiles and fewer in the lower income quintiles than in the lower net worth quintiles; households 55 and over show the opposite pattern (Table 5.5). The joint distribution of income and net worth among quintiles shows the familiar positive correlation, but there is still a great deal of dispersion in net worth within income quintiles (Table 5.6).

Tables 5.7 and 5.9 summarize the data for households with relatively low income and low wealth, both before and after adjusting the income and wealth data for size of household, and using three definitions of wealth. Looking at the estimates before adjustment for size of household, we see that 12.9 per cent of all households were in the bottom income quintile (less than $7,325) and the bottom two net worth quintiles (less than $15,609), while the corresponding figure for households age 65 and over was 20.1 per cent. The percentage for the 65 and over age group exceeds the percentage for each group in the 25–64 age range. Shifting to the bottom three quintiles of net worth minus consumer durables and home equity (less than $5,268) instead of net worth produces fairly small relative changes among age groups. Using the bottom three quintiles of financial assets minus unsecured debt (less than $2,215) produces only small relative changes also. In these three variations, the percentage of households age 65 and over that have both relatively low income and relatively low wealth ranges from 20.1 to 28.9 per cent; in all three cases those percentages are substantially above the percentages for all ages and for each age group in the 25–64 range. Adjusting for size of household decreases the percentages for households 65 and over to a range from 15.4 to 25.0 per cent; those percentages remain above the percentages for all households and for each age group in the 25–64 range, although the differences are reduced.

The proportions of aged households with relatively low income and wealth do not appear to be very sensitive to the particular wealth cutoff points chosen (Table 5.10). Finally, in a comparison between the amounts of wealth and the income cutoff point for the bottom income quintile, it was estimated that about one-fourth of aged households had income in the bottom quintile and financial assets minus debt that would cover that income cutoff for less than 6 months (Table 5.10).

In this chapter we have found that substantial dispersion in amounts of wealth held is present for aged households, even within income groups. A substantial proportion of aged households have both relatively low income and relatively low wealth; that proportion is above the proportion for all ages and for each age group in the 25–64 range. Much work needs to be done to examine in more detail the characteristics of households in the various income–wealth categories. For example, labour force participation, marital status, sex, size of household, and size of social security benefits are among the characteristics that require further examination.[16]

Endnotes

1. The authors are greatly indebted to Sharon Johnson, who prepared the esti-mates, and to Benjamin Bridges, John Hambor, and Thomas Juster for their helpful comments. Any opinions expressed are those of the authors and do not necessarily represent the position of the Social Security Administration.
2. Looking at the aged, Hurd and Shoven (1982) capitalized several sources of income and added those values to estimates of wealth. Thus, income flows were converted into stocks of wealth in their method.
3. Both low-income and high-income households were oversampled slightly. The oversampling was carried out by oversampling housing units in the 1976 Survey of Income and Education that had (1975) income of less than $2,500 or more than $36,999. The oversampling at the top was far less than that used in the 1962 Survey of Financial Characteristics of Consumers.
4. Another problem is that missing asset information and missing income infor-mation were imputed independently.
5. This absence of the extreme upper tail would be expected to have a substantial impact on comparisons between survey aggregates and independent control aggregates.
6. Thus, income from assets is included in income at the same time that

income-producing assets are included in wealth. In effect, this assumes that any unexpected expenses (or loss of income) faced by the household occur at the end of the time period. It should be noted that the non-farm self-employment income estimate is the person's 'draw' from the business, rather than net income from the business.

7. Assets and debts of persons under age 16 are excluded from the estimates shown in this chapter.

8. The asset and debt definitions and terminology used in this chapter were chosen to be as similar as possible to the SFCC definitions and terminology. However, some differences remain. In this chapter, at times 'wealth' is used as a general term when we are not referring to any specific definition.

9. Additional estimates appear in Radner and Vaughan (1984). It should be noted that the income estimates have been revised slightly since that paper was written.

10. The estimates in this chapter exclude the small number of sample cases with negative household income.

11. Using data for Canada and the annuity method of combining income and wealth, Wolfson (1979) found an age pattern of the incidence of 'low income' that is very similar to the age pattern of low income and wealth shown here.

12. The scale values used were; 1 person (under 65), 1.024; 1 person (65 +), 0.943; 1 person (weighted), 1.000; 2 persons (under 65), 1.322; 2 persons (65 +), 1.190; 3 persons, 1.568; 4 persons, 2.009; 5 persons, 2.379; 6 persons, 2.687; 7 persons or more, 3.329.

13. The answer to this question could be sensitive to the choice of the scale. The literature on equivalence scales is extensive. See Vaughan (1984) for a recent discussion and comparison of several equivalence scales.

14. For comparison, in 1979 about 12 per cent of all households and 18 per cent of aged households were considered poor based on money income (US Bureau of the Census 1982, Table 22).

15. This comparison is particularly crude because income from assets is included in income.

16. Radner (1984) has examined some of these characteristics.

References

Beach, C.M. *Distribution of Income and Wealth in Ontario: Theory and Evidence* (Toronto, 1981).

David, M. 'Welfare, Income, and Budget Needs', *The Review of Economics and Statistics*, 41 (Nov 1959), 393–9.

Hurd, M., Shoven, J.B. 'Real Income and Wealth of the Elderly', *American Economic Review*, 72 (May 1982), 314–18.

Irvine, I. 'The Distribution of Income and Wealth in Canada in a Life-cycle Framework', *Canadian Journal of Economics*, 13 (Aug 1980), 455–74.

Moon, M. *The Measurement of Economic Welfare* (New York, 1977).

Murray, J. 'Potential Income From Assets: Findings of the 1963 Survey of the Aged', *Social Security Bulletin*, 27 (Dec 1964), 3–11.

Nordhaus, W.D. 'The Effects of Inflation on the Distribution of Economic Welfare', *Journal of Money, Credit and Banking*, 5 (1973), 465–504.

Pearl, R.B., Frankel, M. 'Composition of Personal Wealth of American Households at the Start of the Eighties', paper presented at the American Economic Association meetings, Washington, DC (Dec 1981).

Pearl, R.B., Frankel, M., Williams, R.C. 'The Effects of Missing Information on the Reliability of Net Worth Data from the 1979 ISDP Research Panel', Survey Research Laboratory, University of Illinois (1982).

Projector, D.S., Weiss, G.S. *Survey of Financial Characteristics of Consumers*, Board of Governors of the Federal Reserve System (Washington, 1966).

—— 'Income–Net Worth Measures of Economic Welfare', *Social Security Bulletin*, 32 (Nov 1969), 14–17.

Radner, D.B. 'An Early Look at the Joint Distribution of Wealth and Income, 1979', paper presented at the American Economic Association meetings, Washington, DC (Dec 1981).

—— 'The Wealth and Income of Aged Households', *Proceedings of the American Statistical Association, Social Statistics Section* (1984).

Radner, D.B., Vaughan, D.R. 'The Joint Distribution of Wealth and Income for Age Groups, 1979', ORS Working Paper No. 33, Office of Research, Statistics, and International Policy, Social Security Administration (March 1984).

Steuerle, E., McClung, N. 'Wealth and the Accounting Period in the Measurement of Means', Technical Paper VI, *The Measure of Poverty*, Department of Health, Education, and Welfare (1977).

Taussig, M.K. 'Alternative Measures of the Distribution of Economic Welfare', Industrial Relations Section, Department of Economics, Princeton University (1973).

US Bureau of the Census *Characteristics of Households and Persons Receiving Selected Noncash Benefits: 1980 (With Comparable Data for 1979)*, Current Population Reports, Series P-60, No. 131 (Washington, DC, 1982).

Vaughan, D.R. 'Family Composition and Poverty Status: Recipient Families and Aggregate Benefits from Selected Public Income Maintenance Programs, Spring 1979', Social Security Administration, Office of Research and Statistics (1983).

—— 'Using Subjective Assessments of Income to Estimate Family Equivalence Scales: A Report on Work in Progress', *Proceedings of the American Statistical Association, Social Statistics Section* (1984).

Vaughan, D.R., Whiteman, C., Lininger, C. 'Quality of the Income and Program Data in the 1979 ISDP Research Panel: Preliminary Findings'. In: David, M. ed. *Technical, Conceptual, and Administrative Lessons of* the Income Survey Development Program (ISDP), Social Science Research Council (New York, 1983), 203-27.

Weisbrod, B.A., Hansen L.W. 'An Income-Net Worth Approach to Measuring Economic Welfare', *American Economic Review*, 58 (Dec 1968), 1315-29.

Wolfson, M.C. 'Wealth and the Distribution of Income, Canada 1969-70', *Review of Income and Wealth*, 25 (June 1979), 129-40.

Ycas, M., Lininger, C. 'The Income Survey Development Program: Design Features and Initial Findings', *Social Security Bulletin*, 44 (Nov 1981), 13-19.

6

Age, Income, and Household Size: Their Relation to Wealth Distribution in the United States

Daphne T. Greenwood

Introduction

This chapter deals with the relationships of age, household size, and income to wealth distribution in the United States. Empirical studies and casual observation indicate that many families become wealthier as they grow older. From this, many infer that a substantial part of observed inequality is due to age. The question of how much of the observed inequality in wealth distribution can be explained by differences in age and household size is addressed in several ways in this chapter. Gini coefficients are calculated within age groups, a modification to the Gini coefficient which removes the inequality within households of the same household size and age is devised and calculated, and age and household size are used as explanatory variables, along with total family income, in a linear regression with net worth as the dependent variable.

When measuring wealth inequality the unit of measurement is generally the household. While this appears to be the best choice of available units, it has the disadvantage of treating all households as equal when some contain only one person and others contain several. However, measuring wealth on a per capital basis would not solve the problem very well since it would treat adults and children as equals. It would also ignore 'economies of consumption' which occur when income and wealth pooling increase the standard of living of two previously single persons.

In the modification to the Gini coefficient used here, adjustments have been made for differences in household size as well as for differences in age. The results indicate that single-person households tend to have lower wealth than larger households, even holding age constant. The combination of age and household size in the adjusted Gini measure yields a coefficient of wealth inequality of 0.76, only slightly lower than the 0.82 of the unadjusted Gini.

Section II of this chapter deals with the methods used to estimate a distribution of wealth, Section III with the relationship of age and household size to net worth, and Section IV with the income-wealth relationship. The distribution of wealth among wealth, income, age, and household size groups is calculated. Standard Gini coefficients are calculated for six age categories, and a modification to the Gini coefficient which takes account of wealth variation by age and household size is applied to 1973 data for the United States of America.

II. Estimation of Wealth from Income Tax Microdata

1. Overview

The wealth estimates presented here are imputations derived from income tax, estate tax, and survey data. A much more extensive discussion of the imputation procedure has been presented by Greenwood (1983). From the income tax return, dividends reported for each family unit were capitalized into the value of corporate stock owned, and interest into the value of debt instruments owned. Property tax paid, divided by the effective property tax rate, yielded estimates of the value of real estate owned. These three components of wealth were thus directly estimated by capitalization.

To estimate net wealth, its relationship to corporate stock, debt instruments, and real estate was calculated by linear regression from a sample of 1972 estate tax returns. The parameters estimated from the estate tax returns were used to impute net wealth to each family record.[1] A frequency distribution of wealth by wealth classes was then constructed.

The data base used was the 1973 microdata file produced by the Office of Tax Analysis (OTA) in the Department of Treasury by merging 50,160 observations from the Current Population Survey (CPS) with 45,030 tax records from the 1973 Individual Income Tax Model. In addition, OTA imputed state and local bond interest and property taxes for tax records which did not itemize.

Although most of the information used in this estimate is from the income tax record, the merged OTA file includes households not required to file a tax return, and permits the construction of a family wealth distribution.

2. Capitalization of Dividends and Interest

Corporate stock values (CSTK) were estimated by capitalizing total reported dividends (DIV) of the *j*th family at the average rate of return (dividend–price ratio) on common stock as in equation (6.1), below.

$$CSTKj = DIVj * \frac{1}{r} \qquad (6.1)$$

For 1973, the economy-wide average rate was 3.4 per cent according to Moody's Investors Service. An analysis of microdata from the 1962 Federal Reserve sponsored survey (SFCC) showed no consistent differences in the rates of return received by families in different income classes, suggesting that the average rate was the best predictor of any family's rate of return, regardless of family income level. Earlier studies by Blume, et al. (1974) found dividend–price ratios to be relatively constant across income class until very high incomes ($50,000 + in 1960) were analysed. Average rates were lower for the upper income group. To the extent that this is true, corporate stock owners are underestimated for high-income groups when applying equation (6.1).

The value of all debt instruments (DINST), or interest-paying assets, of the *j*th family was estimated by capitalizing total reported interest receipts by the average rate paid on savings accounts of 1973, 4.5 per cent, as in equation (6.2).

$$DINSTj = \frac{1}{i} \qquad (6.2)$$

The microdata from the SFCC provided evidence that interest rates did not vary systematically with income class, so that an average rate of interest was the best predictor of any family's rate of interest. This rate was comprised of the rates of credit union deposits, savings and loan deposits, commercial bank deposits, as well as privately held mortgages, municipal bonds, corporate bonds, and US government bonds.

While very large denomination corporate and US government bonds paid higher rates of interest than savings accounts, these represented such a small percentage of interest-bearing assets held by families that they did not have a noticeable effect on the total. Interest on municipal bonds (held almost completely by top wealth holders through the early 1970s, according to estate tax estimates) was much lower—close to the rate paid on bank savings—due to the tax-free status of this income. Since the average rate of interest received by SFCC families in 1962 was close to the rate paid on savings accounts, the 1973 rate on savings accounts was used to capitalize all interest in this estimate. (The much greater variety of interest-bearing assets which are now available requires that more complex methods be used in current estimates.)

3. Estimation of Real-Estate Value

The amount of property taxes paid on real estate was used to estimate real estate by equation (6.3), below:

$$RE_j = PT_j \cdot \frac{1}{eptr} \tag{6.3}$$

where RE = gross real estate wealth
$\quad\quad PT$ = property taxes paid on real estate by jth family
$\quad\quad eptr$ = average effective property tax rate in family's state of residence.

Property taxes are reported by itemizers on their income tax returns, and have been imputed to non-itemizers by the Office of Tax Analysis.[2] Effective property tax rates were calculated for each state from weighted averages of Census of Governments' figures on median *effective* rates (property taxes/market value) collected from recent sales. Although there were variations in the rates by county within states, they were much less than the variations between states.

4. Estimations of a Regression of Net Wealth on Gross Assets

In the early 1970s, when the gross estate of a decedent exceeded $60,000 the executor of the estate was required to file a return with the Internal Revenue Service. Where net wealth (after deduction of debts and mortgages) exceeded $60,000, estates were taxed under a progressive system. The minimum filing requirement has been increased substantially during the last few years, and will soon be $600,000. At the time of this estimate (1973), approximately 7 per cent of the population possessed an amount of wealth sufficient that their estate would be required to file a Federal estate tax return following their death.

Using a stratified sample of individual estate tax returns, a linear relationship between net wealth (gross wealth less all debts) and components of gross wealth was estimated. Since the income tax information available on the OTA file is sufficient to generate estimates of corporate stock, debt instruments, and real-estate wealth, net wealth of each family was estimated as a function of these variables.

Although this relationship was estimated using a variety of functional forms, including log-linear, a simple linear multiple regression with no intercept (equation (6.4), below) yielded the best fit.

$$NW_j = 1.041\ CSTK_j + 1.484\ DINST_j + 0.808\ RE_j$$
$$(17.27) \qquad\qquad (19.76) \qquad\qquad (18.98) \qquad (6.4)$$
$$(0.06) \qquad\qquad (0.08) \qquad\qquad (0.04)$$

This equation yielded an R^2 of 0.86, indicating that only 14 per cent of net wealth is *not* explained by these three assets. Residuals were randomly distributed, showing no correlation of either under-prediction or overprediction with the size of net wealth. All the explanatory variables were significant at the 0.001 level, and the overall F-statistic of 665 indicated strong explanatory power. T-statistics and standard errors are listed in the parentheses.

The estimated coefficients are consistent with our knowledge of portfolio composition. While corporate stock has an estimated coefficient of roughly one, real estate typically carries substantial mortgage debt which reduced its effect on net wealth. It is only its strong correlation with durables, insurance, and so on that makes the coefficient this high. Indirectly measured wealth (all kinds other than corporate stock, real estate, and debt instruments) is mostly strongly correlated with debt instruments, which have a coefficient of 1.48. These assets, by their nature, have no debt associated with them. Prior studies have indicated that savings rates are higher among the self-employed (farmers, small business persons) who would have large amounts of wealth measured only indirectly here.

Separate regressions were run on persons with wealth of between $60–80,000 and over $300,000, but the coefficients were not substantially different in the 1972 estate tax sample. Therefore, the relationship was applied to the entire population, including those with wealth levels below $60,000. It should be noted, however, that the method will underestimate the holdings of many low wealth persons, particularly the elderly, who receive asset income but do not file an income tax return. In addition, it will miss most of the consumer durables in non-homeowner households.

When applied to the 1973 OTA file, this method yields an estimated population total net wealth of $2.6 trillion compared to the national balance sheet household sector total of $3.5 trillion for 1972.[3] This was significantly closer than any of the other functional forms tested. The $3.5 trillion includes over $550 billion in consumer durables and inventories, which are underestimated by this method since some are held by non-homeowners with few or no financial assets. Total corporate stock was estimated at $669.2 billion versus a national balance sheet estimate of $657.1 billion, and total interest-bearing assets were estimated here as $892.6 billion compared to $850.1 billion in interest-bearing instruments. The real-estate total of $774.2 billion is less than the national balance sheet average of $960.4 billion, due in part to homeownership of non-filers which was not accounted for in the estimating procedure.

5. Results of the Wealth Estimate

Table 6.1 indicates the distribution of net worth, income, corporate stock, debt instruments, and real estate for US families in 1973. The net worth share of the top 1 per cent of families is almost one-third of personal wealth, in the upper range of prior estate multiplier estates for the share of the top 1 per cent of individuals (see Smith and Franklin (1974)). The share of the top 10 per cent (those families with net worth over $75,797 in 1973), was approximately 70 per cent. There has been little other information from the twentieth century to compare this rather interesting result with, but it is quite close to the share of the top 10 per cent estimated by both Gallman (1969) and Soltow (1975) for the mid-1800s and by Holmes (1893) near the turn of the century.

Table 6.1. *Cumulative percentages of net wealth, income, and assets held by wealth classes, 1973*

Net wealth percentile	Net wealth	Corporate stock	Debt instruments	Real estate	Census money income
1–35	0.0	0.0	0.0	0.0	16.8
36–40	0.1	0.0	0.1	0.0	20.0
41–5	0.3	0.1	0.5	0.4	24.1
46–50	1.0	0.2	1.0	1.8	28.5
51–5	2.1	0.4	1.8	4.5	33.3
56–60	3.6	0.6	2.7	8.7	38.3
61–5	5.5	0.8	3.7	14.6	43.6
66–70	8.0	1.1	5.1	21.9	49.4
71–5	11.2	1.6	6.9	30.9	55.4
76–80	15.3	2.5	10.0	41.0	61.7
81–5	20.9	3.9	14.9	52.7	68.4
86–90	29.2	7.1	24.2	64.3	75.5
91–5	42.5	14.7	40.6	77.3	83.2
96	46.4	17.5	45.6	80.2	84.9
97	51.3	21.1	52.0	83.3	86.6
98	57.6	28.0	59.5	86.7	88.5
99	67.4	39.7	70.5	91.6	91.3
100	100.0	100.0	100.0	100.0	100.0
Top 1%	32.6	60.3	29.5	8.4	8.7
Top 10%	70.8	92.9	75.8	35.7	24.5

III. Variations in Wealth Holding—Effects of Age and Household Size

1. Theoretical Link Between Age and Wealth

Inequality in the distribution of wealth is often explained by reference to 'life-cycle effects', the variations in income and the savings rate out of that income due to household formation, changes in family size, and retirement. Applying what they term the 'accepted theory of consumer's choice' to the income–consumption relationship, Modigliani and Brumberg (1954) have presented a theory of saving and asset accumulation based on lifetime utility maximiza tion. They identify two motives for saving, the first being the desire to increase the estate of one's heirs. The second, and more immediate, reason for saving is to smooth out the variability of current income and bring it into greater conformity with annual consumption needs. Modigliani and Brumberg argue that both consumption and net worth are heavily influenced by income, age, and income expectations, rather than being functionally related to each other.

Extensions and applications of their theoretical approach of lifetime utility maximization grew into what is called a 'life-cycle hypothesis' of saving and asset accumulation (also, see Ando and Modigliani (1963) and Lydall (1955)). On the basis of this, many have argued that a great deal of conventionally measured inequality is due to differences in position in the life-cycle, or for want of a better proxy, to age differences. Paglin's (1975) claim that inequality is overstated and its downward secular trend missed, rests heavily on this assertion.

2. Wealth by Age Class, 1973

In Table 6.2, where the distribution of households and net wealth is given for six age classes, the mean wealth rises steadily with age. This, I believe, is what has given rise to the myth that age accounts

Table 6.2. *Variations in US wealth inequality by age class, 1973*

Head of household	Mean wealth	Share of household (per cent)	Share of net wealth (per cent)	Standard Gini coefficient	Non-wealth holder (per cent)	Top wealth holder (per cent)
25 and under	$ 9,763	8	2	0.89	77	2
26–35	24,096	20	13	0.84	36	5
36–45	36,454	17	16	0.81	30	10
46–55	43,669	18	21	0.78	26	14
56–65	48,068	17	20	0.75	26	20
Over 65	50,855	20	27	0.84	52	21
All households	$37,711	100	100	0.82	35	14

Table 6.3.   *Relative importance of age class within wealth class, 1973*

Wealth percentile	Per cent in age class					
	25 and under	26–35	36–45	46–55	56–65	Over 65
1–35	12.0	20.0	13.8	13.4	11.6	28.6
36–40	18.9	30.1	16.4	13.9	11.8	8.8
41–45	14.3	27.9	16.3	17.1	13.6	10.9
46–50	11.9	26.8	17.8	17.8	16.2	9.5
51–55	9.9	26.3	19.4	20.7	15.2	8.5
56–60	7.2	26.3	21.1	22.3	14.9	8.3
61–65	5.7	24.4	23.6	23.0	14.4	8.9
66–70	5.4	24.3	23.3	21.8	16.5	8.7
71–75	3.6	21.7	22.5	24.6	18.0	9.7
76–80	2.4	19.6	20.0	25.1	20.2	12.7
81–85	1.7	13.7	17.1	27.2	22.9	17.4
86–90	1.7	12.7	17.5	23.6	23.6	20.9
91–95	1.1	7.8	13.3	21.1	26.4	30.2
96	2.3	5.6	11.3	17.3	27.8	35.8
97	0.7	4.7	8.2	15.6	28.1	42.7
98	0.4	5.3	8.4	14.7	27.8	43.4
99	1.5	4.5	7.0	17.9	24.5	44.5
100	1.8	10.8	18.7	22.2	16.8	29.7
Total	8.0	20.0	17.0	18.0	17.0	20.0

(Percentages may not add to 100 across a class due to rounding.)

for a substantial portion of wealth inequality. Gini coefficients decline with increased age up to age 65, but are nowhere less than 0.75. By this estimate, over half of households headed by someone over 65 hold no measured net wealth. However, the highest percentage (21) of top wealth holders for 1973 are over 65.[4]

Table 6.3 provides a summary of the age profile of each wealth class. For example, close to 29 per cent of both the 'no wealth' class (percentiles 1–35) and the top 1 per cent (over $500,000 in 1973) are made up of households headed by someone over 65. When these two extremes are removed, the importance of the over 65 group increases quite steadily as one goes up the wealth distribution. The elderly are more heavily represented as wealth levels increase. But a large number of elderly households have no wealth or, more likely, net wealth under $10,000 which we are missing in the estimating procedure. It is improbable that all of these individuals are on the brink of death (or have been taken by surprise at their own longevity and in miscalculation spent their assets to zero in anticipation of an earlier death). Lack of accumulated assets among the elderly is more likely to reflect a lifetime of low income.

The sudden drop in the share of households over 65 when we move to the top 1 per cent of wealth holders suggests that age is less important in explaining very high wealth levels than in explaining moderate wealth levels. This is the same phenomenon that Wolff (1981) noted when he improved the R^2 of a regression of net worth on age by omitting the very wealthy from the sample. The life-cycle hypothesis performs best in explaining moderate levels of wealth accumulation.

3. Wealth by Household Size, 1973

A further question which arises when analysing wealth inequality is comparability of the measurement units. Wealth is measured here for households, which may contain one or more adults as well as some children. In comparing the wealth of different households there have not been adjustments for differences in the size of the household. Measuring wealth on a per capita basis would not really be satisfactory, either, since children would be counted equally with adults.

Table 6.4 shows, for 1973, the share of total households and of personal net wealth represented by households made up of one,

Table 6.4.   *Distribution of net wealth and households by household size, 1973*

Household size	Share of total households	Share of net wealth
1	19.4	14.1
2	30.7	36.4
3	17.1	17.0
4	15.6	15.6
5 or more	17.4	17.2

(Percentages do not add to 100 due to rounding.)

two, three, four, and five or more persons. Single-person households hold a share of net wealth considerably less than their share of population, while two-person households hold a higher than proportionate share. These smaller household sizes are heavily dominated by young adults and senior citizens. For larger household sizes, share of wealth is very close to share of household.

4. Modifying the Gini Measure of Inequality for Age and Household Size

In the following section, the method used to adjust the traditional Gini coefficient for both age and household size is outlined. Existing inequality among households is measured relative to a modified comparison line rather than Lorenz's 45° line of absolute equality. The modified comparison line reflects the mean wealth of different age–household size groups. This 'between group' inequality may be due to demographic and compositional effects and thus viewed differently in terms of economic and/or social jsutice.

An adjustment to the Gini coefficient was first made by Paglin (1975), who proposed a comparison line which allowed for age differences in equality of distribution. Paglin argued that since economic theory incorporated differences in accumulated assets over the life-cycle even in an otherwise perfectly egalitarian society, the traditional method of drawing a Lorenz curve and calculating the Gini coefficient considerably overstated inequality. Although he referred to inequality of both income and wealth, only one of Paglin's empirical examples used data on wealth. Using the 1962 survey data on wealth from the SFCC, Paglin computed an adjusted Gini of 0.50 and concluded that wealth is much less concentrated than we have been led to believe. However, his method of calculation was pointed out to be erroneous by Nelson (1977), Johnson (1977), and others in a series of critiques. As outlined later in this paper it subtracted age-related inequality from the numerator of the Gini coefficient without subtracting it from the denominator.

Kurien and others have pointed out that age-related variations include more than pure life-cycle adjustments since in recent history older cohorts have had lower lifetime incomes than the younger are likely to have (1977). The same criticism may be applicable to the household effect if other characteristics which affect wealth holding are associated with household size. The greater wealth of two-person versus one-person households may be due to more than asset pooling. In Kurien's words, the ideal partition would be between 'choice-related variation' and 'differential opportunity' variation. Age and household size incorporate parts of both kinds of variation, and removing the inequality associated with these factors may leave an underestimate of non-choice-related inequality.

In another critique of Paglin, Danziger et al. (1977) give examples of demographic effects on the Paglin–Gini, which are of particular importance when analysing trends in inequality. In particular, the greater the concentration of units in cohorts with wealth greatly different from the average, the larger the age–Gini will be (and therefore, the smaller the Paglin–Gini).

These points should caution us to accept the adjusted Gini as a 'lower bound' estimate on inequality which may be compared with the 'upper bound' of the traditional Gini. A mathematical correction to the Paglin–Gini (which removes age-related inequality from the numerator and denominator) was proposed almost simultaneously by Formby and Seaks (1980) and by Atack and Bateman (1979). This corrected method is used here, with the factor of household size added as well as that of age.

The traditional Lorenz curve, plotted as line C in Fig. 6.1, indicates the cumulative shares of wealth held by percentiles of the population (see Table 6.1), beginning with the lowest wealth households. Since roughly 40 per cent of the population holds no measurable net wealth, the standard Lorenz curve does not depart from the horizontal axis until this point. The conventional Gini measures the entire area between line A, the 45° line of perfect equality, and line C. In contrast, the modified Gini measures the area between line B and the standard Lorenz curve. Line B was constructed by dividing the population of the US households into 30 groups, based on the age of the head of household and the number of persons in the household, as in Table 6.5. Groups are ordered by mean wealth, and the percentage of households which they compose as well as share of net worth which they hold follows. For example, single-person households over age 65 (group 17) constituted 8.3 per cent of all households in 1973, held a mean net wealth of $36,095, and 7.9 per cent of private net wealth, whereas two-person households in the same age group were the highest mean wealth group at $62,553, constituted 9.2 per cent of households, and held 15.3 per cent of net wealth.

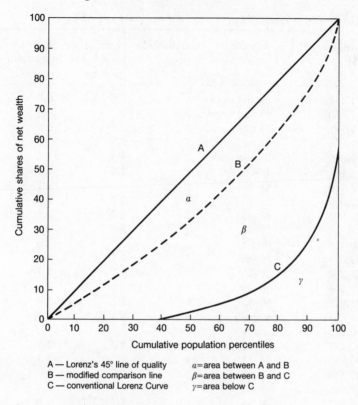

Fig. 6.1   *Illustration of conventional and modified Lorenz curves*

Looking at Table 6.5, one sees that age predominates over household size in establishing position in the wealth distribution, with the lowest five net worth groups all headed by persons 25 and under. The nine highest wealth groups are headed by persons 46 and over. However, single-person households in these upper age groups rank relatively low; seventeenth for over 65, eleventh for 56–65, and seventh for 46–55. This raises questions about these single-person households which cannot be answered from this set of data. Are they predominantly female? Are they single through non-marriage, death of spouse, or divorce? What is their work history? For the younger age groups mean wealth of single- and two-person households is very close. In fact, among the young, wealth does not

Daphne T. Greenwood

Table 6.5. *Wealth by age–household size group, 1973*

Mean wealth ($)	Age class	Household size	Share of households (per cent)	Share of net wealth (per cent)
4,171	25 and under	1	1.6	0.2
7,669	25 and under	5 +	0.3	0.1
9,301	25 and under	3	2.2	0.5
11,584	25 and under	4	0.9	0.3
12,345	25 and under	2	3.5	1.2
14,407	26–35	1	2.4	0.9
17,476	46–55	1	2.3	1.1
21,826	26–35	2	4.2	2.4
21,993	26–35	5 +	4.0	2.4
25,739	26–35	4	5.4	3.7
30,448	56–65	1	3.5	2.8
30,851	36–45	4	4.1	3.3
31,292	26–35	3	4.5	3.7
32,574	36–45	2	1.8	1.6
34,829	36–45	1	1.3	1.2
34,883	over 65	5 +	0.4	0.4
36,095	over 65	1	8.3	7.9
37,797	36–45	3	2.3	2.3
39,747	46–55	3	3.7	3.9
40,430	36–45	5 +	7.3	7.8
43,669	46–55	5 +	4.3	5.0
47,993	46–55	2	4.7	6.0
50,118	56–65	5 +	1.1	1.5
51,460	56–65	2	7.3	9.9
53,720	56–65	3	2.9	4.1
59,067	46–55	4	3.5	5.5
60,239	over 65	4	0.5	0.7
62,253	over 65	3	1.5	2.5
62,428	56–65	4	1.2	2.1
62,553	over 65	2	9.2	15.3

(Percentages do not add to 100 due to rounding.)

vary much for any household size.

Line B was plotted from the cumulation of figures in Table 6.5, in a manner similar to that of the standard Lorenz curve. Beginning with the lowest wealth group, single-person households 25 years of age or under, share of population and share of wealth form the first point on line B. The cumulative shares of the next to the lowest and lowest wealth group are then plotted. The method used differs from Paglin's original suggestion, which understates inequality by computing the P–Gini as the ratio of the area between B and C (β) to the entire area below the 45° line. The MP–Gini used here is the ratio of the area between B and C (β) to the area below B ($\beta + \gamma$).

Where the conventional Gini is measured as

$$\text{Gini} = \frac{\alpha + \beta}{\alpha + \beta + \gamma} \qquad (6.5)$$

the Paglin–Gini would be

$$\text{P–Gini} = \frac{\beta}{\alpha + \beta + \gamma} \qquad (6.6)$$

and has now been more correctly identified as

$$\text{MP–Gini} = \frac{\beta}{\beta + \gamma} \qquad (6.7)$$

When so measured it is 0.76 for the 1973 wealth distribution versus the 0.82 of the standard Gini. The adjustment lowers the Gini inequality measure, but only by six points, or 7 per cent of measured inequality.

IV. Wealth and Income

The correlation levels of income and levels of wealth are far from perfect. Some fairly high-wealth families do not receive a great deal of income flow from their assets (see Steuerle (1982)). Retired persons may receive income from social security or pensions and from assets, but no wage or salary income. In contrast, some high-income families do not have high savings or wealth, particularly if they are young. Dividend and interest income, as reported to the Internal Revenue Service, were used in estimating net wealth for families on the OTA file. The correlation of these with census income, which includes several tax-exempt sources of income, is low. Using a variety of multiple regression forms, I found that age and household size together would account for only 6 per cent of the variation in net wealth while the addition of census income raised the R^2 to 17 per cent.

Table 6.6.   *Simple percentages of net wealth, income and assets held by census money income classes, 1973*

Census class	Net wealth	Census money income	Corporate stock	Debt instruments	Real estate
Lowest 10%	1.8	0.5	1.9	2.1	1.2
11–20	1.8	2.5	1.4	2.4	1.1
21–30	3.7	3.9	2.2	5.2	2.4
31–40	5.1	5.5	2.7	6.5	4.7
41–50	5.5	7.1	3.5	5.8	6.9
51–60	5.9	8.7	3.6	5.7	8.7
61–70	6.4	10.5	3.2	6.2	10.4
71–80	8.3	12.6	4.1	8.0	13.3
81–90	11.4	15.7	6.5	10.9	18.1
91–100	50.1	33.3	70.9	47.2	33.3
Top 1%	24.3	11.2	47.2	20.0	8.1
Top 5%	41.2	23.2	63.5	38.7	22.0

Information on assets by income class is extremely useful in predicting changes in economic behaviour which concern those making tax policy, and provides a basis for evaluating incidence of taxes and tax benefits by wealth and income class. Using the tables and figure which follow one can compare the concentrations of wealth and income over distributions ranked by wealth and income. The standard Gini coefficient for wealth by wealth classes was 0.82 vs 0.46 for income by income classes. Table 6.6 shows the shares of net wealth, income, and assets held by income deciles ranked on a Census family income basis. The top 10 per cent of income-receiving families held 50.1 per cent of net wealth, 70.9 per cent of corporate stock, and one-third of privately held real estate, as well as receiving one-third of the income. For 1973, only 15 per cent of families owned any corporate stock. In Fig. 6.2, two Lorenz curves indicate the cumulative distribution of wealth and income by income class.

1. Conclusion

Differences in total family income are more highly correlated with

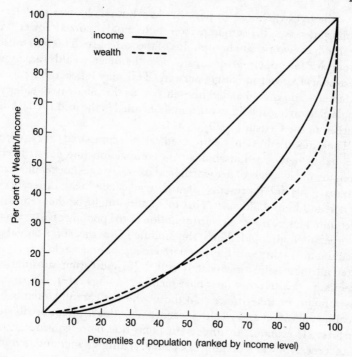

Fig. 6.2 *Lorenz curves of wealth and income by income class, 1973*

variation in family wealth than either age or household size differences, but still do not explain a great deal. Wealth is less concentrated across the income distribution, but only slightly so. While the top 10 per cent of wealth holding families held 70 per cent of net wealth, the top 10 per cent of income recipients held 50.1 per cent of net wealth. Ownership of corporate stock is quite concentrated in either distribution.

Mean wealth rises steadily with age, and the Gini coefficients for inequality of wealth within age group decline up to 65 years of age. But they are still high in each age group, ranging from 0.75 to 0.89. By this estimate, over half of all families headed by someone over 65 years of age hold no wealth, but one-fifth of this group were top wealth holders with assets sizeable enough to require the filing of a Federal estate tax return upon death. In sum, age does not explain a great deal of wealth differences, as other studies have indicated.[5]

While age was more important than household size in determining net wealth, single-person households ranked lower in
wealth than two-person households of the same age. This was most
important for upper age groups, where the mean wealth rankings
were sharply lower for single persons. This may reflect differences
in female- and male-headed households, as the majority of elderly
single-person households were female-headed in the mid 1970s (US
Bureau of the Census (1979) p. 51).

The modified Gini computed here compared measured
inequality between households to a comparison line constructed
from the mean levels of net worth held by thirty age–household size
groups. This line represents inequality associated with differences
in age and household size. This inequality might be theoretically
accounted for by life-cycle accumulation or the pooling of assets in a
two-person household. Thus, the modified Gini measures only the
residual inequality which is unrelated to age or household size. But
after all these adjustments it is still 0.76, indicating substantial
inequality due to other factors as income, savings rates, return on
investment, or inheritance. To those who are careful students of
wealth generation and wealth measurement this is undoubtedly no
surprise. It remains an important point due more consideration
than it receives when making tax policy, setting savings and investment incentives, and creating income maintenance programmes.

Further research should focus on the work history and demographic characteristics of the elderly, as well as separating the 65–75
group from those over 75, in attempting to explain the wide divergence of wealth holdings among the elderly. In addition, estimation
methods need to better account for the assets (particularly real property) of elderly who are not income tax filers. A more recent estimate which is currently in progress attempts to better deal with
these issues.

Endnotes

1. Net wealth, as defined in this estimate, includes all items of durability and realizable cash value, less all debts held by the households. It is equivalent to the
   estate tax measure of wealth, and broader than most survey concepts because it
   includes all debt, as well as personal possessions and the value of equity in life
   insurance, annuities, and retirement funds (where contributions have been paid
   directly by the beneficiary). It does *not* include social security or other pension
   wealth.

2. However, the 1973 file contained no imputations for non-filers, a group which includes many retired persons receiving non-wage income. Thus, assets of this group—small amounts of stock, debt instruments, and particularly, real estate—are unavoidably missed here. A more recent estimate, now in progress, will account for these non-filers when estimating US wealth.
3. The latter figure comes from Ruggles and Ruggles (1982), Table 2.40. It is estimated as the average of the end of the year totals for 1972 and 1973. The Ruggles' figures include consumer durables and household inventories, which are not fully reflected in the OTA data.
4. The use of the term 'top wealth holder' follows Lampman (1962) to refer to persons whose wealth is sufficiently high for a federal estate tax return to be filed.
5. See, for example, Atkinson (1971) or White (1978) for simulation tests of the life-cycle model, and Smith (1975), Mirer (1979), and Wolff (1981) for regression analysis of wealth on age.

References

Ando, A., Modigliani, F. 'The "Life Cycle" Hypothesis of Saving: Aggregate Implications and Tests', *American Economic Review*, 53 (March 1963), 55–84.

Atack, J., Bateman, F. 'The Measurement and Trend of Inequality: An Amendment to a Basic Revision', *Economic Letters*, 4 (1979), 389–93.

Atkinson, A.B. 'The Distribution of Wealth and the Individual Life-Cycle', *Oxford Economic Papers*, 23 (1971), 293–54.

Blume, M.E., Crockett, J., Friend, I. 'Stock Ownership in the United States: Characteristics and Trends', *Survey of Current Business*, 54 (Nov 1974), 16–40.

Danzinger, S., Haveman, R., Smolensky, E. 'The Measurement and Trend of Inequality: Comment', *American Economic Review*, 67 (1977), 505–12.

Formby, J.P., Seaks, T.G. 'Paglin's Gini Measure of Inequality: A Modification', *American Economic Review*, 70 (June 1980), 479–82.

Gallman, R.E. 'Trends in the Size Distribution of Wealth in the Nineteenth Century: Some Speculations.' In: Soltow, L. ed. *Six Papers on the Size Distribution of Wealth and Income, Studies in Income and Wealth*, vol. 33 (New York, 1969).

Greenwood, D. 'An Estimation of US Family Wealth and Its Distribution from Microdata, 1973', *The Review of Income and Wealth*, 29 (March 1983), 23–43.

Holmes, G.K. 'The Concentration of Wealth', *Political Science Quarterly*, 3 (1893).

Johnson, W.R. 'The Measurement and Trend of Inequality: Comment', *American Economic Review*, 67 (1977), 502–4.

Kurien, C.J. 'The Measurement and Trend of Inequality: Comment',

American Economic Review, 67 (June 1977), 517-19.

Lampman, R. *The Share of Top Wealth-Holders in National Wealth, 1922-56* (Princeton, New Jersey, 1962).

Lydall, H. 'The Life Cycle in Income, Saving, and Asset Ownership', *Econometrics*, 23 (April 1955), 131-50.

Mirer, T.W. 'The Wealth-Age Relationship Among the Aged', *American Economic Review*, 69 (June 1979), 435-43.

Modigliani, F., Brumberg, R. 'Utility Analysis and the Consumption Function: An Interpretation of Cross-Section Data.' In: Kurihara, K.K., ed. *Post-Keynesian Economics* (New Brunswick, New Jersey, 1954).

Nelson, E.R. 'The Measurement and Trend of Inequality: Comment', *American Economic Review*, 67 (1977), 495-501.

Paglin, M. 'The Measurement and Trend of Inequality: A Basic Revision', *American Economic Review*, 65 (Dec 1975), 598-609.

Ruggles, R., Ruggles, N.D. 'Integrated Economics Accounts for the United States, 1947-1980', *Survey of Current Business*, 62 (May 1982), 1-55.

Smith, J.D. 'White Wealth and Black People: The Distribution of Wealth in Washington, DC in 1967.' In: Smith, J.D., ed. *The Personal Distribution of Income and Wealth* (New York, 1975).

Smith, J.D., Franklin, S.D. 'The Concentration of Personal Wealth, 1922-1969', *American Economic Review*, 64 (May 1974), 162-7.

Soltow, L. *Men and Wealth in the United States, 1850-1870* (New Haven, Connecticut, 1975).

Steuerle, C.E. 'The Relationship Between Realized Income and Wealth', *OTA Papers* 50, US Department of Treasury (Dec 1982).

US Bureau of the Census *Statistical Abstract of the United States: 1979*, 100th edn (Washington, DC, 1979).

White, B.B. 'Empirical Tests of the Life Cycle Hypothesis', *American Economic Review*, 68 (Sept 1978), 547-60.

Wolff, E.N. 'The Accumulation of Household Wealth Over the Life-Cycle: A Microdata Analysis', *The Review of Income and Wealth*, 27 (March 1981), 75-96.

7

Personal Wealth Distribution in France: Cross-Sectional Evidence and Extensions

Denis Kessler and André Masson

I. Introduction

Almost all possible means for estimating personal wealth distribution have been used in France over the last 10 years. As a result, it seems that our knowledge of wealth accumulation and distribution has improved. Wealth accounts have been computed and are now integrated in the national accounts framework. The size distribution of wealth is now better assessed, each successive study indicating the existence of a somewhat larger inequality of fortune than was previously supposed. Wealth inequality in France seems quite similar to that observed in other developed countries (see Section II).

But to assess the economic and social role of wealth in market industrialized countries—knowing the existence of a possible 'law' of wealth distribution from the international comparison of wealth distribution—it might appear a paradox to say that the measure of personal distribution of wealth seems of little value. To assess the economic and social role of wealth, it is necessary to examine the process of wealth accumulation. The various theoretical approaches (neo-classical or neo-Keynesian) of accumulation behaviour lead to specific ways of interpreting wealth distribution (see Section III).

Theoretical or analytical frameworks for wealth distribution appear quite necessary to (a) pursue sound international comparisons, (b) understand the economic and social forces shaping the distribution of wealth, and (c) analyse the economic and social consequences of wealth inequality.

II. Cross-Sectional Evidence

This section of the chapter is divided into three parts. Part 1 presents briefly the wealth accounts estimates of personal wealth. Those figures seem necessary to estimate the size distribution of wealth. Part 2 presents the four methods that have been used over the last 10 years for estimating the distribution of wealth: direct household sample surveys, income capitalization method, estate duty method, and annual wealth tax files analysis. Part 3 will compare the four methods and show that despite their shortcomings they lead to comparable degrees of instantaneous wealth inequality.

1. The Wealth Accounts Estimates

In order to estimate the size distribution of personal wealth it is necessary to have the best estimates possible of the total amount of wealth held by the household sector. In fact one can argue that the more underestimated is total wealth the less unequal is the wealth distribution. This is the reason why when estimating the size distribution of wealth from a household sample survey it is necessary to use some weighting procedure. But the question is then to dispose of reliable estimates of household wealth coming from other sources. This is true of the French situation in this respect since wealth accounts have now been established and are to become an integrated part of the national accounts framework. Annual estimates of household wealth—as well as the nation's wealth—will soon be available on a regular basis.

The wealth accounts figures have been useful in assessing the global underestimation of wealth accumulation and distribution in France when only sample survey data were available. The wealth accounts now make possible the introduction of realistic 'weights'.

In 1976 the net worth of the wealth of households was 4,700 billion francs, close to two-thirds of the overall wealth of the nation. Three years later at the end of 1979 the net worth of household wealth amounted to 6,656 billion francs. Table 7.1 gives the main assets and liabilities figuring in the wealth accounts. The definition of wealth that has been chosen is rather traditional:

(a) market values in current French francs are used;
(b) durables are excluded but their value has still been computed;

Table 7.1. *Household wealth accounts 1976–1979 (in billions of francs)*

	Assets			Liabilities	
	1976	1979		1976	1979
Land	663	861			
Housing	2,507	3,751			
Other real estate	174	236			
Equipment	154	209			
Inventories	88	114			
Livestock	46	54			
Intangible assets	100	145			
Non-financial total	3,733	5,192			
Cash and money deposits	338	452			
Non-monetary deposits	702	1,109			
Short-term credits	17	30	Short-term credits	85	133
Long-term credits	—	3	Long-term credits	409	710
Insurance reserves	108	164			
Bonds	103	183			
Stocks	208	364			
Financial total	1,477	2,306	*Total credits*	494	843
Overall total	5,210	7,499	*Net value of wealth*	4,716	6,656

Source: Benedetti et al. (1979) for the year 1976 and Milot (1982) for the year 1979.

(c) gold, jewellery, furniture, pieces of art . . . are excluded as well as 'natural resources';
(d) social security wealth and human capital have neither been taken into account nor computed.

2. The Four Methods used to Estimate the Size Distribution of Wealth

Four main methods have been used in France in order to estimate the size distribution of wealth: (a) direct sample surveys; (b) income capitalization technique; (c) estate duty method; (d) annual wealth tax data analysis.

2.1 Direct sample surveys INSEE—the government statistical office—has carried out two direct sample surveys, one in 1973 and the other in 1975. These two surveys were designed to provide estimates of savings. Five thousand households have been surveyed twice on their assets ownership. The difference between the two estimates of wealth was supposed to provide data for a study of savings across households. The collected data have been used to build up the wealth accounts, but have not been published yet. However one can get an idea of the underestimation of wealth in direct sample surveys when considering that the reported wealth in those two surveys amounts only to 50 per cent of the value figuring in the wealth accounts for those given years.

The CREP (Centre de Recherche sur L'Épargne)—a private non-profit organization—has carried out three direct sample surveys in 1975, 1977, and 1980. These surveys were first intended to form a comparison where the same households would be surveyed every 2 years, but this ambitious programme was rapidly abandoned. Sample size is of about 3,000 households each time. As in the INSEE surveys, detailed information on assets ownership has been gathered. But the built-in deficiencies of this approach led to a large underestimation of the value of assets held. To give a few figures, the declared value of stocks represented only 15 per cent of the total value of stock portfolio held by French households and the declared value of bonds amounted only to 10 per cent of the total market value of bonds. But of course the underestimation of assets value is usually smaller for the real assets (for example housing). Another interesting result lies in the fact that the size of underestimation is a positive function of wealth. This contributes to the explanation of why household sample surveys lead usually to a less uneven distribution of wealth than the other methods, even after the application of standard coefficients of revaluation of assets amounts to correct for underreporting.

The 1975 survey led to a wealth distribution where the top decile held about 50 per cent of total household wealth (see Table 7.2). The 1980 survey resulted in a slightly higher degree of inequality. One must note, however, that between 1975 and 1980 better

Table 7.2. *The size distribution of wealth from a CREP sample survey in 1975*

Decile of household	1	2	3	4	5	6	7	8	9	10
Percentage of total wealth	—	0.2	0.5	1.3	2.9	5.4	8.5	12.6	18.5	50.2

estimates of the value of the various assets became available from the wealth accounts.

2.2 Income capitalization method When the government began considering the introduction of an annual wealth tax, the Direction de la Prévision—a division of the Ministry of Finance—was asked to provide detailed information on wealth distribution. The method chosen was the income capitalization technique. Knowing the detailed incomes of taxpayers (from tax returns) and the prevailing rates of return of each asset, it is easy to determine the value of assets held. But this technique was in fact only used to estimate the value of certain assets, that is, shares and stocks, farms and land. For the other assets like housing, each taxpayer of the sample was attributed according to the declared income a certain value of the total amount of the asset considered (this value coming from the wealth accounts).

For a certain number of reasons, all assets cannot be taken into account by the income capitalization technique. The total value of the assets taken into account by this technique represented only 85 per cent of the total personal wealth estimate of the wealth accounts.

The sample consisted of 40,000 taxpayers in 1975. The results obtained are rather striking: the top decile of taxpayers held in 1975 about 57 per cent of gross wealth (see Table 7.3). The poorest half of taxpayers held only 5.5 per cent of total wealth.

According to the income capitalization technique, the Gini coefficient of wealth distribution among taxpayers in 1975 was equal to 0.72 compared to a 0.42 Gini coefficient for the income distribution.

2.3 The estate duty method Only recently the Internal Revenue Service (IRS) resumed collecting detailed information on

Table 7.3. *The wealth distribution in 1975 estimated by the income capitalization technique*

Decile of	1	2	3	4	5	6	7	8	9	10
Taxpayers	0	0.5	1.0	1.5	2.5	3.5	6.5	10.0	17.0	57.5
Households		2.5		2.0	3.0	4.5	7.0	11.0	16.0	54.0

Source: Coutière et al. (1981).

Table 7.4. *Concentration of personal net wealth by the estate duty method, 1977*

Top *x* %	Share of total wealth (in %) indicated by	
	General mortality rates 1966–71	Social class mortality rates
1	22.9	19.1
2	33.3	28.4
3	41.7	35.8
5	53.4	46.6
10	73.2	65.5
20	92.8	85.9

Source: Fouquet and Strauss-Kahn (1981).

inheritances. It has thus become possible to apply the estate duty method to estimate the size distribution of wealth. Five thousand individual records have been gathered. The estimation of wealth distribution concerns the year 1977 (see Table 7.4). A special emphasis through appropriate weighting procedure has been placed on large-scale estates to better estimate the top of the wealth distribution. But one of the major problems of this method lies in the fact that information on assets in estate duty files is rather poor. There are especially difficult valuation problems. Moreover, due to legislation, an important number of inheritances are not recorded.

Using mortality multipliers, it is possible to estimate aggregate wealth. But as it is well-known, different mortality multiplier sets are available. The most appropriate set led to an aggregate wealth amount representing roughly 77 per cent of the net household wealth figuring in the wealth accounts for this year.

The size distribution of personal net wealth will also largely depend on the mortality multipliers set chosen. Table 7.4 gives the concentration of personal net wealth using (a) general mortality rates and (b) social class mortality rates.

The estate duty method leads to estimates of the size distribution of wealth held by individuals and special assumptions on the prevailing mating pattern have to be made in order to assess the size distribution of wealth among households. At one extreme, it can be supposed that men with wealth w marry women with the same wealth so that the household will hold a wealth of $2w$. On the other hand, the assumption can be made that those men marry women without any wealth, in which case the wealth of the household will remain as w. In the first case, the top 1 per cent households would hold 18.7 per cent of total personal net wealth, whereas in the second case they would only hold 12.9 per cent. Of course the 'real' concentration of wealth among households lies somewhere between those two extreme figures.

2.4 Annual wealth tax data   In 1981 the newly elected government introduced an annual wealth tax called 'impôt sur les grandes fortunes'. This tax with a progressive rate is to be paid by all taxpayers with wealth amounting to more than 3 million francs in 1982 after a 2 million francs deduction for the so-called 'professional assets'. We unfortunately have only data on the declared value of estate on the first year when the tax was due. No complete investigation has yet been carried out by the IRS on the declared value of estates filed by the taxpayers. The underestimation might be in the order of 15 to 20 per cent.

The available data coming from the tax returns allow a better understanding of the top of the wealth distribution. (see Table 7.5). It appears clearly that the wealth distribution is even more skewed than previously supposed. The affluent seem less numerous but richer than expected. About 100,000 rich taxpayers have actually filed a tax return for paying the wealth tax. Their global taxable fortune (after the 2 million francs deduction) amounts to 701 billion francs. They indeed represent only 0.45 per cent of all the taxpayers but we can estimate that they hold roughly 9.9 per cent of total personal net wealth. Table 7.5 presents the distribution of wealth among the 100,000 rich taxpayers.

The annual wealth tax data allow us also to improve our

Table 7.5.   *Wealth concentration according to the annual wealth tax returns*

Declared wealth[a]	Number of taxpayers
3–4	35,372
4–5	23,517
5–10	32,118
10–50	9,603
> 50	440

a. After the 2 million francs deduction.

knowledge of the wealth composition of the affluent. It is for instance significant to know that stocks and shares represent 83 per cent of the wealth owned by taxpayers declaring estates ranging between 3 and 4 million francs (after the 2 million francs deduction).

3. Comparison of the Four Methods and their Results

Before comparing the results obtained, it seems necessary to stress the main problems encountered when estimating the size distribution of personal wealth.

3.1 The shortcomings of the four methods   None of the four methods we briefly presented seems optimal. The shortcomings lie in the wealth holder unit considered, the sources used, and the built-in deficiencies of the methods themselves.

As far as the wealth holder unit is concerned, if the estate duty method seems the best one to pick up the upper tail of the wealth distribution, it does not allow a direct estimation of household wealth concentration but only of individual wealth inequality. This wealth holding unit seems less interesting than the household or taxpayer unit since the wealth of an individual depends on his or her marital status and marital legal arrangements. Individual wealth distribution is of rather poor economic or social value. As we have seen, strong assumptions have to be made to estimate from the estate duty data the distribution of wealth among households.

But the taxpayer unit itself is not optimal either. A simple example will show why. When the introduction of the annual wealth tax was considered, a large number of gifts *inter vivos* were made in order to split the estate and hence avoid paying the wealth tax. The observed wealth inequality among taxpayers has thus decreased—and so has the potential tax revenue—but not the 'real' wealth inequality among families. On a theoretical basis the taxpayer unit might be relevant as far as the income distribution is concerned; it might be less relevant for wealth distribution.

Finally the household unit, defined as people living together under the same roof, seems the best of the three units for which wealth distribution data are available. But the household formation and dissolution process is not stable over time and this phenomenon should be taken into account when comparing for instance household wealth distribution over a 10 year period (see Duncan (1983)).

Moreover international comparisons also appear to be questionable because of the important differences in the real meaning of what is a household in the various national economic and social environments.

Concerning the sources, wealth is estimated through a direct declaration by a taxpayer to the IRS using three out of four methods under survey (income capitalization technique, annual wealth tax analysis, estate duty method). The only purpose of the IRS is to collect data in order to determine the amount of taxes to be paid. On a game theory basis, whoever fills in the tax return seeks to lessen the value of income or assets or even to avoid declaring them. The IRS itself is not always interested in market values for certain assets, nor does it always want to know all the assets or incomes of the taxpayers. This is of course the case of non-taxable income or assets. For all these well-known reasons, IRS sources will never be optimal. But it appears that these sources are usually of better quality than the data collected by direct sample surveys. One must emphasize the very classical problem of undervaluation: it seems to us that the main shortcomings of household sample surveys come from the fact that the undervaluation is not a randomly distributed phenomenon. Moreover the weighting procedure does not permit a small sample to be really representative when detailed information is needed.

Concerning the method, each of the four techniques used to estimate the size distribution of wealth has built-in deficiencies that are almost unavoidable. As far as the income capitalization technique is concerned, the major built-in deficiency stems from the assumption of a unique rate of return for each asset whatever its amount is.

This is of course a very restrictive hypothesis that is not verified by available studies. The rate of return for a given asset, appears to be a positive function of its amount. This is particularly true of stock portfolios.

Concerning the estate duty method, we have already stressed the fact that the size distribution of wealth will heavily depend on the mortality multipliers chosen. Since the distribution of age of death is not independent of the distribution of wealth, it is difficult to estimate the wealth distribution without any bias. The main deficiency of the annual wealth tax analysis is that it only deals with the upper tail of the wealth distribution. The existence of a threshold generates 'disturbances' in part of the upper tail distribution. Finally the direct household sample survey method cannot give an accurate account of the first two percentiles of the wealth distribution.

3.2 A comparison of the results of the four methods Each method appears to have specific advantages for describing a given part of the overall wealth distribution. The best method to describe the upper tail of the wealth distribution is the annual wealth tax analysis. But the tax base appears to be too specific (due to deductions, valuation, self declaration, and so on). The estate duty method seems also appropriate to analyse the upper tail of the wealth distribution but unfortunately it is the method that covers the smallest share of total household wealth. The sample survey approach appears especially tailored to study the wealth distribution among middle-class wealth holders but gives poor results both for the upper and lower tails. The income capitalization technique can only give a good description of the distribution of assets generating income. It gives a rather realistic indication of wealth inequality among the richest half of the population but seems quite inappropriate for estimating the assets held by the poorest half of the population.

As it can be seen from Table 7.6, which summarizes the main results of the four methods surveyed, the unit of observation plays an important role. Wealth inequality is larger among individuals than among taxpayers and larger among taxpayers than among households. So one should pay attention to the unit chosen. This choice should be derived from theoretical considerations.

The various methods lead to different degrees of wealth

Table 7.6. *The size distribution of wealth in France: Summary of the main results*

Methods	Year	Unit	Type of wealth	The top x % of wealth holders	Holding y % of total wealth	Gini coefficients	Remarks
I. *Sample Surveys*							
CREP (1975)	1975	Households	Gross	10.0 5.0 1.0	50.2 30.0 13.0	0.71	The CREP 1977 survey led to the same results
CREP (1980)	1980	Households	Gross	12.0 4.0	56.0 29.0	0.70	Gini coefficient for net wealth is 0.72
II. *Income capitalization*							
Coutière et al. (1981)	1975	Taxpayers	Gross	10.0 1.6	57.5 26.0	0.72	Results depend upon the various rates of return
III. *Estate duty method*	1975	Households	Gross	10.0	54.0		
Fouquet and Strauss-Kahn (1981)	1977	Individuals	Net	0.5 1.0 5.0	13.2 19.1 46.6	0.81	Results depend upon the mortality rates chosen
		Households	Net	0.5 1.0 5.0	8.8–13 12.9–18.7 31.3–45.5		Results depend upon mating patterns
IV. *Annual wealth tax*							
Direction de la Prévision (1983)	1981	Taxpayers	Net	0.45	9.9	—	This is a minimum estimate based upon declared values

inequality. It is worth emphasizing the fact that the share of top wealth holders is of similar magnitude when the income capitalization technique, the estate duty method, or the annual wealth tax data analysis is used. Only sample surveys underestimate this share.

The estimation of overall distribution of wealth (decile by decile) differs from one method to another as can be seen by comparing for instance Table 7.2 and Table 7.3. For any economic and social analysis, it is necessary to have a good picture not only of the share of wealth held by the richest deciles or percentiles, but also to know precisely the share (and of course the type) of assets held by the poorest deciles.

Reflecting these different distributions, Gini coefficients range from 0.70 (estimated by a household sample survey) to 0.81 (estimated from estate duty data).

It is tempting to consider the possibility of matching the various sources of data on wealth to get an overall representative wealth distribution. Such a procedure is however quite hazardous: units of account differ, assets coverage varies, and valuation methods diverge. Such a data-matching procedure involves making too many shaky assumptions.

4. Conclusion

The available data show a rather important degree of instantaneous wealth inequality in France. But it is indeed interesting to underline the fact that these estimates of wealth distribution are quite similar to the estimates for other industrialized countries. It seems of course an impossible mission to really have a comparable data set from each country (defined the following way: same assets, same valuation, same unit, same method, same year). This is why it is necessary to be very careful about drawing any definite conclusion from the available country estimates.

It is however striking to see that the observed wealth distributions are quite similar from one country to another (see Table 7.7). This fact points to the possible existence of a somewhat 'unique law of wealth distribution' in industrialized market economies. By law of wealth distribution we do not mean of course a statistical law (such as Paretian, Gamma, or Log-normal) but rather the underlying forces that shape the distribution of wealth.

Table 7.7. *Wealth distribution in eight industrialized countries*

Top x % of wealth holders	Percentage of wealth held							
	France (1977)	Belgium (1969)	United Kingdom (1974)	Federal Republic of Germany (1973)	Denmark (1973)	Sweden (1975)	United States (1972)	Canada (1970)
1.0	19	28	32	28	25	16	25	19.6
5.0	45	47	57		47	35	43	43.4
10.0	61	57	72		60	52		58.0
20.0	81	71	85		75	65		74.0

Source: adapted from Strauss-Kahn (1979). Refer to this article for the national references. The Canadian estimates are from Davies (1979). Those estimates are not fully comparable (unit, method of estimation, assets covered. . .).

Observed inequality in asset holdings in industrial economies could be the outcome of the labour markets (and hence the wage distribution), the capital markets (and hence partially the income distribution), or the so-called political markets (as far as taxation for instance is concerned). The concentration of wealth would also result from the family structures (mating and fertility patterns, or estate division patterns) as well as from the other social structures (including income transfer schemes). In other words, the structure of wealth distribution relies heavily on the structure itself of industrialized market economies. In this perspective, wealth concentration would not only be an outcome of such an economy but also a condition of its existence and functioning.

But in order to check this hypothesis, it is necessary to further analyse the wealth accumulation process rather than study only the cross-sectional distribution of assets. A given instantaneous wealth distribution may indeed result from very different individual accumulation patterns. The next section of this paper deals with a complementary approach to wealth distribution, more rooted in theory.

III. Further Insights into Wealth Distribution

The measure of instantaneous wealth distribution may not be very helpful in assessing the true importance played by wealth. This variable may well be misleading when used to understand the equity and efficiency aspects of wealth. One can indeed argue that the concept itself of instantaneous wealth distribution has no clear economic or social value. Instantaneous wealth distribution seems to lack a theoretical basis. It is therefore necessary—in order to critique the usual measure of instantaneous wealth distribution—to refer to the various theoretical frameworks of wealth accumulation and, correlatively, to specify more closely the subject under investigation. Indeed such an approach will help to propose possible alternate measures of both the distributions of well-being and of economic power.

We shall first consider wealth in the framework of the life-cycle hypothesis. As a reserve for deferred consumption, current non-human wealth is then an indicator of well-being, however incomplete, since future consumption depends also upon human capital.

We shall then consider wealth as an indicator of social status or economic power from a neo-Kaldorian perspective. But for this alternate purpose, current non-human wealth seems too large since only capital assets seem to bring economic power.

We shall finally propose a longitudinal typology of accumulation behaviour relying upon the two previous approaches.

1. *Life Cycle Theory and Wealth Distribution*

Life-cycle models consider the intertemporal allocation of resources over a long time horizon, namely the remaining lifetime as far as the basic model is concerned (see Modigliani (1975)).

The life-cycler is supposed to maximize his utility, derived primarily from his consumption. His preferences are given and he (or she) faces competitive capital markets. The consumer follows a forward-looking behaviour. At a given age, past events are only encapsulated in his present lifetime resources, tastes, and remaining time horizon.

Moreover, preferences are assumed to be autonomous and homogeneous. Autonomous preferences mean that there are no links between the different wealth holding units (individuals, households, or families). The utility derived from consumption for an individual is neither increased nor decreased by the consumption of another individual. Homogeneous preferences mean that wealth holding gives in itself no direct utility: only consumption is supposed to increase the level of utility. In other words preferences are independent on the level of wealth or resources.

Moreover the usual assumptions concerning behaviour—notably the separability of the utility function—lead to an allocation process with an intertemporal two-stage budgeting: one needs only to consider at a given period t the total amount of consumption C_t and assets A_t.

These three characteristics of preferences—autonomy, homogeneity, and separability—make possible a ranking of all individuals on the same unidimensional scale of well-being.

In this behavioural setting, wealth A_t is primarily held for future consumption purposes. It is an important indicator of the present and future consumption capacities of an individual.

More precisely, the distribution of total assets A_t measures the distribution of well-being among a population if one considers the well-being of an individual to be measured by his potential consumption without working in the future.

Current wealth holding of an individual seems therefore easily interpretable in this neo-classical framework, provided appropriate definitions of income, wealth, and consumption are used to make sure that, apart from intergenerational transfers, saving can be identified with the variation of wealth.[1]

However, the economic and social meaning of a degree of instantaneous wealth inequality for welfare comparisons depends upon the variant of the life-cycle model. We will consider the wealth distribution implications of (a) the basic life-cycle hypothesis, (b) the extended life-cycle hypothesis, and (c) the market imperfections and uncertainty.

1.1 Wealth distribution implications of the basic life-cycle hypothesis In a certain no-bequest world with perfect capital markets, the amount of assets A_t will be nil at start and end of life, and for most common sets of preferences and earnings profiles, will peak at the eve of retirement. The age–wealth profile exhibits the standard humped shape.

It is therefore rather meaningless to compare the assets held by people of different ages, since differences in wealth reflect primarily differences in age. This is of course due to the stock nature of wealth: its accumulation requires time.

The relevance—or rather the irrelevance—of current wealth as an indicator of well-being can be assessed when compared with current income (see Masson (1982)). Current income—a flow variable—is also not the best variable to look at in order to appreciate the distribution of well-being in a given society. Current income distribution includes differences in income due to age (seniority) and includes also all transitory variations. This is why it has been proposed to measure the distribution of well-being by using permanent income (eliminating transitory variations) or lifetime income (eliminating age variations).

Compared with current income, current wealth A_t may be supposed to present a relatively smaller transitory component. One can indeed argue that the intracohort mobility is smaller for wealth than for income. However, its variations with age are likely to be more systematic so that cross-sectional wealth inequality will appear to largely overstate well-being inequality assessed on a lifetime basis.

But the main difference between income and wealth is not really due to their stock or flow nature: in the basic life-cycle model it comes from the fact that income is a resource and wealth the result of an allocation of resources.

Wealth results in the basic life-cycle model from an intertemporal allocation process of lifetime earnings. Wealth comparisons are therefore of limited value since they depend largely upon the consumers' preferences (notably intertemporal preferences) and the age—earnings profile.

Two individuals of the same age, having followed the same age–income profile, may hold very different assets amounts. The difference between wealth holdings may therefore not reflect pure differences in well-being but differences in time preferences. As in La Fontaine words, some are cicadas, others are grasshoppers.

It is therefore necessary to search for another indicator of well-being over the long run, less questionable than the amount of current wealth. In this context one can consider the total available resources over the long run, that is, the (discounted) lifetime earnings or initial human capital (or rather earnings abilities). To estimate the current level of well-being of a consumer aged t—no matter his previous earning and consumption behaviour—the relevant measure could be total wealth W_t equal to the sum of assets A_t and human capital present value E_t. Consumption C_t is proportional to W_t. Welfare comparison should then only consider consumers of the same age, or even of same life expectancy.

Since in the elementary life-cycle theory, human and non-human wealth are perfectly substitutable, assets A_t will generally appear as the emerged part of an enormous iceberg W_t.[2] The estimated distribution of well-being measured along these lines will be quite similar to the distribution of (permanent) income.[3]

There is another way to measure the well-being of an individual: instead of converting earnings into a stock, a more appealing way to get a synthetic earnings–wealth measure of current well-being may be to convert A_t into an equivalent flow over the remaining lifetime (see Taussig (1982)). To this annuity value of assets is then added an estimate of (non-property) permanent income in order to get a measure of well-being allowing notably welfare comparisons between households of different ages.

1.2 Wealth distribution implications of the extended life-cycle model   The growing literature on wealth accumulation has labelled 'extended' life-cycle models where individuals receive and leave bequests during their lifetime. Extensions of the life-cycle hypothesis to introduce a bequest motive have followed two main pathways.

The first pathway is simply to add bequest as a new argument besides own consumption in the utility function. Usual hypothesis stipulates separability of bequest and consumption in preferences: the level of bequest is then independent of children characteristics (see Blinder (1974)).

The second way assumes instead that children's consumption (or resources) are arguments of the utility function of their parents, implying that wealth remains as pure deferred consumption (whether for oneself or for heirs) and that the size of bequests depends on the expected income of future generations (see Shorrocks (1979) or Becker and Tomes (1979)).

The conclusions reached in the basic life-cycle hypothesis framework remain largely valid in the extended models except for three major points.

First, current wealth holding is a rather poor measure of well-being since it does not take into account future inheritances or gifts already bestowed.

Second, owing to bequests already received by an individual aged t, part of the current wealth that he owns may be considered as contributing in a particular way to his well-being. On a backward-looking basis, it can be argued that when considering the distribution of current wealth, it would be worth while to distinguish between inherited wealth on one side and self-accumulated wealth on the other side. Even if both kinds of wealth are hard to disentangle, such a distinction would be helpful especially on an economic and social basis. On a forward-looking basis, in the life-cycle framework, a measure of well-being in a world with bequest could be to add to lifetime labour earnings E_0, the discounted sum I_0 of inheritances and gifts received. Current wealth A_t remains therefore endogenous as the outcome of the allocation of total initial resources $I_0 + E_0$. In the same way, total wealth $W_t (= E_t + A_t)$ can be replaced by $E_t + A_t I_t$, with I_t standing for inheritances and gifts to be received from t onwards.

Third, the presence of altruism in the utility function complicates the choice of the wealth holding unit in inequality measures. In the extended life-cycle model, the household seems still to be the appropriate unit for welfare comparisons for a large part of the population. But when bequest plays a very important role in the process of wealth accumulation, the relevant wealth holding unit seems to be the family in its dynastic meaning. If we consider the dynastic family, any *inter vivos* gifts or inheritances have no effect on the distribution of well-being.

1.3   Wealth distribution implications of market imperfections and uncertainty   Of the considerable developments of the life-cycle hypothesis devoted to the effects of capital market imperfections, risk, and uncertainty, a very sketchy outline will be sufficient for our purpose (see Kessler and Masson (1987)). All the recent models rest on the main assumptions of the life-cycle hypothesis: forward-looking behaviour, isolated units, separability conditions allowing consideration only of total consumption C_t and total assets A_t at age t.

To assess the role of capital market imperfections and uncertainties on the status of current wealth A_t, three aspects can be distinguished. First, liquidity or borrowing constraints (such as to assume the non-negativity of wealth) or a rate of return positively correlated with wealth will lead to an accumulation profile $\bar{A}_t$ instead of A^*_t obtained if capital markets were perfect—and correspondingly to $\bar{C}_t$ instead of C^*_t. Second, in a world of imperfect information and risk, the consumer will have to form expectations of his future resources, rates of return, and preferences over his remaining lifetime. In the more general case, he will only foresee the distributions of these variables. According to his attitude towards risk (notably his degree of risk aversion) he will initially plan an age–wealth profile $\hat{A}_t$ instead of $\bar{A}_t$. Third, in a dynamic setting, he consumes so as to follow an age–wealth profile A_t resulting from his luck and the successive revisions of his initial plans.

There may indeed be a large gap between the reference amount of wealth A^*_t in a certain world with perfect capital markets and the actual amount of wealth A_t in the imperfect world. The difference $A_t - A^*_t$ will depend upon a set of interactions between preferences (and especially risk aversion), degrees of information for different variables, various market imperfections, and finally luck.

Current wealth A_t therefore presents two components: A^*_t is derived from preferences and lifetime income and is endogenous to each individual. But the difference $A_t - A^*_t$ is largely out of the control of the consumer and reflects factors such as market failures that exert naturally an effect on the level of well-being. The more capital market imperfections and uncertainties, the more the share $(A_t - A^*_t)/A_t$ will be high. One should therefore be cautious when interpreting current wealth distribution: assets held by an individual represent not only past resource allocation choices due to his preferences, but reflect also the various market failures out of his control. Therefore, a share of his current wealth equal to $A_t - A^*_t$ should appear separately from human capital when measuring well-being. It is however obvious that this share $(A_t - A^*_t)/A_t$ will be difficult to assess empirically.

Moreover empirical measures of well-being will need to include precisely the respective weights given to the contribution of wealth and to the contribution of income. These weights will depend in turn upon the degree of substitutability between assets A_t and human capital present value E_t.

Uncertainty and market imperfections will indeed limit the degree of substitution between A_t and E_t. Besides deferred consumption, assets A_t fulfil specific functions not assumed by income. Assets can be held for precautionary motives, for speculative motives, or as a liquidity reserve or even for direct use (consumer durables).

The main difficulty comes from the variability of this degree of substitution between A_t and E_t. Friedman's solution in favour of a high uniform discount rate for earnings up to 33 per cent (corresponding to a 3-year time horizon) does not seem satisfactory at a micro level. The degree of substitution between A_t and E_t depends upon a large number of variables such as age, uncertainty, and information. The degree of substitutability will be low when market imperfections and uncertainties are prevalent.

Imperfect markets and uncertainty do not lead to a clear-cut conclusion on the best measure of well-being. In the presence of strong imperfections and general uncertainty, the distribution of A^*_t is almost impossible to measure and the distribution of current wealth A_t is more relevant as a measure of well-being than in a perfect certain world. Besides, it will often appear preferable to measure well-being with a bi-dimensional income and wealth indicator, when studing carefully the correlation between the two distributions (especially within age cells, see note 3).

2. A Neo-Kaldorian Asset-Grouping Approach to Wealth Distribution

In the previous section, we followed the neo-classical approach of consumer behaviour: wealth was held only for differed consumption purposes. Current wealth distribution in itself had little equity or efficiency meaning. In this section we follow what could be labelled the neo-Kaldorian approach to wealth accumulation. Wealth is no longer a substitute for income; wealth is no longer held only for future consumption. In this alternate approach, the distribution of wealth serves notably to assess the distribution of social roles and status, the distribution of economic and social power. The society is no longer homogeneous but split into specific groups. Wealth is no longer homogeneous and distributions of specific assets are considered separately. After reviewing the main types of assets, we will focus on a simple asset-grouping approach inspired by the two-class neo-Kaldorian model.

2.1 The heterogeneity of wealth   Let us start by stressing of course that the neo-classical theory admits that there are different types of assets composing wealth, distinguished according to their physical or financial nature, riskless or risky characteristics, rates of returns and liquidity, and so on. The composition of non-human wealth of a given individual is traditionally derived in the neo-classical theory from attitudes towards risks and returns.

More recently other factors affecting wealth composition have been emphasized. King and Leape (1984) focus on differential tax treatment and the role of information. More generally assets may differ according to legal or institutional arrangements or by the degree of economic and financial knowledge required to manage them properly. Bernheim et al (1984) separate 'bequeathable' from 'non-bequeathable' assets since only the former will play a role in the complex relationship linking parents and children.

Neo-classical theory has also provided useful insights into the differences between non-human and human wealth. Of course the former copes better with uncertainty than the latter. The former is exchangeable and the latter is not. Moreover returns to assets and human capital result from different production functions. Time cost in the form of foregone leisure plays an important role when human capital is used to acquire resources. Investment in non-human and human wealth takes different forms. Human capital investment requires more time than investment in assets. Finally the rates of return on both types of investments differ greatly.[4]

But even if there are differences between the various non-human assets, it is always possible to sum them up in the neo-classical models and to provide a measure of wealth. Since assets are always 'comparable', there is no problem in comparing the amount of wealth held by someone holding only stocks and someone holding only cash. If both amounts are equal in money terms, neo-classical theory will consider both types of wealth to be identical. The under-lying reason for doing so is easy to find: with perfect markets, money can buy stocks and stocks can be sold.

One can argue that assets are heterogeneous, and that it is mis-leading to sum them up. If this is true, it is necessary to compare distribution of wealth asset by asset (or rather asset category by asset category).

The heterogeneity of assets may come from the wealth holding motives. There are indeed other criteria to differentiate assets that are usually not taken into account by the neo-classical theory— recall the numerous motives explaining saving (and therefore wealth accumulation) in Keynes' *General Theory*. Moreover the bequest motive is not limited to the transmission of purchasing power. Many explanations of savings behaviour do not rest on the usual neo-classical postulates of consumption behaviour (auto-nomous preferences, forward-looking behaviour and so on).

To take one example, we can refer to the French wealth accum-ulation behaviour. A noticeable part of the population does not follow the traditional forward-looking behaviour as in the life-cycle theory. Certain wealth holders in France follow a rather 'backward-looking' behaviour since there are more heirs than accumulators. They manage the wealth they have inherited rather than accumulate wealth. This is why there are certain assets called 'biens de famille', because they cannot really be sold by someone inheriting them but can only be bequeathed to the next generation.

But there are numerous other wealth holding motives such as social prestige or status, economic power, or influence referring to interdependent preferences and relative positions in the social hierarchy or to the role played in the process of production. It seems difficult to introduce these motives in the life-cycle model.

Moreover wealth holding motives become totally incompatible with neo-classical theory when they are based upon population heterogeneity and more specifically upon class divisions. It must be recalled that for some authors, assets held are the main factors of social stratification.

2.2 A neo-Kaldorian approach to wealth composition   Rather than considering only the distribution of current wealth, it might seem interesting to try to elaborate a typology of wealth holdings based upon the nature of assets owned. The purpose in elaborating such a typology is of course to understand the economic and social meaning of wealth.

This typology of the population rests upon a typology of assets. A major prerequisite for defining different categories of assets is a limited degree of substitutability between assets. As we have seen previously, all assets are imperfect substitutes for one another. Before trying to elaborate such a typology, it must be stressed that there is no unique asset grouping. The most appropriate classification, as the best concept of wealth, depends always on the precise aim of the study.

Tony Shorrocks's aim (this book, pages 29–50) is portfolio theory testing and improvement: his classification of assets relies heavily upon variables like risk, return, and liquidity. Our objective is somewhat different since we investigate the possibility of deriving an alternate approach to the current wealth distribution in order to measure both the distribution of well-being and of economic power. This explains the greater emphasis put on wealth holding motives (usually not considered in life-cycle models) in the following classification of both human and non-human wealth:

(a) human capital, including social security wealth, which is interpreted here as a claim on the income of future generations;
(b) life insurance, life annuities, pensions rights, and so on, which have limited fungibility and satisfy life-cycle needs (and eventually a bequest motive for certain types of insurance) but are all funded by financial and material assets (in contrast to social security wealth or human capital);
(c) liquidities and quasi-liquidities, used for transactions and precautionary balances: cash, checking accounts, savings accounts, time deposits, short-term bonds and money market funds;
(d) durable goods;

(e) own home and other residential housing;
(f) stocks and shares, bonds or securities, investment in real estate, which are financial or tangible assets held both for capital gains and income yields;
(g) business equity (unincorporated, professional, or productive capital including farms and agricultural land and forests).

Note that this classification of assets in six groups (plus human capital) is not really different either from Shorrocks's typology (in this book) or from Wolff's typology (1981) derived mainly from consideration of asset concentration.

To emphasize the economic role of wealth as a factor of production, and therefore as a factor of society stratification, two kinds of assets A could be distinguished: S-wealth on one side and K-wealth on the other side (with $A = S + K$).

S-wealth covers assets held for future consumption (in the short, medium, and long runs), for liquidity, precautionary, and transaction purposes. S-wealth is usually the assets held by low- and medium-wage earners in a country like France. S-wealth includes the assets (b) to (e) in the classification proposed above.

K-wealth includes assets held mainly for their returns (capital gains and capital income) and also productive and professional assets. K-wealth includes the assets (f) and (g). This K-wealth represents capital goods, used directly in the production process either in combination with human capital (farmers, self-employed, professionals, and the like) or alone (in the case of financial assets).[5]

Altogether wealth can therefore be divided in three components: human capital H-wealth, S-wealth, and K-wealth.

This typology may be helpful in understanding the overall accumulation process since one can argue that savings in S-assets or in K-assets are quite different. S-wealth accumulation behaviour follows roughly the life-cycle model presented above. The age–S-wealth profile exhibits a more or less pronounced hump-shaped pattern. When there are S-wealth bequests, they can be considered residual or contingent due to lifetime uncertainty and market imperfections (see Davies (1981)). Of course, the relative share of S-assets decreases with the level of A.

K-wealth accumulation behaviour is less likely to follow the usual life-cycle pattern. K-wealth holding fulfils motives such as economic and social power that are less easily saturated than consumption needs. Since K-wealth is not primarily held for future self-consumption, its accumulation over the life-cycle does not show a typical pattern as S-wealth accumulation does. One of the reason for this lies in the fact that K-wealth is more likely to be transferred between generations through bequests than S-wealth. But since the probability of receiving a bequest increases with age, K-wealth is usually rising with age throughout the lifetime.

As a consequence K-wealth inequality should be higher than S-wealth inequality and K-asset distribution is likely to be highly concentrated.

2.3 Some empirical evidence of the S–K division of assets   Evidence on the distinction between S- and K-wealth accumulation behaviours is notably available in France and in the US (see Wolff (1981) and (1983)). We will first present some evidence on life-cycle accumulation behaviours and then some evidence on the share of S- and K-wealth held for different amounts of fortune.

With the help of a simulation accounting model, synthetic longitudinal wealth profiles have been reconstituted over the period 1949–75 for French households belonging to different cohorts and to eight occupational groups (see Masson (1983)). Cohort analysis led then to the following characteristics for age–wealth effects over the period. Unstable age effects over the post-war period were found for small-scale self-employed, especially farmers. Various stable hump-shaped patterns were obtained for wage earners. But wealthy self-employed do not seem to run down their portfolio during retirement, which is evidence of a strong propensity to bequeath or of the existence of wealth holding motives different from the life-cycle hypothesis.

The results are quite in line with those obtained with different methods and for different countries, by Shorrocks (1975) for Britain, Wolff (1981) for the US, and King and Dicks-Mireaux (1982) for Canada. They are consistent with the S–K division hypothesis.

Table 7.8 presents the degree of concentration for different wealth assets and is directly comparable to Wolff's results for the US (1983, Tables 3 and 4). The same conclusions emerge: S-wealth is, as predicted, more concentrated than income, but far less than K-wealth. Moreover figures are strikingly similar in the two countries with two exceptions: US Gini coefficients for owners are only 0.585 for S-wealth (0.67 in France) and 0.795 for K-wealth

Table 7.8. *The concentration of different components of household wealth*

Type of wealth	Share held by top 10%	Gini coefficient (total population)	Gini coefficient (owners only)
Current income	30%	0.50	0.46
S-Wealth	45%	0.70	0.67
A-Wealth	54%	0.73	0.71
K-Wealth	78%	0.86	0.69

Source: Panel CREP, 1975.

(0.69 in France) indicating a higher degree of capital concentration in the US.[6]

More relevant information comes however from the S–K composition of wealth according to the level of total assets A. Table 7.9 gives the share of portfolio held in different assets for households grouped in A-wealth deciles and parallels Table 5 in Wolff (1983). Again the results are quite similar in France and in the US. The shares held in K-assets rise regularly with the level of wealth A and are much higher among the richest households. Inversely the percentages decrease monotonically with A for some S-assets. But in both countries an inverse U-shape form is found for the shares held in time and savings deposits and residential housing although the percentages of these assets in portfolios of rich households are below average.

Owing to composition effects however, relative shares are not always easy to interpret and further insights into the S–K allocation process of wealth A can be obtained by analysing, for various assets, the rate of ownership among households ranked by A-wealth decile (Table 7.10). Most S-assets appear largely diffused in the population whereas K-asset ownership is restricted to the richest group.[7] Besides, a more precise picture of the distribution of S-wealth and K-wealth within the population ranked by A-wealth decile can be derived from Table 7.11. In this table are reproduced the shares held by each wealth decile in the total amount of three S-assets and three K-assets. Results are rather striking: no decile up to the seventh one owns at least one-tenth of one asset; in the eight first deciles, S-asset shares are always higher than K-asset share; in the

Table 7.9. *The percentage composition of household disposable wealth by wealth decile*

Wealth decile	Checking account	Time and savings deposits (incl. bonds)	Residential housing	Investment real estate and land	Stocks, shares, and obligations	Business equity (including farms)	Total
S–K type	S	S	S	K	K	K	
1	67.5	28.7	—	—	3.7	—	100
2	57.8	41.3	—	—	—	0.9	100
3	34.4	63.3	1.7	—	0.6		100
4	21.5	62.8	9.0	4.0	1.2	1.5	100
5	7.4	27.0	57.5	2.6	1.5	4.0	100
6	5.2	17.5	64.0	5.7	2.1	5.4	100
7	4.6	16.3	67.9	3.3	2.5	5.4	100
8	3.1	13.1	68.2	3.1	3.8	8.7	100
9	3.4	10.9	43.1	19.3	5.5	17.8	100
10	2.4	8.4	22.8	32.6	9.1	24.7	100
Total	5.7	10.1	37.8	21.6	6.6	18.2	100

Source: Panel CREP, 1977.

Table 7.10. *Rate of asset ownership by wealth decile*

Asset	S–K type	1	2	3	4	5	6	7	8	9	10	Total population
Checking acounts	S	66.4	86.7	80.3	83.2	78.8	86.4	91.1	94.3	92.0	98.1	85.7
Bank savings deposits	S	8.3	10.8	15.8	27.0	13.8	22.1	35.5	41.2	32.8	39.8	24.5
CNE savings deposits	S	34.1	54.1	81.0	74.6	69.2	65.5	66.2	76.8	81.7	76.1	68.0
Housing savings arrangements	S	1.3	7.6	8.8	15.1	14.9	11.3	16.2	21.8	22.0	26.1	14.6
Short-term bonds	S	—	—	—	0.5	9.9	12.0	10.9	7.9	26.8	32.2	10.2
Owner occupied housing	S	—	—	1.4	11.7	58.2	67.6	79.4	80.9	80.3	83.7	46.7
Other residential housing	S	—	—	—	1.1	7.2	10.9	7.3	15.0	20.8	26.8	9.1
Obligations	K	—	—	—	—	0.7	3.4	2.9	4.9	8.3	12.7	3.4

Stocks and shares	K	0.2	0.5	1.2	1.9	2.4	2.5	6.0	5.9	13.5	27.9	6.4
Investment real estate	K	—	—	—	0.4	0.2	4.4	0.8	4.4	16.3	41.3	7.1
Unincorporated non-farm business equity	K	—	—	—	1.6	5.1	3.3	5.4	10.6	19.5	23.4	7.0
Farm equity	K	—	1.5	—	0.2	2.5	7.5	6.5	4.4	17.0	31.0	7.3
Land	K	—	0.2	0.1	9.6	6.5	8.9	8.9	3.7	18.2	23.1	8.3

Source: Panel CREP, 1977.

Table 7.11. *Percentage held by each wealth decile in the total amount of various assets*

Wealth decile	Checking account	Time and savings deposits (incl. bonds)	Residential housing	Investment, real estate, and land	Stocks, shares, and obligations	Business equity (including farms)
S-K type	S	S	S	K	K	K
1	0.6	—	—	—	—	—
2	2.7	0.6	—	—	—	—
3	4.2	2.3	—	—	—	—
4	6.3	5.4	0.3	0.3	0.2	—
5	6.1	6.6	4.5	0.3	0.7	0.7
6	7.4	7.4	8.6	1.3	1.6	1.5
7	9.8	10.4	13.7	1.2	2.9	2.3
8	9.4	11.9	19.9	1.6	6.3	5.2
9	17.2	18.3	21.0	15.4	15.2	18.1
10	36.3	37.1	32.0	79.9	73.1	72.2
Total	100.0	100.0	100.0	100.0	100.0	100.0

Source: Panel CREP, 1977.

ninth decile shares held in different assets are very similar; the last decile owns around a third of S-assets and more than 70 per cent of K-assets.

Beyond current wealth-A inequality, the previous observations provided further insights into the nature and meaning of the distribution of wealth and are largely consistent with the hypothesis of the S–K dichotomy. This hypothesis requires of course further empirical and theoretical investigation with a greater emphasis placed on different wealth holding motives and especially bequest behaviour (see Kessler and Masson (1979a) and (1979b)).

For instance, since K-assets are dominant in bequests, non-human wealth receipts over the course of one's life, I_0, can be expected to follow a fairly autonomous process relative to human capital. Hence I_0-wealth inequality may be thought to adequately characterize unequal 'life chances' (see Atkinson (1971)). In an intergenerational perspective, it should be further complemented by a measure of the degree of intergenerational wealth mobility.

3. Towards a Typology of Wealth Accumulation Behaviour

Given the existence of three different types of wealth—human capital, S-wealth, and K-wealth—and their very specific nature and distribution among households, the population can be split into three subgroups (see Wolff (1981)). The first group is composed of people holding only human capital. The second group holds mainly S-wealth. The third group holds not only human capital and S-wealth but also large amounts of K-wealth. To distinguish the second and the third group it is necessary to consider a threshold of K-assets ownership (see Vaughan (1979)).

But this segmentation of the population into three classes relies too heavily on the neo-Kaldorian approach and neglects some of the important life-cycle analysis insights. One can therefore refine the previous segmentation of the population by taking into account the following elements.

First, a typology of wealth accumulation behaviours must be longitudinal. It must consider the life-cycle wealth profiles rather than the assets held at a given time.[8]

Second, the fact that to hold throughout the life-cycle only small amounts of wealth (or rather of S-wealth) is not always clear evidence against life-cycle behaviour. This profile can result from strong market imperfections and uncertainty. It may also be the outcome of insurance schemes like social security (Kessler and Masson (1987)).

Third, there is a large variety of behaviour among those accumulating only S-assets. It is possible, with the help of life-cycle theory, to distinguish several groups of 'life-cyclers'.

Fourth, an accumulation behaviour typology must take into account bequest behaviour. This bequest behaviour depends in turn upon the family structure (including of course intergenerational relations, mating, and fertility patterns).

A typology regarding those four conditions has been proposed (see Kessler and Masson (1984)). The two most important criteria are, on the one hand, the nature of wealth held and, on the other hand, the time horizon.

Wealth is divided into H-wealth, S-wealth, and K-wealth. Time horizons are short-sighted (myopic individuals), medium-sighted (life-cyclers), or far-sighted (intergenerationalists).

The combination of the two criteria leads to nine possible cases but only five of them are relevant.

Type 1 households (or rather individuals) are short-sighted and own only small amounts of S-assets. Moreover their human capital wealth is quite uncertain and they are usually dependent on social or family assistance.

Type 2 households are life-cyclers, but whose accumulation behaviour is impeded by strong liquidity constraints, uncertainties, and lack of information. They hold only limited amounts of S-assets.

Type 3 households are genuine life-cyclers. Their age–wealth profile is hump-shaped. They hold mainly S-assets. They make small bequests, or contingent bequests (owner-occupied housing).

Type 4 households follow an extended life-cycle model: their non-human wealth is mainly composed of S-assets but the bequest motive is rather strong.

Type 5 households hold, besides H-wealth and S-wealth, K-assets. The bequest motive is generally strong. The families are likely to take a dynastic form.

This typology is of course open to criticism. It is certainly more relevant for European countries than for North American countries. It needs further study, especially concerning the link between family structures (including mating and fertility

Table 7.12. *A wealth accumulation typology of the French population*

Type	Population share (%)	A-Wealth share (%)	K-Wealth share (%)	S-Wealth share (%)
Type 1	20–25	5	—	< 10
Type 2	10		—	
Type 3	near 40	15–20	—	55
Type 4	> 10	15–20	20	
Type 5	10	55–60	75	30–35
Others	5–10	5–10	5	< 5

behaviours) and accumulation behaviour.[9] The outcome of such a study could help to better sketch the frontiers between the five patterns of wealth accumulation behaviours.

In spite of its shortcomings, we have tried to split the French households population into these five types of behaviours (see Kessler and Masson (1984)). The results are very preliminary (see Table 7.12).

4. Conclusion

There is no unique way to statistically measure inequality and various indexes have been proposed. There is no unique way either to define and value wealth. There is no unique way finally to interpret wealth distribution in terms of economic efficiency or equity. Ways followed depend upon the specific aim pursued.

It might be suggested that this variety of approaches is an obstacle for a clear understanding of the economic and social role of wealth. To our point of view however, the confrontation of concepts and theories is fertile. In this field also, the melting pot seems to succeed.

Endnotes

1. All variables are in after tax real terms. The identity between savings and change in wealth supposes that:
   (a) consumption includes the flow of services derived from durables;
   (b) rate of return and property income include both income yields and capital gains but are net of capital depreciation;

(c) A is net worth with liabilities defined as the sum of discounted future repayments in real terms instead of current equity (assuming perfect capital markets).

2. In this vein Feldstein (1976) proposes to add non-human wealth A_t to social security wealth SSW_t, that is the discounted sum of future benefits. This procedure is debatable since SSW is a very peculiar asset which is not fungible and originates from compulsory saving. Feldstein's argument however is more empirical and says that, for wealth inequality comparisons over time, the variable $A + SSW$ plays today an equivalent role to assets A alone in earlier times (when social security did not exist). But social security, as a substitute for assets, should then depress saving (Feldstein (1974)), an implication which is in contradiction with most empirical evidence.

3. The contribution of assets in well-being inequality can be adequately assessed from the distribution, within age cells, of the ratio of wealth to permanent income. Such data have been gathered only for Canada by King and Dicks-Mireaux (1982) who supply elaborate cross-sectional estimates of permanent income based upon 'full-time' employment. Their results show a high dispersion of this ratio at each age and, moreover, little correlation of this ratio with the level of permanent income.

4. Becker and Tomes (1979) and Tomes (1981) have also assumed that parental investments in the human capital and material wealth of their children have different marginal intergenerational rates of return. This element appears central in their models to account for the low degree of intergenerational wealth mobility (compared with that of income): indeed the transmission of assets is the privileged buffer against intergenerational regression towards the mean in abilities or in income.

5. Wolff (1981) and (1983) propose a similar decomposition of assets in S-wealth and K-wealth for the US. However certain fixed claim assets, that is time and savings deposits, bonds and securities, are considered K-assets in Wolff's study but S-assets in ours. This discrepancy may partly reflect national differences in the nature of such assets or in the attitudes of households towards them. In France at least there will be general agreement concerning the S-nature of time and savings deposits. Moreover the S-category should include most bonds which satisfy life-cycle and retirement needs and are, for that reason and others, concentrated in old households' portfolios. As risky assets with a variable price, French 'obligations' are more of a K-type.

6. Our more narrow definition of K-assets (see note 5) may explain part of the difference in the Gini coefficients.

7. Note however that a criterion of S–K asset differentiation based upon diffusion in A-wealth brackets will have difficulties separating S-assets which are not 'necessities' such as short-term bonds and other residential housing.

8. For instance the lower class includes only households that are expected to remain poor most of their life (see King and Dicks-Mireaux (1982) for a discussion along these lines).

9. For instance it is likely that two sub-groups will appear in type 5: the first less wealthy one is composed of nuclear families while the richest group is formed of dynastic or extended families where wealth is often kept in indivision or collective management. Indeed a privileged way used by very rich French families to

keep their social position is through their daughters' marriage to competent managers.

References

Atkinson, A.B. 'The Distribution of Wealth and the Individual Life Cycle', *Oxford Economic Papers*, 23 (1971), 239–54.

Atkinson, A.B., Harrison, A.J. *Distribution of Personal Wealth in Britain* (Cambridge, 1978).

Becker, G.S. 'A Theory of Social Interactions', *Journal of Political Economy*, 82 (1974), 1063–93.

Becker, G.S., Tomes, N. 'An Equilibrium Theory of the Distribution of Income and Intergenerational Mobility', *Journal of Political Economy*, 87 (1979), 1153–89.

Bedford, N.M., McKeown, J.C. 'Comparative Analysis of Net Realizable Value and Replacement Costing', *The Accounting Review* (April 1972), 333–8.

Benedetti, A., Consolo G., Fouquet, A. 'Les comptes de patrimoine', *Economie et Statistique* (Sept 1979).

Bernheim, B.M., Schleifer, A., Summers, L. 'Bequests as a Means of Payment', *NBER Working Paper*, no. 1030 (1984).

Blinder, A.S. *Towards an Economic Theory of Income Distribution* (Cambridge, Massachusetts, 1974).

Centre de Recherche Economique sur L'Epargne 'Les comportements financiers et le patrimoine des ménages.' Mimeo (Nov 1981).

Coutière, A., Hatem, F., Mantz, P., Pontagnier, C. 'La concentration du patrimoine des foyers', *Economie et Statistique* (Oct 1981).

Davies, J.B. 'On the Size Distribution of Wealth in Canada', *Review of Income and Wealth*. 25 (1979), 237–60.

—— 'Uncertain Lifetime, Consumption and Dissaving in Retirement', *Journal of Political Economy*, 89 (1981), 561–77.

Duncan, G.J. 'The Implications of Changing Family Composition for the Dynamics Analysis of Family Economic Well-Being'. in: Atkinson, A.B., Cowell, F.A. (eds.) *Panel Data on Incomes* (London, 1983).

Feldstein, M. 'Social Security, Induced Retirement and Aggregate Capital Accumulation', *Journal of Political Economy*, 82 (1974), 905–26.

—— 'Social Security and the Distribution of Wealth', *Journal of the American Statistical Association*, 71 (1976), 800–7.

Fouquet, A., Strauss-Kahn, D. 'The Size Distribution of Personal Wealth in France: A First Attempt at the Estate Duty Method.' Mimeo (1981).

Kessler, D., Masson, A. 'Transmission, accumulation et immobilité intergénérationelles des patrimoines', *Consommation*, 3–4 (1979a), 77–105.

176   *Denis Kessler and André Masson*

—— 'Les transferts intergénérationnel l'aide, la donation et l'héritage', *CNRS Report* (1979b).

—— 'Combien exist'il de modèles d'accumulation patrimoniale?' Mimeo (1984a).

—— 'On the Distributional Consequences of life Cycle Models', in: Kessler, D., Masson, A. (eds), *Modelling the Accumulation and Distribution of Wealth,*' Oxford (1987).

King, M.A., Dicks-Mireaux, L. 'Asset Holding and the Life Cycle', *Economic Journal*, 92 (1982), 247–61.

King, M.A., Leape, J. 'Household Portfolio Composition and the Life Cycle', Contribution to the Seminar on *Modelling the Accumulation and Distribution of Wealth*, Paris (1984).

Lillard, L. 'Inequality: Earning vs. Human Wealth', *American Economic Review*, 67 (1977), 43–53.

Masson, A. 'Profils diachroniques et inégalités: l'exemple de l'accumulation patrimoniale', in Kessler, D., Masson, A., Strauss-Kahn D. eds. *Accumulation et répartition des patrimoines* (Paris, 1982).

—— 'A Cohort Analysis of Wealth–Age Profiles Generated by A Simulation Model (France 1949–1975).' In Atkinson, A.B., Cowell, F.A. eds. *Panel Data on Incomes* (London, 1983).

Milot, J.P. 'Le patrimoine en 1979', *Economie et Statistique* (June 1982).

Modigliani, F. 'The Life Cycle Hypothesis of Saving Twenty Years Later.' In: Parkin, M., Nobay, A.R. eds. *Contemporary Issues In Economics* (1975).

Olson, M., Bailey, M. 'Positive Time Preference', *Journal of Political Economy*, 89 (1981). 1–25.

Shorrocks, A.F. 'Age–Wealth Relationship: A Cross-section and Cohort Analysis', *Review of Economics and Statistics*, 57 (1975), 155–63.

—— 'On the Structure of Intergenerational Transfers Between Families', *Economica* (1979), 415–26.

Strauss-Kahn, D. 'Eléments de comparaison internationale des patrimoines des ménages', *Economie et Statistique* (Sept 1979).

Taussig, M.K. 'Wealth Inequalities in the US.' In: Kessler, D., Masson, A., Strauss-Kahn, D. eds., *Accumulation et répartition des patrimoines* (Paris, 1982).

Tomes, N. 'The Family, Inheritance, and the Intergenerational Transmission of Inequality', *Journal of Political Economy*, 89 (1981), 928–58.

Vaughan R.N. 'Class Behaviour and the Distribution of Wealth', *Review of Economic Studies*, 47 (1979), 447–65.

Wolff, E.N. 'The Accumulation of Household Wealth over the Life Cycle: A Microdata Analysis', *Review of Income and Wealth*, 27 (1981), 75–96.

—— 'The Size Distribution of Household Disposable Wealth in the United States', *Review of Income and Wealth*, 29 (1983), 125–46.

III OTHER TOPICS IN ESTIMATING HOUSEHOLD WEALTH

8

Lifetime Coverage: The Adequacy of Canada's Retirement Income System

Michael C. Wolfson[1]

I. Introduction

One of the major issues in recent debates on pension reform in Canada is the adequacy of the pension arrangements now in place. Currently, many of Canada's elderly live below the poverty line and there have been major pressures to expand public pension programmes. Since these arrangements are still maturing, a key question is whether they can be expected to generate adequate retirement incomes in the future. This chapter provides a detailed analysis of the expected adequacy of current pension arrangements.

One of the fundamental objectives of Canada's pension system is that individuals should be able to avoid serious disruption in their living standards upon retirement. This objective implies that a key criterion in assessing the adequacy of the pension arrangements now in place is the extent to which individuals and families can in fact expect to maintain their pre-retirement living standards after retirement. This chapter highlights an analysis of pension adequacy in terms of this criterion or fundamental objective.

The analysis requires a number of assumptions or judgements that are clearly matters of public policy. For example, how much of a decline in living standards upon retirement constitutes a 'serious disruption'? What is a practical way to measure 'living standards'? What kinds of saving behaviour should be assumed for the future elderly? What government programmes or kinds of saving should be considered as part of Canada's retirement income system?

The answers to these questions are generally beyond the scope of this chapter. Nevertheless, specific answers must be assumed for the analysis to proceed, and this has been done. The sensitivity of the results to alternative assumptions is examined subsequently.

In this analysis, the expected adequacy of the pension system will be measured in terms of net replacement ratios. These ratios indicate the extent to which post-retirement consumption 'replaces' pre-retirement consumption; in other words, the numerator of the ratio is post-retirement consumption and the denominator is pre-retirement consumption. A net replacement ratio of one thus represents complete replacement or full maintenance of living standards. A ratio less than one indicates a decline in living standards.

If an individual worked, but did no saving at all, and never belonged to an occupational or employer-sponsored pension plan

Table 8.1a. *The definition of the net replacement ratio*

Numerator: post-retirement consumption	Denominator: pre-retirement consumption
Plus items[a]	*Plus items*
GIS	Labour earnings
OAS	
C/QPP	
Minus items	*Minus items*
Federal and provincial income taxes	Federal and provincial income taxes
	C/QPP premiums
	Unemployment insurance premiums
	Work-related expenses (5 per cent of earnings)

a. The Guaranteed Income Supplement (GIS) is essentially a guaranteed annual income for the 65 and over population. Benefits are currently bout 15% of the average wage for a single person and 25% for an elderly couple. Benefits are subject to a 50% tax back rate based on the previous year's net income for tax purposes. The Old Age Security (OAS) pension is a virtually universal demo-grant for the 65 + population and amounts to about 14% of the average wage. Both GIS and OAS are ordinarily CPI indexed and financed out of general federal revenues. The Canada and Quebec Pension Plans (C/QPP) provide earnings-related retirement pension of 25% of career average earnings (where the full career earnings base is updated by an index of average wages before being averaged) up to an intended ceiling of 25% of the average wage. These plans are financed on a pay-go basis by a payroll tax.

(legally referred to as a Registered Pension Plan or RPP), his net replacement ratio for purposes of this analysis would be defined as shown in Table 8.1a.

These items, of course, still represent an approximation to the concept of consumption. For example, work-related expenses are only a rough average, and consumer durables (for example furniture and appliances) purchased and used prior to retirement but also used after retirement have been ignored as an element of post-retirement consumption.

Individuals could choose to save some portion of their income during working years either in a savings account or by purchasing a house, and could then draw upon the accumulated savings after retirement by buying an annuity, making withdrawals from a savings account, continuing to live in or selling their house. They may also belong to an RPP. In these cases, the components of their net replacement ratio as just defined would have to be augmented as shown in Table 8.1b.

The resulting definition of the *net* replacement ratio in Tables 8.1a and 8.1b should be clearly distinguished from the concept of the gross replacement ratio. For example, the C/QPP provide (roughly speaking) benefits equal to 25 per cent of updated career

Table 8.1b. *Refinements to the definition of the net replacement ratio*

Numerator: post-retirement consumption	Denominator: pre-retirement consumption
Additional plus items	*Addition plus items*
RP (pension) benefits	Investment income
Investment income	Interest income
Interest income	Imputed rent on equity
Interest portion of	in owner-occupied housing
annuity income	
Imputed rent on owner-	*Additional minus items*
occupied housing	
Dissaving	Saving
Drawing down savings	Bank deposits
Capital portion of	House downpayment, capital
annuity income	portion of mortgage
Sale or reverse annuity	payments
mortgage on house	RPP contributions

average earnings, while an RPP might provide a maximum pension of 70 per cent of final average earnings. In both of these cases, the replacement ratios (that is, 25 per cent and 70 per cent) are gross rather than net; they take no account of income taxes, transfers, premiums, contributions, and so on. The concern in this analysis, however, is with *net* replacement ratios which more accurately reflect a household's consumption opportunities.

All the items in the two tables above are considered explicitly in this analysis for the final calculation of expected net replacement ratios. One of the principal reasons for the focus on net replacement ratios is to take some account of the view that the income needs of the elderly are lower than those of the working age population. This is clearly true insofar as the elderly no longer have to make pension contributions, save for retirement, incur work-related expenses, bear the costs related to raising children, or pay off a mortgage. It is also true to the extent that other sources of income like OAS and C/QPP come into pay after reaching age 65, as well as special income tax provisions such as the additional personal exemption for those over age 65. The net replacement ratio above takes all these factors into account.

However, some have argued further that after taking all these items into account, the elderly still need less income. For example, some have suggested that while expenditures for food and shelter remain relatively constant as a proportion of income, expenditures for furniture, automobiles, clothes, and other consumer goods fall. Some have also argued that the increase in leisure time after retirement compensates for a reduction in money income. Finally in the latter years of the retirement period, individuals may be confined to a nursing home where their ability to spend money on personal consumption is very limited. On the other hand, others have noted that the elderly may need more income in order to enjoy their additional leisure time; that the elderly experience new costs in hiring people to do tasks that in earlier years they did themselves; and that increased spending on bus and cab fares offsets at least in part any reduction in the costs of using a car.

These considerations all affect the question of what constitutes a 'serious disruption in living standards'. Since this question is a matter of judgement, the results of the analysis will be presented so as to accommodate differing views by showing results for expected net replacement ratios generally ranging from 75 per cent to 100 per cent, in other words expected declines in living standards ranging up to 25 per cent.

It should be noted that there are still some omissions in the net replacement ratio defined above. For example, some provincial governments provide top-ups to the GIS, and these have been excluded, as have social assistance benefits, and various pro-grammes providing in kind benefits such as subsidized rental accommodation. These omissions are relatively small, both in terms of aggregate expenditures and given that the focus in this analysis is on middle-income groups.

It might be argued (for example by the Canadian Labour Congress) that the net replacement ratio as defined above is too comprehensive. For example, why should GIS benefits be included if the focus is on the adequacy of pensions? The GIS, according to this view, is not a pension programme and it might be argued that an adequate pension system would result in many fewer people being eligible for GIS. On the other hand, GIS benefits clearly exist and it would not seem reasonable to suppose that the programme will be eliminated. The present trend, in fact, is that the GIS has been growing relative to the OAS.

Another example where the above definition may be considered too comprehensive concerns the extent to which the retired popula-tion should be expected to draw down their personal wealth—either accumulated savings or equity in an owner-occupied house. The current elderly do not appear to draw upon their accumulated wealth very much; instead they tend to consume the investment income and bequeath the capital to younger generations (see Wolfson (1977), Foot and Treffler (1983)). This implies that rela-tively low levels of dissavings are currently typical post-retirement (contrary to much economic theorizing).

None the less, for purposes of this analysis, it is assumed that a substantial proportion of personal wealth—whether in the form of personal savings or owner-occupied housing—is drawn upon in retirement. This assumption, by taking into account most sources of income available to the elderly, presents their potential consump-tion opportunities in the most favourable light that could reason-ably be expected. The analysis shows that even with this comprehensive definition of consumption opportunities, consider-able numbers of middle income Canadians are still likely to experience declines in their living standards upon retirement. The results of a number of sensitivity analyses have also been presented. These show the extent of the declines in living standards if there is little or no utilization of personal (non-pension) wealth in retirement. In these latter circumstances, the declines in living standards are considerably greater.

II. Overview of the Analysis

The analysis draws upon diverse sets of data and several earlier studies, and then attempts to weave these various strands together. Thus, it may be helpful at the beginning to have a brief sketch of the main strands and how they fit together.

The principal criterion to be used in assessing the adequacy of the pension system, the net replacement ratio, has just been discussed. In the first phase, a model was developed to simulate the lifetime impact of the current *public* pension system. This model allowed estimates to be made of the extent to which OAS, GIS, and C/QPP would maintain living standards in the future; in other words, estimates were made of the net replacement ratios that individuals and couples could expect if they did no personal saving and were never covered by an RPP. These estimates assume that the C/QPP are mature (that is, that the age cohort entered the labour force after 1966 when the C/QPP were introduced and that the Year's Maximum Pensionable Earnings or YMPE which had been lagging has in fact caught up to and equals the average wage), and that the structure of these programmes remains unchanged. It was also assumed that the OAS would retain its current relative role instead of being price indexed, that is, OAS benefits would remain a constant proportion of the average wage or, equivalently, of the maximum C/QPP pension.

The result of these simulations is a set of net replacement ratios for households over a range of pre-retirement earnings levels. Many are considerably less than one, indicating that a significant gap can be expected between the living standards that will be provided by mandatory Canada-wide basic public pensions, and pre-retirement living standards. This is of particular note for those in middle income ranges. Those in the lowest income groups pre-retirement can, in fact, expect net replacement ratios greater than one, mainly because of the minimum income guarantees provided by OAS and GIS. Those in the upper income ranges would also experience declines in living standards upon retirement if they made no other provisions. However, the situation of the wealthy will not be a concern in this analysis.

The assumption that the OAS will be updated to maintain its relative role is significant. The anticipated gap between pre- and post-retirement living standards taking only mandatory public programmes into account would be large if the OAS did not maintain in a general way its relationship to average wages. The analysis proceeds on the basis that the OAS will be updated, though the sensitivity of the results to this assumption is also considered.

The second phase of the analysis is devoted to estimating the prospective impact of individual saving, home ownership, and employer-sponsored pension plan (RPP) benefits on net replacement ratios. In order to assess the expected amounts of such private sources of retirement income, fairly detailed analyses have been made of patterns of private pension plan benefit accruals and accumulated household wealth.

A key feature of these analyses is that they are carried out in terms of distributions. The analysis does not consider merely the average level of private retirement income for a given subgroup of the population. Rather, numbers of households at all points in a range of levels of private retirement income (that is, frequency distributions) are estimated. This renders the analysis somewhat more complex, but greatly enhances its realism and the quality of the results. Three steps are involved.

First, in the case of private pension benefits, the typical effective sizes of current pension plans, rates of coverage, and vesting rules were determined. These were then entered as parameters of the detailed Monte Carlo simulation model of labour force mobility and pension benefit accrual. The output of this model was then an expected distribution of pension benefits expressed in terms of gross replacement ratios. Alternative distributions of expected private pension benefits based on three reform scenarios were also simulated.

Second, the 1977 Statistics Canada Survey of Consumer Finances, the most recent available, was drawn upon to provide a detailed picture of the distribution of non-pension personal wealth that individuals and families could expect to have as they entered retirement. These distributions of wealth were combined with assumed yields and patterns of dissaving after retirement to generate distributions of prospective pre-tax retirement income. Separate distributions were computed by earnings range and tenure category (owner or renter). Again, all the distributions were expressed in terms of gross replacement ratios.

Third, these distributions of retirement incomes expressed in terms of prospective gross replacement ratios were converted into distributions of net replacement ratios. This was based, for example, on the tax payable on the RPP benefit post-retirement and the tax deductibility of RPP contributions pre-retirement.

Finally, these various distributions were brought together to allow an overall assessment of the range of replacement ratios that current working age cohorts can expect after retirement. This analysis necessarily contains a range of assumptions, both technical and policy related. A number of these policy-related assumptions were mentioned in the section on the definition of adequacy; another is the assumed wage indexing of OAS. The final phase of the analysis examines the sensitivity of the basic results to various key assumptions.

1. The Lifetime Model

The starting point for the analysis is projections of the net replacement ratios to be expected from the public part of the retirement income system. The simulation model is designed to estimate over a household's or family's lifetime the year by year impact on consumption both pre- and post-retirement of personal saving, home ownership, RPP membership, income taxes, and public programmes (GIS, OAS, C/QPP, family allowances), in other words all the items mentioned earlier regarding the definition of the net replacement ratio. These estimates are for a specified set of households, where this set is chosen in order to be generally representative of Canadian households currently of working age. The main elements of the specification are the households' demographic characteristics and their lifetime employment income profiles.

The demographic characteristics have been set for three main family types—individuals who remain single throughout their lives, married couples who always have one earner, and married couples who always have two earners. These are clearly simplified cases, but they generally span the range of possibilities. For example, the situation of a couple where one spouse is in and out of the labour force from one year to the next would be an intermediate one, as would the case of a couple whose marriage broke down.

The employment income profiles have also been specially chosen. They were derived from detailed data on CPP contributors' sex, earnings, and ages so as to represent all Canadians with income from employment. Individuals or families were ranked in increasing order of earnings (by sex at each age) and then divided into equal groups of 10 per cent of the total population within each age–sex group—that is, earnings deciles. Then it was assumed that there is no income mobility across deciles over the entire working career (ages 18 to 64—clearly a strong assumption, but a simple polar case for the dispersion in lifetime earnings). Thus, for example, the third representative one-earner couple has an age–earnings profile based on the average earnings of males in the earnings range between the twentieth and thirtieth percentiles within each 5-year age range. As a result, the model enables projections to be made for various income groups where these groups can be defined with some precision. Since the focus of this analysis is middle-income households, attention will in the end be confined to the third to eighth deciles among each of the three households types.

Table 8.2 shows the results of a simulation run focusing only on the public portion of the pension system. For example, a fifth decile (that is, fortieth to fiftieth percentile) two-earner couple can expect to have annual earnings (in 1982 dollars) on average over their working career of about $29,200 and to pay income taxes averaging about $4,500. If the couple does no saving at all and never belongs to a pension plan, their pre-retirement disposable income will average about $22,100 (after also taking account of C/QPP and UI premiums and work-related expenses). In turn, their post-retirement consumption will be derived entirely from public sources, and will be about $13,900 in the first year. The resulting net replacement ratio in this case is thus 58.1 per cent.

As the first stage of the analysis, the basic level of income maintenance from public programmes must be estimated. Table 8.2 above referred to two-earner couples. Table 8.3 presents expected net replacement ratios from this model for the three different household types; single individuals, one-earner couples, and two-earner couples.

In the net replacement ratios for the surviving spouse, no

Table 8.2. *Selected components of pre- and post-retirement consumption for representative two-earner couples by earnings group assuming no savings or private pension plan coverage (annual averages, 1982 $000s)*

Earnings group (percentiles of population ranked by earnings)	Average pre-retirement			First-year post-retirement					Net replacement ratio
	Earnings	Income taxes	Consumption	OAS	GIS	C/QPP	Consumption		
0–10%	14.1	0.6	12.4	5.8	2.6	3.9	12.2		98.2
10–20	17.5	1.3	14.8	5.8	2.2	4.7	12.6		85.3
20–30	21.5	2.3	17.3	5.8	1.6	5.7	13.1		75.7
30–40	25.8	3.5	20.0	5.8	1.1	6.8	13.7		68.2
40–50	29.2	4.5	22.1	5.8	0.8	7.3	13.9		62.8
50–60	32.6	5.6	24.1	5.8	0.7	7.6	14.0		58.1
60–70	36.0	6.8	26.1	5.8	0.6	7.7	14.0		53.8
70–80	39.2	8.0	28.0	5.8	0.7	7.6	14.0		50.1
80–90	44.1	9.9	30.8	5.8	0.7	7.5	14.0		45.5
90–95	53.0	13.4	35.6	5.8	0.5	8.0	14.2		39.9
95–100	76.6	24.2	47.2	5.8	0.4	8.3	14.3		30.3

Table 8.3. *Net replacement ratio (%) for representative family types by earnings group based on OAS, GIS, and C/QPP and assuming no savings or private pension plan coverage*

Earnings group (percentiles of population)	Type of family unit					
	Single individual	One-earner couple		Two-earner couple		
		First year of retirement	Surviving spouse	First year of retirement	Surviving spouse	
0–10%	205.9	349.4	196.8	102.5	61.4
10–20	113.1	173.0	97.1	93.8	55.3
20–30	85.4	121.2	67.9	80.9	47.5
30–40	72.3	102.1	57.1	71.2	41.8
40–50	64.8	91.6	51.2	65.9	38.6
50–60	56.8	80.7	45.1	59.8	35.1
60–70	50.3	71.5	40.0	54.6	32.0
70–80	44.4	63.4	35.4	51.0	29.9
80–90	37.6	54.2	30.3	45.7	26.8
90–95	31.0	44.8	25.0	38.9	22.7
95–100	20.1	29.5	16.5	27.5	16.0

adjustment for differences in family size has been made, mainly because such an adjustment is basically a matter of judgement. Nevertheless, many would consider a net replacement ratio for a surviving spouse of 60 to 67 per cent of that for the couple immediately following retirement to represent full maintenance of living standards during the retirement period. In fact, these figures show the surviving spouse's replacement ratios to be about 56 per cent and 59 per cent of the couples replacement ratio for one- and two-earner couples respectively (that is, the ratios of the figures in the last column to those in the second last column are all about 59 per cent). The 56 per cent and 59 per cent numbers are thus lower than the 60 to 67 per cent often used as a benchmark.

Table 8.3 shows that among the three types of family units, one-earner couples can expect the highest levels of net replacement from public programmes in each income group (initially while both spouses are alive). The main reason for these higher net replacement ratios is the second OAS benefit post-retirement combined with there being only one earner pre-retirement (that is, a relatively larger numerator than single individuals, and a relatively smaller denominator than two-earner couples, in making up the net replacement ratio).

Table 8.3 suggests further that the bottom 20 per cent of single individuals, the bottom 40 per cent of one-earner couples, and the bottom 10 per cent of two-earner couples might consider themselves to be *worse off* if they saved for retirement or belonged to an RPP. The reason is that their post-retirement consumption can already be expected to be more than 100 per cent of their pre-retirement consumption without any saving or RPP benefits (leaving aside the question of the appropriate level of net replacement for surviving spouses).

On the other hand, those in the middle quintile (fortieth to sixtieth percentile) can expect a net replacement ratio in their first year of retirement in the 56.8 to 91.6 per cent range, depending primarily on their family status. Thus, without any private saving or RPP benefits to augment the public programmes, many in this middle-income group could expect significant declines in living standards upon retirement.

III. Private Sources of Retirement Income

The next main step in the analysis is to determine the amount of private source income that is likely to be available after retirement. These income sources can be divided into five main categories: accumulated savings, owner-occupied housing, RPP benefits, continued employment past age 65, and intra-family transfers. The option of continued employment has not been considered, since it is contrary to the basic premise of a retirement income system. No data exist on the last category, intra-family transfers, so it has not been included in the analysis. Thus, to the extent that the future elderly can count on continued employment income or financial support from their children or other relatives, the amounts they would need from the other three sources in order to provide an adequate retirement income are reduced. Looking at it a different way, the results from this analysis of expected declines in living standards will be overstated.

A further problem is that only very limited data are available jointly on RPPs and personal non-pension wealth (that is, savings and owner-occupied housing). The analysis will therefore deal first with RPPs, then with personal non-pension wealth, each separately, and then estimates will be made of expected distributions of retirement income from these two sources jointly.

A major consideration in this part of the analysis is that distributions of wealth and expected RPP benefits are unequal. In this area particularly, the use of average levels of wealth and expected RPP benefits can be seriously misleading, simply because so many households are far above or far below the average.

The main determinants of expected RPP benefits are the extent of RPP coverage, the typical levels of pension benefits for those who are covered, vesting rules, anticipated rates of inflation and the degree of inflation protection of pension benefits, and patterns of labour force mobility. In order to estimate expected distribution of RPP benefits, that is, the distribution of private pension wealth, these factors must be combined in a complex dynamic model, one that follows individuals through their working years, keeping track of the periods when they are covered by an RPP, and accumulating benefits as they become vested. Several scenarios for the reform of the private pension system were considered, based on the results of the Task Force Report (1979, Appendix 8).

The other main private sources of prospective income in retirement are from savings and home ownership—the stock of non-pension wealth accumulated by a household during its working years which it can then draw upon after retirement. This wealth may take the form of saving deposits, bonds, company shares, equity in a business, and equity in an owner-occupied home.

The basic empirical question is how much personal non-pension wealth are Canadian families likely to have as they enter retirement in the future, and how is it likely to be distributed. One reasonable alternative is to project from the current situation. The basic assumption is that current levels of wealth relative to earnings and current patterns of the distribution of wealth (that is, relative shapes of the density functions) will persist.

To the extent that any trends are evident that seem to contradict this basic assumption, they can be factored into the interpretation of the final results. For example, personal sector saving rates in Canada as conventionally reported have increased dramatically over the past decade. If this represents a long-run shift in household saving behaviour, it would mean that the expected replacement ratios derived in this analysis were too low. However, this increase in saving rates has not been nearly as great when corrected for inflation (that is, for the decline in the real value of nominal personal sector assets like bonds and Guaranteed Investment Certificates). Also, it may not represent any fundamental shift in lifetime saving behaviour insofar as it reflects instead the baby boom bulge in the age structure, or increased precautionary saving during the current period of economic weakness.

Another example concerns housing. It may be that the incidence of home ownership will decline in coming decades. Alternatively, there may be a continuing shift in the forms of home ownership from single family dwellings towards condominiums. The latter kind of trend would be compatible with the basic assumption being made. The former trend could imply that the estimates of expected income from private saving and home ownership are too high.

A third example concerns the evolving role of public pensions. It has been argued that public pensions are at least in part a substitute for personal wealth. To the extent that this is true, and to the extent that recent levels of personal wealth embody savings behaviour dating back before the inception of the C/QPP and GIS, then these levels will represent overestimates of future levels of personal wealth. In turn, this would imply that the estimates in this analysis of expected income in retirement from personal wealth will be too high; insufficient account will have been taken of the extent to which enlarged public pensions displace personal wealth accumulation. (This factor is largely taken into account for RPPs because the extent to which their benefits are integrated with the C/QPP has been taken into account.)

The most recent source of data on the distribution of personal wealth in Canada is the Statistics Canada Survey of Consumer Finances for 1977 (henceforth the SCF). This survey collected detailed data on the assets, including RRSPs (Registered Retirement Savings Plan, similar to IRAs and Keogh plans in the US) and debts of a large stratified sample of Canadian family units as of May 1977, as well as their incomes for the year 1976, and whether or not they were covered by an RPP. These SCF data have provided the basis for the estimated replacement incomes Canadian families can expect during retirement from their personal savings and home ownership.

Since the focus in the analysis is on replacement adequacy, these distributions of personal non-pension wealth have to be converted to common units with public and private pension plan wealth, that is, expected replacement ratios. Essentially, the analysis is an attempt to determine the shape of the joint distribution of public pension, private pension, and private non-pension wealth. However, instead of using stocks of dollars as the numeraire, the common unit of measurement will eventually be net replacement ratios.

The analysis of the private non-pension wealth data began by singling out all those family units (single individuals and couples) where the age of the family's head was 50 to 64, the major source of income of the family was from earnings (that is, employment or self-employment income), and the family head or spouse was the principal earner. In this way, the focus could be on the wealth positions of families just prior to retirement, and on those families where income replacement is a reasonable concern (that is, excluding the poor whose major source of income is government transfers, and the very wealthy who can live on the income from their capital).

These family units were then quite finely disaggregated by several variables expected to have a significant relationship with the distribution of personal wealth. In particular, separate wealth distributions (at the decile level) were tabulated for this group of family units broken down by earnings ranges, and then these joint wealth–earnings distributions were disaggregated by 5-year age ranges, whether or not they were home owners, and whether or not they were covered by an RPP. Based on inspection of these cross-tabulations, it was concluded that the finer 5-year age breakdown and the breakdown by RPP coverage status were not generally significant to the analysis. As a result, more aggregated and hence statistically robust wealth distributions, broken down only by earnings range and tenure, were ultimately used.

RPP coverage, the closest proxy available for private pension plan wealth, did not appear inversely correlated with non-pension wealth, particularly in the bottom half of the wealth spectrum. This is significant for a later stage of this analysis. Conventional economic theory suggests that private pension wealth in the form of expected RPP benefits should largely be a substitute for other forms of personal wealth. Thus, RPP coverage should be associated with lower levels of average personal wealth. This was only clearly apparent in the top 20 per cent of the wealth spectrum for savings other than in an owner-occupied house. It was not clearly apparent for the bottom half of the wealth spectrum and, indeed, in a significant number of cases equity in owner-occupied housing was positively rather than negatively related to RPP coverage.

An explanation for these observed patterns could be that there is a minimum level of savings by families that is not related to retirement planning; rather, saving at these low levels may be precautionary or habitual. Because it is for different purposes, this extent of saving is generally unaffected by RPP coverage. It is only when a family has accumulated substantial wealth that the potential of substitutability with RPP coverage becomes meaningful.

This view is made more plausible when the question of how to transform these savings and house equity to earnings ratios to estimates of replacement income is addressed below. Basically, a ratio of less than 1.0 corresponds to the replacement that would be generated by less than 5 years of service in a 'good' pension plan, so that accumulated savings or house equity are still quite small in such cases in comparison to a reasonable amount of private pension wealth.

A further interesting item was the apparent positive correlation between RPP coverage and home ownership throughout the upper-middle earnings range and in the top wealth quintiles of the other two earnings ranges. Perhaps in these cases, both home ownership and RPP coverage are related to a third factor such as a more stable career pattern with a larger employer.

Since the overall results of the analysis will depend only on the savings and house equity to earnings ratios in the first two or three quintiles (that is, those people least likely to have sufficient private means to fill the gap between the income replacement provided by the public pension system and full maintenance), it was considered reasonable to ignore the inverse correlation between RPP coverage and the savings to earnings ratio in the top quintile. Instead it was assumed that the savings to earnings and house equity to earnings ratios are not generally correlated with the RPP coverage.

The results also indicate that there are large and systematic differences between owners and renters. Homeowners are not only better off by the net equity in their homes; they also have substantially higher savings in almost all cases. Home ownership thus indicates a more basic difference in levels of wealth. Because of the significance of the disaggregation by tenure, this division is retained in the subsequent analysis.

The prospective retirement income resulting from accumulated non-pension wealth was derived by considering savings and net equity in owner-occupied housing separately within each decile of the wealth distribution. Family units in each earnings range and tenure group were distributed in terms of their level of (non-pension) wealth, and within each wealth decile of the distribution, the savings and home-ownership components were tabulated separately. This was done to enable the analysis to consider drawing upon these two forms of wealth in different ways during retirement.

Savings were defined to exclude cash on hand, the value of automobiles, and half the amounts in checking accounts and other liquid assets less personal debts, since these were not considered retirement savings. (These exclusions amount to just over 10 per cent of average net worth.)

Because of evidence (presented in the documentation of the SCF microdata tape) that there was substantial underreporting of the wealth components making up savings as defined here, these data from the SCF were scaled up to 150 per cent of their reported values. While this is a rough adjustment, it generally insures that any underreporting in the SCF will not cause the results of this analysis to overstate the expected gaps in maintenance of living standards.

The savings data were then converted to gross replacement ratios by assuming that upon retirement these accumulated savings were used in a manner generally equivalent to the purchase of a fully indexed joint and survivor annuity. The resulting expected distributions of income from saving, expressed in terms of gross replacement ratios, are shown in Table 8.4.

Gross replacement ratios resulting from home ownership were computed based on the assumption that on average, half the net equity value of the house was liquidated and used in a manner generally equivalent to the purchase of a fully indexed joint and survivor life annuity. Liquidating half the house corresponds roughly to situations where the house is sold half way through the retirement period, or a reverse annuity mortgage on half the value of the house is acquired at retirement. The other half of the house was assumed to continue to yield benefits in the form of net imputed rental income, in order to put homeowners on the same footing as renters in the analysis. The resulting expected distributions of gross replacement ratios are shown in Table 8.5.

Table 8.4. *Expected distributions of gross replacement ratios (%) from personal savings by earnings range and tenure based on the 1977 SCF for all family units aged 50 to 64 with employment the principal source of income*

Wealth decile	Lower-middle earnings		Middle-middle earnings		Upper-middle earnings	
	Own	Rent	Own	Rent	Own	Rent
1	− 0.1	− 0.8	0.9	− 1.1	0.8	− 1.9
2	2.6	0.9	3.1	− 0.9	1.5	0.2
3	4.3	0.9	2.7	0.6	2.2	0.4
4	6.0	0.9	3.0	0.8	3.5	1.1
5	6.4	0.9	3.9	0.8	4.2	3.0
6	6.2	2.9	5.5	0.8	3.9	5.5
7	8.4	5.4	8.4	1.9	5.0	5.8
8	11.4	5.4	11.6	3.7	7.7	9.5
9	42.5	8.9	21.8	7.5	14.2	14.5
10	134.1	21.2	89.9	27.4	63.8	32.3

Table 8.5. *Expected distributions of gross replacement ratios (%) from home ownership by earnings range and tenure based on the 1977 SCF for all family units aged 50 to 64 with employment the principal source of income*

Wealth decile	Lower-middle earnings		Middle-middle earnings		Upper-middle earnings	
	Own	Rent	Own	Rent	Own	Rent
1	2.9	0.0	3.8	0.0	2.8	0.0
2	6.4	0.0	5.3	0.0	4.5	0.0
3	9.0	0.0	7.1	0.0	5.5	0.0
4	10.4	0.0	8.0	0.0	6.8	0.0
5	11.8	0.0	9.8	0.0	7.7	0.0
6	14.6	0.0	11.1	0.0	8.3	0.0
7	16.8	0.0	12.1	0.0	9.5	0.0
8	19.8	0.0	13.2	0.0	9.9	0.0
9	16.6	0.0	13.4	0.0	10.6	0.0
10	16.2	0.0	13.7	0.0	9.7	0.0

The assumptions regarding owner-occupied housing are quite important to the overall results of this analysis. For example, some may feel that it is inappropriate to expect the elderly to draw at all upon the capital value of their homes. An alternative assumption, for example, would be to include only the imputed rent on the net equity of the house.

Not drawing at all on the capital value of owner-occupied housing would, however, result in lower expected replacement ratios from personal wealth. The assumption being made here thus tends to show the current retirement income system being more adequate. The sensitivity of the overall results to this assumption is considered below, as well as sensitivity to the particular choice of interest rates and hence annuity factors, and sensitivity to the valuation of imputed rent.

The figures in Tables 8.4 and 8.5 illustrate how unequally income from non-pension wealth is likely to be distributed. Taking homeowners in the 'middle-middle' earnings range, for example, those in the top wealth decile can expect about 90 per cent gross replacement from their savings alone (third column, bottom row of Table 8.4), leaving aside their equity in a house, and RPP and public pension benefits. However, 90 per cent of renters in the same earnings range can expect less than 10 per cent gross replacement from their non-pension wealth when they enter retirement (fourth column of Table 8.4).

One caveat regarding these prospective retirement incomes from personal saving and home ownership should be noted. The distributions in Tables 8.4 and 8.5 assume a completely certain real rate of return during the post-retirement period. However, in fact there will likely be considerable volatility in these rates of return. Thus, the distributions likely understate the dispersion in prospective gross replacement ratios.

So far the analysis has focused on gross replacement rates for each of the three kinds of private savings. Table 8.6 shows the implied net replacement rates from total 'personal wealth', defined as the sum of RPP benefits, savings, and housing. As expected, homeowners have systematically higher prospective net replacement rates.

IV. Combining Net Replacement Ratios from Public and Private Sources

As the final stage of the analysis, it is now possible to bring together the two sets of net replacement ratios—those for public pension benefits as in Tables 8.2 and 8.3, and those for personal wealth as in Table 8.6. The objective is to determine what proportions of family units can expect to achieve at most a given net replacement ratio taking account of both the public programmes and accumulated personal wealth.

The final results of the analysis are shown in Table 8.7 under a range of assumptions. The figures in row 1 show that under the 'Current Situation', almost one-half can expect at least a 5 per cent decline in net living standards upon retirement (that is, a net replacement ratio of at most 95 per cent), close to one-third at least a 15 per cent decline, and about one in six at least a 25 per cent decline. The corresponding fractions under the 'Full Cost Reform' scenario (row 2) are about one-third, one-fifth, and one in ten.

The proportions failing to exceed the various levels of net replacement under the 'low cost reform' and 'minimal reform' scenarios are shown in the third and fourth rows of Table 8.7. As might be expected, these figures are between the first two sets of results.

Table 8.6. *Expected distributions of net replacement ratios (%) from total personal wealth*[a] *by earnings range and tenure*

Wealth decile	Lower-middle earnings		Middle-middle earnings		Upper-middle earnings	
	Own	Rent	Own	Rent	Own	Rent
1	9.3	0.5	11.0	− 0.3	8.9	− 0.4
2	19.4	2.1	17.0	1.2	15.4	3.2
3	24.8	5.1	22.0	3.6	19.3	7.3
4	29.5	7.3	26.9	6.5	23.3	10.8
5	34.6	10.3	31.7	9.8	27.3	14.8
6	40.4	13.9	36.8	13.8	32.7	19.4
7	46.4	18.5	43.7	18.9	37.9	24.4
8	58.4	23.2	50.3	25.3	44.5	31.3
9	81.5	29.1	64.1	33.8	57.0	40.6
10	182.6	38.4	142.9	46.0	113.3	56.6

a. This is defined as the sum of RPPs, savings, and home ownership, where RPPs are assumed to be distributed independently of income from savings and housing.

The results are particularly sensitive to the assumption that the OAS will maintain its relative role. Rows 5 to 8 of Table 8.7 show the results if instead the OAS maintains its real purchasing power but falls as a proportion of the average wage and hence relative to the C/QPP. (The income-tested GIS part of the guaranteed annual income for the elderly however is assumed to maintain its relationship to the average wage.) In this case, over 40 per cent of families and individuals could expect a drop of at least 25 per cent in net living standards upon retirement. With 'full cost reform' of RPPs, this figure would be 28.2 per cent. Thus, the question of the form of indexing for the OAS demogrant portion of the elderly's guaranteed annual income is far more significant—by at least 2.5 times in terms of proportions expected to fail to achieve various net replacement ratios—than the potential impact of regulatory reform for occupational pension plans (RPPs).

A second alternative assumption concerning the public programmes is examined in rows 9 to 12. Here, the OAS is assumed to maintain its relative role, the base case assumption, but GIS is ignored. The results in these rows thus show the expected declines in net replacement ratios if GIS is *not* considered part of the pension system. These results show that 5 to 6 per cent more middle-income family units would experience various declines in net replacement if they could not rely on GIS (for example, 21.1 rather than 15.9 per cent comparing rows 9 and 1 for a 25 per cent decline in net replacement ratios). Under the 'full cost reform' scenario for RPPs, about 3½ per cent more middle-income family units would experience various declines in net replacement without any GIS (comparing rows 10 and 2). Thus, GIS as currently structured would continue to play a substantial role for middle-income households even if RPPs were substantially reformed and upgraded.

Another assumption to which the results are quite sensitive is the treatment of home ownership. Rows 13 to 16 show the sensitivity of the initial results to alternative assumptions. (Rows 14 and 1 are identical.) The results in row 13 assume that all equity in an owner-occupied house is fully annuitized upon retirement. As a result, 3 to 5 per cent fewer family units would experience the declines in net replacement shown in row 1. Alternatively, row 15 shows the results assuming that none of the net equity in owner-occupied housing is drawn upon during retirement. Instead homeowners are assumed to derive benefits in retirement only from the net imputed rental income on their homes. Under this assumption, which is in line with the Task Force Report, one in five could expect a decline of at least 25 per cent in net living standards under the 'current situation'. Finally, row 16 shows the results if housing is ignored completely, with neither net equity nor imputed rent taken into account. Under this assumption, 28 per cent of middle-income family units could expect at least a 25 per cent decline in living standards upon retirement. Overall, annuitizing owner-occupied housing and thus assuming this form of wealth is drawn upon fully during retirement, instead of ignoring home ownership, makes a difference of about 20 percentage points in the proportion of middle-income households who can expect various declines in net living standards upon retirement. Thus, the treatment of owner-occupied housing is second only to the question of the indexing of the OAS in assessing the prospective adequacy of Canada's retirement income system. It is far more significant than regulatory reform of private pensions and the debate on whether or not GIS should be considered part of the pension system.

Rows 17 to 20 illustrate the impact of regulatory reform of RPPs just as in rows 1 to 4 except that only the imputed rent aspect of

Table 8.7. *Final simulation results and selected sensitivity analyses.*
Percentages of middle-income family units expected to face various declines in net replacement upon retirement

Row	Public programmes[a]	RPP reform[b]	Drawing upon accumulated		Minimum expected decline in net replacement ratios (%)					
			Savings[c]	House[d]	25	20	15	10	5	0
1	Base	Current	Base	Base	15.9	22.3	30.0	37.6	45.2	52.0
2	Base	Full cost	Base	Base	9.2	13.7	19.6	26.1	33.1	40.5
3	Base	Lower cost	Base	Base	9.9	14.9	21.2	28.4	35.8	43.4
4	Base	Minimal	Base	Base	13.5	19.6	27.3	35.1	43.3	50.6
5	OAS–CPI	Current	Base	Base	41.2	49.6	57.2	64.3	70.6	75.3
6		Full cost	Base	Base	28.2	36.1	44.3	52.2	59.4	65.9
7		Lower cost	Base	Base	30.7	39.2	47.6	55.6	62.6	69.0
8		Minimal	Base	Base	38.4	47.5	55.8	63.4	69.9	74.8
9	No GIS	Current	Base	Base	21.1	28.8	36.2	43.6	51.1	58.1
10	No GIS	Full Cost	Base	Base	12.0	17.3	23.2	29.6	36.5	43.7
11	No GIS	Lower cost	Base	Base	13.0	18.7	25.2	32.2	39.7	47.2
12	No GIS	Minimal	Base	Base	17.7	25.0	32.8	40.6	48.6	56.3
13	Base	Current	Base	All ann.	12.7	18.2	25.2	32.3	39.2	46.0
14	Base	Current	Base	Base	15.9	22.3	30.0	37.6	45.2	52.0
15	Base	Current	Base	Imp. rent	20.3	27.6	35.9	44.0	51.6	58.5
16	Base	Current	Base	Ignore	28.0	36.2	44.9	53.2	60.6	66.6

Table 8.7. (*Cont*):

Scenario assumed

Row	Public programmes[a]	RPP reform[b]	Drawing upon accumulated		Minimum expected decline in net replacement ratios (%)					
			Savings[c]	House[d]	25	20	15	10	5	0
17	Base	Current	Base	Imp. rent	20.3	27.6	35.9	44.0	51.6	58.5
18	Base	Full cost	Base	Imp. rent	11.9	17.3	24.1	31.2	39.0	46.6
19	Base	Lower cost	Base	Imp. rent	12.9	18.8	26.2	34.0	42.1	49.8
20	Base	Minimal	Base	Imp. rent	17.3	24.5	33.1	41.7	49.9	57.4
21	Base	Current	r = 3%	r = 3%	13.7	19.5	26.7	33.9	41.0	47.9
22	Base	Current	Base	Base	15.9	22.3	30.0	37.6	45.2	52.0
23	Base	Current	r = 1%	r = 1%	18.6	25.5	33.8	41.7	49.5	56.3
24	Base	Current	Base	Base	15.9	22.3	30.0	37.6	45.2	52.0
25	Base	Current	Inv. inc.	Base	18.3	25.3	33.8	41.8	49.7	56.5
26	Base	Current	Inv. inc.	Imp. rent	23.5	31.4	40.4	48.9	56.7	63.5
27	Base	Current	Inv. inc.	Ignore	32.4	40.9	50.1	58.5	65.4	71.2
28	OAS–CPI	Current	Base	Base	41.2	49.6	57.2	64.3	70.6	75.3
29	OAS–CPI	Current	Base	Imp. rent	48.9	57.2	64.6	71.4	76.4	80.2
30	OAS–CPI	Current	Inv. inc.	Imp. rent	54.5	63.0	69.9	75.9	80.4	84.0
31	OAS–CPI	Current	Inv. inc.	Ignore	64.9	72.0	77.6	82.5	86.1	88.6
32	OAS–CPI	Full cost	Base	Base	28.2	36.1	44.3	52.2	59.4	65.9
33	OAS–CPI	Full cost	Inv. inc.	Imp. rent	38.7	48.1	56.8	64.7	71.4	76.8

34	OAS–CPI	Full cost	Inv. inc.	Ignore	49.3	58.5	66.4	73.4	78.9	83.1
35	No GIS	Current	Inv. inc.	Imp. rent	30.5	39.3	48.0	56.2	63.5	70.0
36	No GIS	Full cost	Inv. inc.	Imp. rent	17.6	24.4	31.7	39.5	47.4	55.1
37	No GIS	Lower cost	Inv. inc.	Imp. rent	19.1	26.5	34.6	43.1	51.4	59.2
38	No GIS	Minimal	Inv. inc.	Imp. rent	26.0	35.0	44.2	53.2	61.5	68.9

a. Three alternative scenarios have been considered for the public programmes. The 'base' assumption is the basic one described in the main text. In particular, OAS and GIS are assumed to maintain their relationship to the AIW (Average Industril Wage), in effect each to be wage indexed; and full account is taken of GIS. Under the alternative 'OAS–CPI' assumption, OAS remains price indexed but falls relative to the AIW. (The maximum GIS benefit remains wage indexed; but the combined OAS + GIS guarantee falls relative to the AIW.) Under the third alternative, 'No GIS', GIS is completely ignored while OAS maintains its relationship to the AIW.

b. The four scenarios can be summarized as follows: (i) Vesting occurs after 40 years of age and 5 years of service in the 'current' scenario but at 25 years of age and 2 years of service in the others. (ii) Indexing of benefits is assumed to be complete in the 'full cost' and 'lower cost' scenarios but partial in the other two. (iii) Coverage is assumed to be 100 per cent of public workers in all scenarios, 60 per cent of private workers in the first three scenarios, and 50 per cent in the 'minimal' scenario. (iv) Unit benefit reductions to offset the costs of reform are assumed to be zero in the first two scenarios but 10 per cent for public workers and 25 per cent for private workers in the last two scenarios.

c. The 'base' assumption is that virtually all savings are used to purchase a joint and two-thirds survivor annuity at retirement assuming a 2% real yield, effectively implying full CPI indexing of the stream of annuity payments. The '$r = 3\%$' and '$r = 1\%$' cases are identical to the 'base' case except that the annuity factors are based on 3% and 1% interest rate assumptions respectively. The 'inv. inc. scenario assumes instead that savings (other than in RRSPs which must, by law, be annuitized) are drawn upon only to the extent of the real investment income they yield at a rate of 2%.

d. The 'base' assumption is that half of the equity in owner-occupied housing is annuitized by purchasing a joint and two-thirds survivor annuity based on a 2% yield, and that the other half yields a stream of imputed net rental income at a real rate of 2%. The '$r = 3\%$' and '$r = 1\%$' cases are identical to the 'base' case except that 3% and 1% yields are used instead both for the annuity factors and the imputed rent. The 'imp. rent' case assumes that none of the net equity is annuitized; instead the whole value of owner-occupied housing is drawn upon during retirement only to the extent of an annual 2% yield in the form of imputed net rental income. Finally, the 'ignore' case assumes a zero contribution of equity in owner-occupied housing to post-retirement consumption.

owner-occupied housing is taken into account. Compared to the
base assumption where half of the equity is assumed to be drawn
upon, the RPP reforms appear somewhat more important.

Rows 21 to 23 illustrate the sensitivity of the results to alternative
interest rate assumptions for annuitizing private non-pension
wealth upon retirement. (Rows 1 and 22 are identical.) This is of
lesser importance than any of the other factors considered so far.

Rows 24 to 27 consider various steps towards ignoring both
owner-occupied housing and the capital portion of other private
non-pension wealth. In row 27, for example, housing is completely
ignored and only (real) investment income is considered. Measured
this way, almost a third of middle-income households could expect
a decline of at least 25 per cent in living standards upon retirement.

If, in addition, the OAS did not maintain its relative position
(that is, it was CPI indexed, row 31), the one-third figure would rise
to almost two-thirds. Thus, by ignoring most personal wealth, and
taking the current statutory treatment of OAS, Canada's pension
system does look seriously inadequate. Even with an optimistic
scenario for RPP reform (row 34), this would still be the case.

Finally, Table 8.8. provides a more detailed picture of the results
in the base case scenario, row 1 of Table 8.7. It shows the proportions of households facing various declines in net replacement disaggregated by family type and income decile, and for a wider range
of net replacement ratios. This table shows that among family
types, one-earner couples can expect the highest net replacement
ratios and single individuals the lowest, with two-earner couples in
between but closer to single individuals. By deciles within the
middle-income group, lower-income deciles can expect uniformly
higher net replacement ratios. This is principally a consequence of
the flat demogrant OAS which is proportionally of greater significance at lower levels.

Endnotes

1. Currently, Director, Social and Economic Studies Division, Statistics Canada.
   This chapter is based largely on 'Background Note No. 4', which was published
   by the Government of Canada to improve public understanding and encourage
   public discussion of some of the more detailed and technical issues that arise
   from the federal 'Green Paper' *Better Pensions for Canadians*, Ottawa, Dec 1982.
   Many details which are omitted in this paper are contained in Background Note

Table 8.8. *Further details on base case final simulation results: percentages of middle-income family units expected to attain at most various net replacement ratios by decile and family type*

Family type	Decile	Maximum expected net replacement ratio (%)										
		50	60	70	75	80	85	90	95	100	110	120
Never married single individuals	3	0.0	0.0	0.0	0.0	0.0	0.0	10.6	19.8	28.3	45.1	62.8
	4	0.0	0.0	0.0	7.5	16.6	25.2	32.7	41.6	51.1	67.4	77.3
	5	1.6	1.6	8.6	13.8	22.1	31.5	41.1	50.4	59.4	73.2	82.2
	6	1.6	6.3	18.6	27.7	37.2	46.6	55.9	64.0	70.5	81.1	86.7
	7	1.0	10.5	30.9	43.0	53.3	62.1	70.4	77.2	81.1	87.1	88.6
	8	6.1	20.8	45.1	54.9	63.7	71.8	77.9	81.8	85.6	87.9	89.4
	average	1.7	6.5	17.2	24.5	32.2	39.5	48.1	55.8	62.7	73.6	81.2
One-earner couples	3	0.0	0.0	0.0	0.0	0.0	0.0	0.0	0.0	0.0	0.0	0.0
	4	0.0	0.0	0.0	0.0	0.0	0.0	0.0	0.0	0.0	16.9	33.0
	5	1.6	1.6	1.6	1.6	1.6	1.6	1.6	6.6	12.0	28.1	47.0
	6	1.6	1.6	1.6	1.6	1.6	7.6	12.9	20.6	29.8	48.7	65.4
	7	1.0	1.0	1.0	4.3	8.7	17.1	27.9	40.2	51.1	68.7	80.2
	8	1.0	1.0	7.0	13.8	23.3	35.5	47.4	56.7	65.5	78.7	86.4
	average	0.9	0.9	1.9	3.6	5.9	10.3	15.0	20.7	26.4	40.2	52.0
Two-earner couples	3	0.0	0.0	0.0	0.0	0.0	9.7	18.9	27.5	34.7	53.9	69.2
	4	0.0	0.0	0.0	9.3	18.4	27.1	34.3	43.7	53.3	68.9	77.9
	5	1.6	1.6	7.4	12.7	20.2	29.4	39.0	48.3	57.5	71.7	81.6
	6	1.6	2.0	13.8	22.1	31.5	41.1	50.4	59.4	66.6	79.3	85.0
	7	1.0	5.9	20.3	32.6	44.6	54.5	63.4	71.5	77.8	85.5	87.9
	8	1.0	9.3	29.2	41.4	52.0	60.9	69.4	76.4	80.6	87.0	88.4
	average	0.9	3.1	11.8	19.7	27.8	37.1	45.9	54.5	61.7	74.4	81.7

Table 8.8. *(Cont)*:

Maximum expected net replacement ratio (%)

Family type	Decile	50	60	70	75	80	85	90	95	100	110	120
Weighted average	3	0.0	0.0	0.0	0.0	0.0	5.6	12.4	18.7	24.0	37.5	48.9
	4	0.0	0.0	0.0	6.4	13.0	19.2	24.5	31.1	38.0	54.1	65.2
	5	1.6	1.6	5.9	9.8	15.3	22.0	28.8	37.0	45.1	59.7	72.0
	6	1.6	2.5	11.1	17.2	24.0	32.5	40.8	49.2	56.9	71.0	79.8
	7	1.0	5.3	16.5	26.2	35.9	45.2	54.5	63.6	70.8	81.0	85.8
	8	1.8	8.7	25.3	35.7	45.7	55.4	64.5	71.7	77.1	84.8	88.0
	average	1.0	3.0	9.8	15.9	22.3	30.0	37.6	45.2	52.0[a]	64.7	73.3

a. Same as first row in Table 8.7.

No. 4 and its annexes. Any views expressed as well as any errors are those of the author alone and are not necessarily those of the Government of Canada.

References

Foot, D., Treffler, D. 'Life-Cycle Saving and Population Aging.' Working Paper no. 8308, Department of Economics and Institute for Policy Analysis, University of Toronto (1983).

Government of Canada *The Retirement Income System in Canada: Problems and Alternative Policies for Reform* the 'Task Force Report', (Ottawa, 1979).

—— *Better Pensions for Canadians* (Ottawa, 1982).

—— 'Background Note No. 4—Lifetime Coverage.' Mimeo. (Ottawa, 1983).

Statistics Canada, Public Use Sample Micro Data Tape for the 1977 Survey of Consumer Finance, 'Income, Assets, and Debts of Economic Family Units.' Ottawa.

Wolfson, M.C. *The Causes of Inequality in the Distribution of Wealth—A Simulation Analysis* Ph.D. Thesis, Cambridge University (1977).

9

The Effects of Pensions and Social Security on the Distribution of Wealth in the US

Edward N. Wolff[1]

This chapter simulates a 'lifetime' wealth distribution, which includes pension, social security, and human capital wealth, as well as traditional or disposable elements of household wealth. Calculations are made for the United States in 1969. Three concepts of household wealth are developed. The first is what I call 'household disposable wealth', which includes the traditional components of the household portfolio. The second is 'household reserve wealth', where it is assumed that the reserves of pension funds are included as part of the household portfolio along with traditional assets. Various assumptions are made to assign pension reserves to individual households. The third is lifetime wealth, which is defined as the present value of the discounted stream of expected net income flows. This measure includes the net value of pension and social security income (that is, future benefits less future contributions), as well as disposable wealth. Different simulations are run for various assumed growth rates for income and benefits to generate estimates of pension and social security wealth. Also, various assumptions are used in computing future social security benefits relative to contribution growth rates. Moreover, it is argued that, for consistency, this measure must also include the present value of lifetime earnings, or 'human capital wealth'. The sample is divided by age, sex, race, and education level to estimate lifetime earnings. A fourth measure is also developed for analytical purposes, called 'household accumulations', defined as the sum of disposable wealth and the accumulated value of pension and social security contributions. This measure is used to compute household wealth distribution if retirement benefits were based directly on contributions into the retirement systems.

Three main conclusions emerge from this study. First, pension wealth is less equally distributed than disposable wealth, but its magnitude is very low compared to disposable wealth. Its addition to household disposable wealth has virtually no impact on wealth inequality. Second, social security wealth is more equally distributed than disposable wealth, and is close in magnitude to disposable wealth. Its inclusion in the household portfolio results in a significant reduction in measured wealth inequality. Third, human capital wealth is distributed more equally than disposable wealth but less equally than social security wealth and is strongly correlated with the latter. However, its magnitude is substantially greater than either. Its addition to household disposable wealth causes a significant reduction in measured inequality. The addition of social security wealth to the sum of disposable and human capital wealth causes a further but much more moderate decline. Finally, overall inequality in household lifetime wealth is dominated by two components: household disposable wealth, because of its high inequality, and human capital wealth, because of its size.

It might be helpful to contrast these results with those of a 1976 study by Martin Feldstein. He defined social security wealth (SSW) as the present value of expected social security benefits when retired.[2] Using the 1962 Survey of Financial Characteristics of Consumers, Feldstein imputed SSW to all families with a male head of household between the ages of 35 and 64. He found that the aggregate value of SSW for these households is $382 billion, compared to an aggregate value of fungible wealth of $711 billion. Thus, SSW amounts to 54 per cent of fungible wealth for these families. As a result of its large magnitude and its more equitable distribution than fungible wealth, the inclusion of SSW in the household balance sheet greatly reduces the inequality of household wealth. In particular, the top 1 per cent of wealth holders in the 35 to 64 age bracket owned 28.4 per cent of fungible wealth in 1962 but only 18.9 per cent of total wealth. The top 4.1 per cent of families held 44.6 per cent of fungible wealth but only 30.8 per cent of total wealth. Moreover, the Gini coefficient for fungible wealth among families in the 35 to 64 age class is 0.72, while the Gini coefficient for total wealth is 0.51. The inclusion of social security wealth as a household asset thus results in about a 30 per cent reduction in the measured concentration of household wealth.

I find a similar difference between the concentration of disposable wealth (Feldstein's fungible wealth) and that of lifetime wealth (Feldstein's total wealth). The Gini coefficient for disposable wealth is 0.73 and that for lifetime wealth is about 0.51. However, the similarity in results hides a major difference in the method used. Whereas Feldstein added only gross social security wealth to fungible wealth to derive total wealth, I include net pension and human capital wealth along with net social security wealth in my concept of lifetime wealth. As a result, most of the difference between the concentration of disposable and lifetime wealth is due to the incorporation of human capital in the latter measure, not social security wealth.

The chapter is divided into six parts. The first discusses the various measures of household wealth, as well as the definitions of pension, social security, and human capital wealth. In the second part, results are presented on the distribution of household wealth, and, in part three, overall wealth inequality is decomposed by component. Part four analyses social security by age and wealth class, and in part five, results are presented on wealth inequality by age class. Conclusions are drawn in the last section of the chapter.

I. Measures of Household Wealth

Three concepts of household wealth are developed in this chapter. (a) Household disposable wealth (HDW) is the traditional concept of household wealth, including assets (and liabilities) that have a current market value and that are directly or indirectly marketable (fungible). It represents the portion of wealth over which households have discretion. Household disposable wealth excludes non-tradable or non-saleable accumulation rights such as social security wealth and most forms of pension wealth. These two forms of wealth are really entitlements controlled by an outside party and their disposition is not at the discretion of the individual household. However, this measure does include the cash surrender value of a pension plan, since this form of wealth is directly convertible into cash.

(b) Household reserve wealth (HRW) is a slightly broader concept of household wealth and includes both marketable and fungible assets and asset reserves held by a third party for the benefit of individuals and households. In this measure, the full reserves of pension funds are included in household assets instead of their cash surrender value. The rationale for a reserves notion of wealth is that the assets accumulated in these funds are held for the benefit of households, since the stream of income from these reserves provides personal income to retired workers.[3] Pension funds are therefore similar to many kinds of trust funds whose capital value is not directly available to the beneficiaries but whose income is.

In a reserves concept of household wealth, only the actual accumulations of the pension funds are included in household wealth, rather than the fully funded pension liability. The difference, or the 'unfunded' portion of pension liabilities, does enter the lifetime wealth measure.

(c) Lifetime wealth (HLW) is the third definition of household wealth and is the neo-classical concept of the present value of the discounted stream of future net income flows. This is the concept of total wealth that Feldstein adopted in his 1976 study. In principle, all forms of future income should be included in computing HLW. These include property income, labour earnings, private pension income, and government transfers such as social security benefits, unemployment benefits, welfare payments, disability payments, medical payments, food stamps, and the like. The first four are by far the biggest and, for simplicity, I shall ignore the others.[4] The first component of HLW, the present value of the future stream of net income from household assets (less liabilities), is presumably already captured in HDW. That is to say, if all capital markets are perfect, then the current market value of household assets (liabilities) should equal the present value of their corresponding income (payment) flows.[5] HDW thus, in theory, capitalizes the future net income flows emanating from disposable assets and liabilities.

The second component of HLW is the capitalized value of future labour earnings, usually referred to as 'human capital'. Unlike disposable assets, there are no capital markets to assign a market value to human beings based on expectations of their future earnings. However, with some crude assumptions, one can estimate human capital for current workers.

The last two components are pension and social security wealth. The two are now on equal footing, because their value depends on expected future benefits and contributions, irrespective of the mode in which they are accumulated. Pension wealth is defined as the present value of discounted future pension benefits less the present value of discounted future pension contributions. In similar fashion, social security wealth is defined as the present value of the discounted stream of future social security benefits less the present value of future social security contributions. Future entitlements for both pensions and the social security programme depend on many factors, such as the health (and survival) of a company, productivity growth, and other macroeconomic factors, and future legislation.[6] Estimating the value of such forms of wealth, like human capital, depends on relatively crude assumptions about the future state of the economy.[7]

The concept used in computing pension and social security wealth is their *net* value. The gross value of each is defined as the capitalized value of future benefits. The net value is the difference between this and the capitalized value of future contributions. The reason for using the net value instead of the gross value is that the neo-classical notion of wealth requires the capitalized value of the net addition to the future income stream from the various sources of income. If benefits were exactly determined by contributions (as in a defined benefit pension plan), there would be no net addition to wealth, since the future benefits would already be captured in human capital. To include the future benefits in this case would be to double-count. Thus, an addition to this form of wealth from pensions or the social security system would occur only if a given group of retirees received a 'bonus' over and above their accumulated contributions. For the social security system, this has been historically true, at least up to now, through legislative fiat. The underlying economic conditions that allowed this were labour force participation patterns, the age distribution, the start-up of the system in 1937, sustained productivity growth since the Second World War, and the pay-as-you-go nature of the social security system. Certain 'defined benefit' pension plans also have this feature, where benefits are determined by a formula involving years of service and company earnings history, rather than by the worker's contributions into the pension fund. In this regard, the social security system is treated as a defined benefit plan.[8]

For analytical purposes, a fourth measure is developed, which I call 'household accumulations' or HHA. In the reserves concept of wealth, pension funds represent the actual accumulations of savings made by employees and employers for the benefit of workers. Total household reserves thus represent the total savings accumulated for the benefit of the household sector held either directly by households or indirectly in the hands of a third party. Social security contributions are also made by employees and employers for the benefit of workers. The difference between pension and social security contributions is that the latter are not accumulated as reserves whereas the former are. This difference is due to the pay-as-you-go nature of the social security programme.

One can construct a hypothetical measure of household wealth, which I call household accumulations, which equals the sum of household reserves and the accumulated contributions made by employees and employers to date into the social security system. This latter portion represents the savings-equivalent of these social security contributions if the contributions were put into a savings account or pension reserves. Like a savings plan or a pension fund, these contributions are accumulated over time with the going interest rate. This treatment of household wealth places social security contributions on an equal footing with private pension contributions. In particular, social security contributions are treated as if they are made into a 'defined contribution' pension plan, the benefits from which are based directly on the contributions. Total household accumulations thus represent what the total wealth held by or for the benefit of the household sector would have been if social security contributions were placed in pension reserves.[9]

1. Definitions and Notations

In more formal terms, the accounting framework for each form of wealth can be stated, as follows. First, define HDWX as the sum of (a) owner-occupied housing and other real estate; (b) consumer durables; (c) household inventories; (d) bank deposits and other liquid assets; (e) bonds and other securities; (f) corporate stock; (g) equity in unincorporated businesses; (h) trust fund equity; and (i) the cash surrender value of life insurance policies less the sum of (i) mortgage debt and (ii) other household debt.

Let us now define the various forms of pension and social security wealth as well as human capital wealth. (Technical details on the imputation procedures can be obtained from the author.)

1. PDW, or 'pension disposable wealth', is defined as the cash surrender value of pension plans. Ruggles and Ruggles (1982)

estimate the total cash surrender value of pension reserves in 1969
at $7.0 billion. Though only a small number of pension policies
have the option of conversion from an annuity into a lump-sum
payment, it is impossible to identify such plans in my sample. A
pension reserve amount is calculated for each pension beneficiary
(see below), and the total cash surrender value of pension reserves is
distributed proportionally to estimated reserves among pension
beneficiary households.[10]

2. PRW, or 'pension reserve wealth', is the value of reserves
held in the pension system which is imputed to each household.
Ruggles and Ruggles (1982) estimate the total reserves of the
pension system at $140.3 billion in 1969, and this I use as a control
total. Separate imputations are provided for pension beneficiaries
in 1969 and those (currently) at work in 1969. For beneficiaries, it is
assumed, as was generally true in 1969, that pension benefits (PB)
remain fixed in nominal terms. The 10-year treasury bill rate in
1969, r, is used as the discount rate. (Its value was 6.67 per cent.)
PRW for beneficiaries is imputed as:

$$PRW_b = \int_0^{LE} PBe^{-rt}\, dt \qquad (9.1)$$

where LE is the conditional life expectancy.

For current workers, a two-stage imputation is necessary. The
first stage assigns pension coverage. From Skolnik (1976) and
Kotlikoff and Smith (1983, Table 3.1.1), the total number of
covered workers is estimated at 36.5 million. From the President's
Commission of Pension Policy (1980a, 1980b), information is
obtained on relative coverage rates by incomes class, industry of
employment, age, and sex of worker. Based on these data, pension
coverage is randomly assigned among workers. In the second stage,
accumulated earnings (EA) from the start of working life to the
present are estimated for each covered worker. These are based on
human capital earnings functions, which are imputed separately by
sex, race, and schooling level. Past earnings are accumulated on the
basis of real growth in average earnings and the discount rate is the
average yield on high-grade corporate bonds. PRW for covered
workers is then given by:

$$PRW_b = \alpha_p\, EA$$

where the parameter α_p is chosen so that total PRW aligns with the control total of \$140.3 billion.

3. PLW, or 'pension lifetime wealth', is the present value of the projected stream of future (lifetime) pension benefits less contributions. Since, among pension beneficiaries, there are no future contributions into pension plans, then

$$PLW_b = PRW_b.$$

For covered workers, it is assumed that the full incidence of future contributions falls on their human capital (see below). As a result, PLW becomes identical to PRW, with one qualification. If the pension plan is underfunded, it is assumed that the shortfall in reserves is ultimately paid by workers in the form of additional contributions. From Kotlikoff and Smith (1983, Table 5.7.2), the median funding ratio β_p among Fortune 1000 companies was 0.93 in 1980. Using this figure, I assign:

$$PLW_w = \beta_p PRW_w.$$

4. SSLW, or 'social security lifetime wealth', is the present value of the projected stream of future (lifetime) social security benefits less contributions. Two scenarios are used to project social security benefits and contributions. Scenario A assumes that benefits grow at a constant rate and taxes are raised or lowered to pay for them. Scenario B assumes that social security tax rates are fixed and benefit growth rates vary to equate annual contributions with total annual benefits. Varied assumptions are also made in regard to future real earnings growth (k^*).

My imputation procedure essentially follows Feldstein (1974). For current social security beneficiaries,

$$SSLW_b = \int_0^{LE} SSBe^{(g^* - r^*)t}\, dt \tag{9.2}$$

where SSB is the family's social security benefit in 1969, LE is based on the greater of that of the husband or wife in the case of a married couple, g^* is the expected rate of growth of real social security benefits, and r^* is the real treasury bill rate in 1969 on a 10-year bill. Among workers, social security coverage is based on the person's 1969 employment status. It is assumed that a worker in the nth percentile of the size distribution of labour earnings of workers of his age A receives at retirement (at age 65) a social security benefit SSBR given by:

$$SSBR_n = SSB_n \, e^{g^* (65-A)} \tag{9.3}$$

where SSB_n is the nth percentile of social security benefits among beneficiaries currently of age 65. The present value of future social security benefits, GSSLW, of a worker in the nth percentile is then given by

$$- \quad GSSLW_{w,n} = SSBR_n \int_0^{LE} e^{g^* t} \, e^{-r^* (t + A_r)} \, dt \tag{9.4}$$

where $A_r = 65 - A$ is the years to retirement. SSLW, or (net) social security lifetime wealth, is the difference between GSSLW and the discounted stream of future social security contributions, $SSCW_w$:

$$SSLW_w = GSSLW_w - SSCW_w.$$

SSCW depends on future social security tax rates.

To impute SSLW, assumptions must be made about future social security benefits and tax rates. The two are not independent, and I assume that total social security benefits equal total social security contributions in each (future) year. Two scenarios are employed in the imputation procedure.

Scenario A. The annual rate of real growth of social security benefits, g^*, is preset. Based on historical experience, three values for g^* are simulated: (a) 0.01, (b) 0.02, and (c) 0.03. Moreover, also on the basis of historical experience, two values are preset for the rate of growth of average real earnings, k^*: (a) 0.01 and (b) 0.02. Then, from information on the projected number of social security beneficiaries and covered workers, the necessary social security tax rate γ_Y in each future year to maintain balance between total social security benefits and contributions can be computed.[11] SSCW is then given by:

$$SSCW_w = \sum_{t=A}^{65} \gamma_t \hat{E}_t \, (1 + k^* - r^*)^{(t-A)} \tag{9.5}$$

where $\hat{E}_t$ is projected earnings for the worker based on a human capital earnings function, where real earnings growth is assumed to be zero (see below).

Scenario B. In this approach, I preset the social security tax rate γ_y at its 1969 level. To estimate security benefits in each future year, assumptions must be made regarding the rate of growth of real earnings growth. As before, I assume values of 0.01 and 0.02 for k^*.[12]

5. SSA, or 'social security accumulations', is a hypothetical measure of the accumulated contributions made by employees and employers into the social security system on behalf of each individual. Separate imputations are required for workers and beneficiaries. For current workers, it is assumed that each was continuously employed from the end of schooling and that their coverage status was the same as in 1969. From human capital earnings functions and historical data on past rates of growth of real average earnings, I first estimate past earnings $E_{i,y}$ for each worker i in year y. Define γ_y to be either twice the employee social security tax rate in year y or the self-employed tax rate in year y, depending on the employment status of the worker, and $SSMAX_y$ to be the maximum taxable wage base in year y. The social security wage base, SSWAGE, in year y for a covered worker with earnings $E_{i,y}$ is then given by:

$$SSWAGE_{i,y} = MIN [E_{i,y}; SSMAX_y]$$

where MIN indicates the minimum value of the two arguments. Then social security accumulations for covered workers are given by

$$SSA_w = \sum_{t=A_0}^{A} \gamma_t SSWAGE_t/(1 + r^*)^t \qquad (9.6)$$

where A_0 is the age at which work began.

For current beneficiaries, the appropriate concept is the present value of benefits that would be strictly calculated as an annuity on the person's accumulated contributions. Unfortunately, there is no information available on past earnings or contributions into the social security system. The imputation used is essentially the reverse of the procedure used in imputing GSSLW. It is assumed that a retiree in the nth percentile of social security benefits for his age group was also in the nth percentile of the earnings distribution at retirement (assumed to be at age 65). $SSA_{w,n}$ is then computed for a worker of age 65 in the *n*th percentile of the earnings distribution. This value is then appropriately discounted, depending on the year of retirement of the beneficiary, to obtain $SSA_{b,n}$. In general, $SSLW_b$ is considerably in excess of SSA_b, because of increased benefits from the social security system.[13]

6. HK, or 'human capital wealth', is the present value of the stream of future expected labour compensation. For consistency with PLW and SSLW, labour compensation is defined to include all fringe benefits, including the employer's contribution to both the social security system and pension plans. As noted above, human capital earnings functions are estimated for each worker based on sex, race, and schooling to obtain $\hat{E}_{i,y}$, future expected earnings for each worker *i* in year *y*, assuming no growth in average real earnings. Then,

$$ HK = \int_0^{A_r} \hat{E}(t)\, e^{(k^* - r^*)t}\, dt $$

where, as before, values of 0.01 and 0.02 are used for k^*.

7. Household wealth. The three concepts of wealth can now be defined. Household disposable wealth (HDW) is given by:

$$ HDW = HDWX + PDW. \qquad (9.7) $$

Household reserve wealth (HRW) is defined as:[14]

$$ HRW = HDWX + PRW, \qquad (9.8) $$

and household lifetime wealth (HLW) becomes

$$ HLW = HDWX + PLW + SSLW + HK. \qquad (9.9) $$

Finally, the hypothetical measure household accumulations (HHA) is given by:

$$ HHA = HDWX + PRW + SSA. \qquad (9.10) $$

II. The Composition of Aggregate Wealth and Overall Wealth Inequality

Table 9.1 presents aggregate household balance sheets for the various measures of household wealth. All calculations are

Table 9.1. *Aggregate household wealth by measure and component*[a]

Wealth measure	Assumptions		Scenario[b] (A or B)	HDWX ($)	Pension wealth ($)	Social security wealth ($)	Human capital ($)	Total household wealth ($)	Ratio SS WLT/Total
	Real earnings growth	Social Security benefits growth							
1. HDW	—	—	—	2,904.00	7.00	—	—	2,911	—
2. HRW	—	—	—	2,904.00	140.00	—	—	3,044	—
3. HLW	0.01	0.01	A	2,904.00	137.00	2,083.00	12,259	17,383	0.120
	0.01	0.02	A	2,904.00	137.00	3,364.00	12,259	18,664	0.180
	0.01	0.03	A	2,904.00	137.00	5,649.00	12,259	20,949	0.270
	0.02	0.01	A	2,904.00	137.00	2,083.00	14,344	19,468	0.107
	0.02	0.02	A	2,904.00	137.00	3,364.00	14,344	20,729	0.162
	0.02	0.03	A	2,904.00	137.00	5,649.00	14,344	23,034	0.245
	0.01	—	B	2,904.00	137.00	1,194.00	12,259	16,494	0.072
	0.02	—	B	2,904.00	137.00	2,001.00	14,344	19,386	0.103
4. HHA	—	—	—	2,904.00	140.00	288.00	—	3,332	0.086
5. Feldstein (1976)[c]	—	—	—	711.00	—	382.00	—	1,093	0.349

a. All values are in billions of (1969) dollars.

b. Scenario A assumes that social security benefits grow at a constant rate over time. Scenario B assumes that social security tax rates are fixed over time.

c. Feldstein's results are based on the 1962 Survey of Financial Characteristics of Consumers. Only households with males between the ages of 35 and 64 are included in his calculations.

performed with the MESP data base (see Wolff (1980) and Wolff (1983) for a description), and valuations are made as of 31, December 1969, from information provided in the 1970 Census Public Use sample, the 1969 Internal Revenue Service Tax model, and previous wealth imputations. Total household disposable wealth amounted to 2.9 trillion dollars in 1969. The cash surrender value of pension plans was $7 billion, a trivial proportion of HDW. Pension reserves in 1969 totalled $140 billion, or 5 per cent of household reserve wealth. Pension wealth was thus relatively small compared to other components of household wealth.

In contrast, social security wealth was of approximately the same magnitude as household disposable wealth. In comparison, Feldstein found that in 1962 social security wealth totalled about half the volume of fungible wealth. This suggests that social security wealth was increasing relative to traditional household wealth over the 1960s. Moreover, estimates of social security lifetime wealth show considerable variation, depending on the assumptions used to generate the imputations. In Scenario A, SSLW increases by 60 to 70 per cent for each percentage point rise in the assumed annual growth rate of social security benefits. On the other hand, the aggregate value of SSLW is found to be independent of the assumed growth rate of real labour earnings, since total SSLW depends only on the assumed value of social security benefits and the implied value of social security contributions. The growth rate of real earnings determines only what the necessary tax rate must be to generate the needed social security contributions.

In Scenario B, the aggregate value of SSLW increases by about two-thirds each percentage point increase in the annual growth rate of labour earnings. There are two reasons for this. First, social security entitlements and, hence, *gross* social security lifetime wealth (GSSLW) vary directly with earnings growth, when the tax rate is fixed. Second, though social security contributions will also increase as benefits do, if the two are assumed equal on a year-by-year basis, only current covered workers are assigned this liability. Future workers, who are included in the projections and hence used to balance total contributions with total benefits in future years but who are not represented in the 1969 sample, cannot be assigned this liability. Hence, even in a pay-as-you-go social security system, where total contributions balance with total benefits on an annual basis, total (net) SSLW will still be positive.

An interesting contrast is provided by the estimates of total social security accumulations (line 4). Estimated hypothetical social security 'reserves' would have amounted to $288 billion in 1969. This is about twice the value of pension reserves in 1969 and about 10 per cent of the aggregate value of household disposable wealth and of social security lifetime wealth.

The final component of household wealth is human capital. It is considerably larger in magnitude than household disposable wealth or social security wealth—in the order of four to five times as great. Moreover, its aggregate value also varies with the assumed growth in real labour earnings, increasing by about 15 per cent for each percentage point increase in annual earnings growth.

The ratio of social security wealth to total household wealth also shows considerable variation, depending on the assumptions used. The proportion ranges from 7 to 27 per cent. Of the eight calculations shown in Table 9.1, the median value is 0.14. Moreover, the ratio of social security accumulations to household accumulations is 9 per cent. In contrast, Feldstein calculated a 0.35 ratio of (gross) social security wealth to total household wealth, a proportion considerably higher than mine, since human capital was not included in his measure of household wealth.

Measures of overall wealth inequality are presented in Table 9.2. The Gini coefficient for household disposable wealth, the traditional measure of household wealth, is 0.73. The Gini coefficient for household reserve wealth is slightly lower, at 0.72. Gini coefficients for household lifetime wealth are considerably lower, ranging from 0.49 to 0.51 in the estimates shown. On the surface, these results are quite similar to those of Feldstein, who found that the addition of social security wealth to fungible wealth lowered the 1962 Gini coefficient from 0.72 to 0.51. However, it should be recalled that Feldstein's total wealth measure does not include human capital. Finally, the Gini coefficient for household accumulations is 0.66, lower than that of HDW but higher than those for household lifetime wealth.

A breakdown of wealth inequality by component allows a further analysis of the sources of total wealth inequality. The Gini coefficient for HDWX is almost identical to that for HDW, since the two wealth measures differ by only 0.2 per cent (from the exclusion of pension cash surrender value from the former). Inequality in the holdings of pension wealth is uniformly greater than that of

Table 9.2. *Gini coefficient estimates of wealth inequality by component and wealth measure*

Wealth measure	Real earnings growth	Social security benefits growth	Scenario[a] (A or B)	HDWX	Pension wealth	Social security wealth	Human capital	HDWX + PEN WLT	HDWX + SS WLT	HDWX + HUM CAP	Total household wealth
1. HDW	—	—	—	0.73	0.97	—	—	0.73	—	—	0.73
2. HRW	—	—	—	0.73	0.87	—	—	0.72	—	—	0.72
3. HLW	0.01	0.01	A	0.73	0.88	0.43	0.61	0.72	0.51	0.55	0.50
	0.01	0.02	A	0.73	0.88	0.48	0.61	0.72	0.49	0.55	0.50
	0.01	0.03	A	0.73	0.88	0.55	0.61	0.72	0.50	0.55	0.49
	0.02	0.01	A	0.73	0.88	0.43	0.62	0.72	0.51	0.56	0.52
	0.02	0.02	A	0.73	0.88	0.48	0.62	0.72	0.49	0.56	0.51
	0.02	0.03	A	0.73	0.88	0.55	0.62	0.72	0.50	0.56	0.50
	0.01	—	B	0.73	0.88	0.53	0.61	0.72	0.60	0.55	0.51
	0.02	—	B	0.73	0.88	0.47	0.62	0.72	0.54	0.56	0.51
4. HHA	—	—	—	0.73	0.87	—	—	0.72	0.67	—	0.66
5. Feldstein (1976)[b]	—	—	—	0.72	—	—	—	—	—	—	0.51

a. Scenario A assumes that social security benefits grow at a constant rate over time. Scenario B assumes that social security tax rates are fixed over time.

b. Feldstein's results are based on the 1962 Survey of Financial Characteristics of Consumers. Only households with males between the ages of 35 and 64 are included in his calculations.

HDWX. In the case of PDW, the cash surrender value of pension plans, the reason for the high inequality is the small percentage of households (only 5 per cent) that hold this form of wealth. Among holders, the Gini coefficient is only 0.41. For both PRW, pension reserve wealth, and PLW, pension lifetime wealth, the high degree of inequality is due to two factors. The first is that half of all households do not hold this form of wealth. The second is that, among holders, the average value of PRW (and PLW) is about 20 times greater among pension beneficiaries than among individuals currently at work (in 1969). This is due, in large measure, to the assumptions used in the imputation procedure, whereby beneficiaries are assigned the full capitalized value of their annuity and the remaining reserves are divided among covered workers.[15] The Gini coefficient for PRW among pension beneficiaries separately is only 0.47 and that among covered workers is only 0.38.

Social security lifetime wealth is more equally distributed than HDWX. Gini coefficients for SSLW range from 0.43 to 0.55, in comparison to a value of 0.73 for HDWX. The degree of inequality in the distribution of SSLW, imputed under the assumptions of Scenario A, rises as the assumed rate of social security benefit growth (g^*) increases from 1 to 3 per cent per year. However, there is no apparent correlation between the two, since the Gini coefficient for SSLW is slightly higher for g^* equal to 0 than for g^* equal to 0.01.[16] Inequality in the distribution of SSLW computed under Scenario B is greater for real earnings growth (k^*) of 1 per cent per year than 2 per cent. Here, too, there is no apparent correlation between the two, since the Gini coefficient for SSLW is greater at k^* equal to 0.03 than a value of k^* of 0.02.[17] Finally, the distribution of social security accumulations (SSA) is more equal than that of SSLW (across all parameter values). This result may at first glance appear surprising, since social security benefit formulas in 1969 were such as to redistribute social security benefits relative to social security contributions in favour of the low wage earner. However, the equalizing effect implicit in the benefit formula is apparently more than offset by the disequalizing effect from differences in conditional life expectancies, particularly on the basis of age.

The distribution of human capital wealth is less equal than social security wealth but more equal than fungible wealth. The reason its distribution is more unequal than social security wealth is that, as defined, HK is the present value of *future* earnings, not total lifetime earnings. Therefore, HK is generally greater for younger age cohorts than older ones, even though older workers have greater annual earnings. As a result, the Gini coefficient for HK is greater than that for annual earnings—about 0.62 compared to 0.49.[18] The distribution of social security wealth, on the other hand, is largely determined by the distribution of annual earnings, because of the offsetting effects of the (equalizing) social security benefit formula and (disequalizing) differential life expectancies.[19]

The next two columns of Table 9.3 show the effects of adding pension wealth and social security wealth each separately to HDWX. The addition of pension wealth of all three forms (PDW, PRW, and PLW) to HDWX causes virtually no change in measured inequality, even though pension wealth is more unequally distributed than HDWX. There are two reasons for this. First, pension wealth is small relative to HDWX (the ratio of PRW to HDWX is 0.05). Second, pension wealth is almost uncorrelated with traditional household wealth (the correlation coefficient between HDWX and PRW is 0.01 as shown in Table 9.3).

In contrast, the inclusion of social security wealth with traditional wealth causes a marked reduction in measured wealth inequality from 0.73 to the range 0.49 to 0.60, depending on the assumptions made. These results are comparable to those of Feldstein, who found that the Gini coefficient fell from 0.72 to 0.51 after the inclusion of social security wealth. The large effect of social security wealth on measured inequality is due to three factors. First, it is more evenly distributed than traditional wealth. Second, its magnitude is very close to that of traditional household wealth. The exception is Scenario B when earnings growth is 1 per cent per year and aggregate SSLW is only 41 per cent of HDWX. It is for this reason that the reduction in the Gini coefficient from the addition of SSLW to HDWX is the smallest of all the cases. Third, social security wealth is almost uncorrelated with traditional household wealth (see Table 9.3). This, in turn, is due to two offsetting tendencies. First, within age cohort, both traditional wealth and social security wealth are generally correlated with labour earnings and, as a result, positively correlated with each other. Second, the mean value of traditional wealth rises across age cohorts, whereas the mean value of social security wealth generally rises with age until middle-age and then declines (see Section 4 for more details). As a result, HDWX and SSLW are generally negatively correlated

Table 9.3.   *Correlation coefficients between selected components of household wealth*

Wealth component	Assumptions			HDWX	Pension wealth[b]	Human $k^* = 0.01$	Capital $k^* = 0.02$
	Real earnings growth	Social security benefits growth	Scenario[a] (A or B)				
1. HDWX	—	—	—	—	—	—	—
2. PRW	—	—	—	0.01	—	—	—
3. PLW	—	—	—	0.01	—	—	—
4. SSLW	—	0.01	A	-0.03	0.04	0.34	0.32
	—	0.02	A	-0.03	0.03	0.43	0.42
	—	0.03	A	-0.03	0.03	0.44	0.43
	0.01	—	B	0.00	0.06	-0.09	—
	0.02	—	B	-0.02	0.05	—	0.14
5. SSA	—	—	—	-0.05	0.04	—	—
6. HK	0.01	—	—	-0.03	-0.03	—	—
	0.02	—	—	-0.03	-0.03	—	—

a. Scenario A assumes that social security benefits grow at a constant rate over time. Scenario B assumes that social security tax rates are fixed over time.

b. Pension lifetime wealth (PLW) is used in all cases, except for line 5, where pension reserve wealth (PRW) is used.

across age cohort.[20] Finally, the inclusion of social security accumulations (SSA) with traditional household wealth causes the Gini
coefficient to fall from 0.73 to 0.67. Though SSA is more evenly
distributed than SSLW, it is uncorrelated with HDWX (the correlation coefficient is − 0.05) and it is much smaller in magnitude
than SSLW, accounting for its smaller impact.[21]

The addition of human capital wealth to traditional wealth
results in a drop of the Gini coefficient from 0.73 to about 0.55,
despite the fact that the Gini coefficient for human capital is about
0.62 (next to last column). There are two explanations for this.
First, human capital is much larger in magnitude than HDWX (of
the order of four to five times as large). Second, the two are essentially uncorrelated (the correlation coefficient is − 0.03). This, in
turn, is due to two factors. First, by construction, human capital
tends to decline with age, since years left to work fall with age,
whereas HDWX increases with age (see Section 4 for more details),
inducing a negative correlation between the two. Second, the two
components are positively correlated with labour earnings within
age cohort and, as a result, with each other.[22]

III. Decomposition of Overall Wealth Inequality

The contribution of each of the components of household wealth to
overall wealth inequality can be analysed more rigorously using a
decomposition of the coefficient of variation measure. As noted in
the discussion above, there are three factors which affect the contribution of a wealth component to total wealth inequality. The first is
the magnitude of the component relative to total wealth. The
greater the relative magnitude, the greater its effect on total wealth
inequality. The second is the degree of inequality within the component itself. This also has a positive relation to overall wealth inequality. The third is the correlation of the component with the other
components of wealth. The greater the correlation, the greater the
effect on overall wealth inequality.

These relations can be formalized as follows. Suppose household
wealth W is divided into two components, X_1 and X_2:

$$W = X_1 + X_2.$$

The coefficient of variation of wealth, CV, is given by:

$$CV \equiv SD/\overline{W}$$

where SD is the standard deviation of wealth and $\overline{W}$ is mean wealth. From the standard formula,

$$V = V_1 + V_2 + 2C_{12}$$

where V is the variance of wealth, V_1 is the variance of X_1, and C_{12} is the covariance between X_1 and X_2, and from

$$\overline{W} = \overline{X}_1 + \overline{X}_2$$

it follows that

$$CV^2 = p_1^2\,CV_1^2 + p_2^2\,CV_2^2 + 2p_1 p_2\,CC_{12}$$

where $p_1 = \overline{X}_1/\overline{W}$, CV_1 is the coefficient of variation of X_1 and CC_{12} is the 'coefficient of covariation' between X_1 and X_2, defined as

$$CC_{12} \equiv C_{12}/(\overline{X}_1.\overline{X}_2).$$

The decomposition can be easily extended to the case of n wealth components.
Let:

$$W = X_1 + X_2 + \ldots + X_n.$$

Then,

$$CV^2 = \sum_i p_i^2\,CV_i^2 + \sum_{i \neq j} \sum p_i p_j\,CC_{ij}.$$

The square of the coefficient of variation of wealth is thus decomposable into a weighted sum of the squares of the coefficient of variation of its components and the coefficients of covariation, where the weights depend on the proportion of each component in total wealth.

Decompositions are shown for four measures of household lifetime wealth and for household accumulations (see Table 9.4). The first line of each decomposition shows the value of each component; the second line shows its corresponding weight; and the third line shows the 'contribution' of each component to overall wealth inequality, where the contribution is defined as the product of the value and the weight. The decompositions of HLW indicate quite

Table 9.4. The decomposition of the coefficient of variation of wealth by component and for selected measures of wealth

Wealth measure	Coefficient of variation squared			Coefficient of covariation			Total
	CV² (HDWP)c	CV² (SSLW)	CV² (HK)	CC (HDWP & SSLW)	CC (HDWP & HK)	CC (SSLW & HK)	CV² (HLW)
1. HLW (k* = 0.01; g* = 0.01; Scen. A)a							
Value	29.34	0.84	1.54	-0.12	-0.21	0.39	—
Weight	0.03	0.01	0.50	0.04	0.25	0.17	1.00
Contrib.b	0.90	0.01	0.77	-0.01	-0.05	0.07	1.69
2. HLW (k* = 0.01; g* = 0.02; Scen. A)a							
Value	29.34	1.03	1.54	-0.17	-0.21	0.55	—
Weight	0.03	0.03	0.43	0.06	0.21	0.24	1.00
Contrib.b	0.78	0.03	0.66	-0.01	-0.05	0.13	1.55
3. HLW (k* = 0.01; Scen. B)a							
Value	29.34	1.45	1.54	0.00	-0.21	-0.13	—
Weight	0.03	0.01	0.55	0.03	0.27	0.11	1.00
Contrib.b	1.00	0.01	0.85	0.00	-0.06	-0.01	1.78

4. HLW ($k^* = 0.02$; Scen. B)[a]

	CV² (HDWX)	CV² (PRW)	CV² (SSA)	CC (HDWX & PRW)	CC (HDWX & SSA)	CC (SSA & PRW)	CV² (HHA)
Value	29.34	1.14	1.63	−0.10	−0.22	0.19	—
Weight	0.02	0.01	0.55	0.03	0.23	0.15	1.00
Contrib.[b]	0.72	0.01	0.89	0.00	−0.05	0.03	1.60

Addendum:

5. HHA

Wealth measure	CV² (HDWX)	CV² (PRW)	CV² (SSA)	CC (HDWX & PRW)	CC (HDWX & SSA)	CC (SSA & PRW)	CV² (HHA)
Value	31.91	19.76	0.44	0.31	−0.20	0.13	—
Weight	0.76	0.00	0.01	0.07	0.15	0.01	1.00
Contrib.[b]	24.24	0.03	0.00	0.02	−0.03	0.00	24.27

a. k^* is the growth rate of real earnings; g^* is the growth rate in social security benefits; and 'Scen.' refers to the Scenario.
b. The contribution (contrib.) is the product of the value term and the corresponding weight.
c. HDWP is defined as the sum of HDWX and PLW.

Edward N. Wolff

clearly that there are only two components that contribute appreciably to overall wealth inequality. The first is the high degree of inequality in the distribution of HDWX, which, despite its very low weight, contributes to about half of overall inequality in HLW.[23] The second is the large magnitude of human capital wealth, which, despite its relatively low inequality, also contributes to about half of overall inequality. The distribution of social security wealth has very little effect on overall inequality because of its very small weight. Finally, the cross-terms also contribute very little to overall inequality, despite their high weights in several cases, because of the relatively low values of the coefficients of covariation.

In comparison, overall inequality in household accumulations is almost totally dominated by the distribution of HDWX, which accounts for three-quarters of the total weight. The only other component with a significant weight is the cross-term between HDWX and social security accumulations, but since their coefficient of covariation is relatively low, the contribution of this term is approximately zero.

IV. Social Security Wealth by Age and Wealth Class

Further analysis reveals some of the reasons for the low correlations of traditional wealth with social security wealth and other components of expanded wealth. Table 9.5 shows mean wealth by age class for the various components of household wealth. The mean value of traditional household wealth, HDW, rises with age across all cohorts, though the increment among the last three age cohorts is relatively small. Mean pension lifetime wealth (and, by implication PRW, since the two differ by a constant proportion) has a hump-shaped distribution, peaking in the 45–54 age group. This age pattern is due to three factors. First, the percentage of families that hold pension wealth (that is, either expect pension benefits or currently receive pension benefits) rises sharply between the youngest age group and the 25–34 age group, peaks at 64 per cent for 45–54 age group, falls off to 51 per cent in the 55–64 age group, and then again to 16 per cent in the oldest age group. Second, the mean value of *gross* pension wealth (the discounted value of future pension benefits) among pension wealth holders is relatively

Table 9.5. *Mean wealth by component and age class*

Wealth component	Assumptions			Mean wealth by age class[b]						
	Real earnings growth	Social security benefits growth	Scenario (A or B)[a]	All	Under 25	25–34	35–44	45–54	55–64	Over 64
1. HDW	—	—	—	45,768	17,047	30,050	34,380	55,029	58,878	61,891
2. PRW	—	—	—	2,221	698	1,170	2,016	3,549	2,962	2,014
3. PLW	—	—	—	2,012	639	1,057	1,811	3,210	2,675	1,854
4. SSLW	—	0.01	A	32,826	30,691	32,196	36,824	39,364	34,354	22,480
	—	0.02	A	53,017	60,883	61,909	63,179	61,974	50,025	25,543
	0.01	—	B	18,820	5,436	8,175	19,031	25,872	26,137	20,391
	0.02	—	B	31,540	21,357	25,629	36,488	40,923	36,447	22,576
5. SSA	—	—	—	4,536	2,081	4,101	5,465	5,686	5,048	3,394
6. HK	0.01	—	—	193,188	369,084	404,450	277,531	157,393	51,648	2,978
	0.02	—	—	226,036	464,126	488,436	316,606	121,267	53,959	3,098
7. HLWX[c]	—	0.02	A	100,686	78,569	93,016	99,369	120,212	111,578	88,716
	0.01	—	B	66,489	23,122	39,281	55,222	84,110	87,690	83,563
	0.02	—	B	79,209	39,043	56,736	72,678	99,162	98,000	85,749
8. HLW	0.01	0.02	A	293,874	447,652	497,465	376,900	277,605	163,226	91,694
	0.02	0.02	A	326,722	542,694	581,451	415,975	241,480	165,537	91,813
	0.01	—	B	259,678	392,206	443,731	332,753	241,503	139,338	86,541
	0.02	—	B	305,245	503,169	545,172	389,284	220,429	151,959	88,847

Table 9.5. *(Cont)*:

Wealth component	Assumptions			Mean wealth by age class[b]						
	Real earnings growth	Social security benefits growth	Scenario (A or B)[a]	All	Under 25	25–34	35–44	45–54	55–64	Over 64
9. HHA	—	—	—	52,206	19,767	35,208	41,656	63,924	66,601	66,566
Memo: Ratio of social security wealth to total wealth										
10. SSLW/HLW	0.01	0.02	A	0.180	0.136	0.124	0.168	0.223	0.306	0.279
	0.02	0.02	A	0.162	0.112	0.106	0.152	0.257	0.302	0.278
	0.01	—	B	0.072	0.014	0.018	0.057	0.107	0.188	0.236
	0.02	—	B	0.103	0.042	0.047	0.094	0.186	0.240	0.254
11. SSA/HHA	—	—	—	0.087	0.105	0.116	0.131	0.089	0.076	0.051

a. Scenario A assumes that social security benefits grow at a constant rate over time. Scenario B assumes that social security tax rates are fixed over time.

b. The age class is based on the age of the head of household.

c. HLWX is defined as HDWX + PLW + SSLW.

constant across age groups. Third, the mean value of pension liabilities declines with age group and for retirees is zero (since there are no more pension contributions to be made). The increase in mean pension wealth with age through the 45–54 age group is thus due to the increasing proportion of households with pension wealth and the decline in pension liabilities. The fall in mean pension wealth thereafter is due to the declining percentage of households with pension wealth.

Average social security wealth has a very similar hump-shaped pattern with age, with the peak occurring in either the 45–54 or the 55–64 age group. There are three factors involved. First, unlike pension wealth, the per cent of households holding social security wealth is relatively constant across age groups, at about 90 per cent. Second, average *gross* social security wealth tends to decline with age because future earnings growth is, in each of the cases shown here, greater than the (real) discount rate. Third, future social security liabilities will decline with age, since the number of working years left before retirement declines. Apparently the third factor dominates the second until middle-age, causing mean SSLW to advance with age. After that point, the second factor dominates the third, causing mean social security wealth to decline with age. Mean social security accumulations also has a hump-shaped pattern with respect to age. The reason is that, by definition, accumulations of social security contributions will generally rise with working life. The fall-off in the 55–64-year-old cohort is likely due to their lower average earnings over their working life, and the decline in the last age cohort is from the dissipation of their social security 'reserves' during retirement. Mean human capital wealth generally declines with age, since, by construction, its value is based on the number of years left to work.

Panel 7 of Table 9.5 shows the mean value of the sum of HDWX, PLW, and SSLW across age cohorts. It also follows a hump-shaped pattern across age groups, peaking at the 45–54 or 55–64 age group and following very close the pattern of SSLW across age groups. In contrast, the age pattern of mean HLW is dominated by that of human capital, rising slightly between the first two age groups and then falling off rapidly with age. Finally, mean household accumulations (HHA) rises with age until age group 55 to 64 and then levels off.

The importance of social security wealth in the household

portfolio can now be analysed by age cohort. Under the assumptions of Scenario A, SSLW as a proportion of total household wealth generally increases with age until the 55–64 age group and then declines moderately in the oldest age cohort. The major reason for this pattern is the sharp decline of human capital wealth with age. The moderate decline of SSLW in HLW in the oldest age group is due to the sharp decline in their social security wealth. If we exclude human capital wealth from total household wealth, then social security wealth declines in importance in the household portfolio with age, because of the increasing value of traditional household wealth.

In contrast, under the assumptions of Scenario B, SSLW rises as a proportion of HLW across all age cohorts, including the oldest; and more steeply than in Scenario A. This difference is due to the more rapid rate of increase of SSLW with age under Scenario B and the less pronounced fall-off in average social security wealth in the oldest age cohort. The ratio of SSLW to the sum of HDWX, PLW and SSLW is hump-shaped with respect to age, peaking in the 35–44 age group. Finally, the ratio of social security accumulations to HHA is also hump-shaped across age groups, also peaking in the 35–44 age cohort, because of the sharp increase in mean HDW between this cohort and the older ones.

Table 9.6 presents similar results by traditional wealth (HDW) class. The mean value of social security lifetime wealth and social security accumulations rises between the lowest wealth (HDW) class and the second lowest wealth class and then declines as HDW increases. This pattern accounts for the low correlation between SSLW and HDW (see Table 9.3). On the other hand, human capital wealth tends to decline with HDW, due to its dependence on age. As a result, household lifetime wealth tends to remain relatively constant across the first four wealth classes and then rises with HDW across the last two classes, as traditional wealth begins to dominate human capital. Moreover, as a consequence, SSLW increases as a proportion of HLW across the first two wealth classes, falls off gradually across the next two, and then declines sharply as a per cent of HLW across the upper two wealth classes. In contrast, social security accumulations as a proportion of household accumulations declines continuously with HDW. These results indicate that social security wealth is very unimportant in the household portfolio for the upper wealth classes.

Table 9.6. *Mean wealth by component and wealth class*

Wealth component	Assumptions			Mean value by wealth (HDW) class[b]						
	Real earnings growth	Social security benefits growth	Scenario[a] (A or B)	All	0–25K	25–50K	50–100K	100–250K	250–500K	Over 500K
1. PRW	—	—	—	2,221	1,476	3,226	3,597	3,878	5,199	4,443
2. PLW	—	—	—	2,012	1,331	2,923	3,275	3,545	4,762	4,048
3. SSLW	—	0.01	A	32,826	31,262	39,130	33,768	30,892	27,210	19,639
	—	0.02	A	53,017	52,301	61,122	50,319	46,006	37,661	26,482
	0.01	—	B	18,820	16,269	24,593	23,005	21,446	19,168	14,253
	0.02	—	B	31,540	29,265	38,952	33,904	31,253	26,046	18,901
4. SSA	—	—	—	4,536	4,452	5,307	4,393	3,793	3,222	2,276
5. HK	0.01	—	—	193,188	213,307	192,000	134,680	105,803	119,099	98,450
	0.02	—	—	226,036	252,960	218,442	151,547	118,607	134,779	110,782
6. HLWX[c]	—	0.02	A	100,686	63,471	98,636	122,996	199,149	378,632	1,886,518
	0.01	—	B	66,489	27,438	62,106	95,683	174,589	360,139	1,874,289
	0.02	—	B	79,209	40,435	76,465	106,582	184,396	367,017	1,878,937
7. HLW	0.01	0.02	A	293,874	276,778	290,635	257,676	304,952	497,731	1,984,968
	0.02	0.02	A	326,722	316,431	317,078	274,544	317,756	513,411	1,997,300
	0.01	—	B	259,677	240,745	254,106	230,363	280,392	479,238	1,972,739
	0.02	—	B	305,245	293,394	294,907	258,129	303,003	501,797	1,989,719

Table 9.6.   *(Cont):*

Wealth component	Assumptions			Mean value by wealth (HDW) class[b]						
	Real earnings growth	Social security benefits growth	Scenario[a] (A or B)	All	0–25K	25–50K	50–100K	100–250K	250–500K	Over 500K
8. HHA	—	—	—	52,206	15,767	43,123	77,392	157,269	344,630	1,862,707
Memo: Ratio of social security wealth to total wealth										
9. SSLW/ HLW	0.01	0.02	A	0.180	0.189	0.210	0.195	0.151	0.076	0.013
	0.02	0.02	A	0.162	0.165	0.193	0.183	0.145	0.073	0.013
	0.01	—	B	0.072	0.068	0.097	0.100	0.076	0.040	0.007
	0.02	—	B	0.103	0.100	0.132	0.131	0.103	0.052	0.009
10. SSA/HHA	—	—	—	0.087	0.282	0.123	0.057	0.024	0.009	0.001

a. Scenario A assumes that social security benefits grow at a constant rate over time. Scenario B assumes that social security tax rates are fixed over time.

b. Wealth class is based on household disposable wealth (HDW). 'K' refers to $1,000s.

c. HLWX is defined as HDWX + PLW + SSLW.

V. Wealth Inequality by Age Cohort

The last issue to be addressed is whether social security and human capital wealth have the same effect on wealth inequality within age cohorts as across the whole population. Results on wealth inequality by component are shown in Table 9.7. Line 1 shows the Gini coefficients for the distribution of traditional household wealth within age cohort. Surprisingly, the distribution of HDW is almost as unequal within age cohort as within the full population. Traditional wealth inequality is at its lowest for the 35–44 age cohort, with a Gini coefficient of 0.60. The Gini coefficient falls by 0.10 between the first two age cohorts, increases across the next three age cohorts, reaching its maximum of 0.81, and then falls to 0.73 in the 65 and over age cohort.[24]

Social security lifetime wealth also tends to be as unequally distributed within age cohort as within the whole population. Under Scenario A, the Gini coefficient for SSLW increases from 0.41 for the under 35 age cohort to 0.52 for the 55–64 age cohort and then declines to 0.45 for the 65 and over age group. The distribution of SSLW among preretirement families in Scenario A depends primarily on two factors: the distribution of labour earnings and the distribution of conditional life expectancies. Among age cohorts under 65, there is relatively little variation of conditional life expectancies. As a result, the increasing inequality in SSLW across age cohorts under 65 is almost entirely due to the increasing inequality in labour earnings (its Gini coefficient increases from 0.36 in the youngest age cohort to 0.50 in the 55–64 age cohort). The distribution of SSLW in the 65 and over age cohort is primarily due to the distribution of social security benefits and of conditional life expectancies. The distribution of social security benefits is more equal than that of labour earnings but the variation in life expectancies among the over 65 age group is considerably greater than that within younger age cohorts.

The age pattern for inequality in SSLW computed under Scenario B is very similar to that computed under Scenario A, except for the youngest age cohort, which has the highest degree of inequality under Scenario B. Because of the assumed constant social security tax rate in Scenario B, young workers in the upper quartile or so of the earnings distribution will actually pay more into the social security system than they will receive in benefits and will

Edward N. Wolff

Table 9.7. *Gini coefficient estimates of wealth inequality by age cohort*

Wealth component	Assumptions			All	Under 35[b]	35–44	45–54	55–64	Over 64
	Real earnings growth	Social security benefits growth	Scenario[a] (A or B)						
1. HDW	—	—	—	0.73	0.70	0.60	0.67	0.81	0.73
2. PRW	—	—	—	0.87	0.87	0.78	0.81	0.84	0.94
3. PLW	—	—	—	0.88	0.87	0.79	0.82	0.85	0.94
4. SSLW	—	0.02	A	0.48	0.41	0.44	0.46	0.52	0.45
	0.02	—	B	0.47	0.51	0.42	0.43	0.48	0.42
5. SSA	—	—	—	0.37	0.36	0.29	0.32	0.37	0.35
6. HK	0.02	—	—	0.62	0.36	0.41	0.47	0.62	0.92
7. HDWX + SSLW	—	0.02	A	0.48	0.41	0.40	0.46	0.57	0.58
	0.02	—	B	0.53	0.52	0.41	0.48	0.59	0.58
8. HDWX + HK	0.02	—	—	0.56	0.35	0.38	0.44	0.61	0.72
9. HLW	0.02	0.02	A	0.51	0.33	0.36	0.41	0.52	0.56
	0.02	—	B	0.51	0.33	0.36	0.41	0.53	0.57
10. HHA	—	—	—	0.66	0.63	0.52	0.60	0.73	0.68

a. Scenario A assumes that social security benefits grow at a constant rate over time. Scenario B assumes that social security tax rates are fixed over time.

b. The age class is based on the age of the head of household.

therefore have negative SSLW. (This effect is more pronounced for $k^* = 0.01$ than for $k^* = 0.02$.) The resultant inequality in the distribution of SSLW is therefore substantially higher within the youngest cohort than the other cohorts.

The age pattern of inequality in the distribution of social security accumulations is very similar to that of SSLW computed under Scenario B, though the reasons are somewhat different. The distribution of SSA among the working population depends on two factors: the distribution of *annual* labour earnings and the distribution of number of years at work. The increasing inequality in SSA across the middle three age cohorts is due to the increasing degree of inequality in annual labour earnings. The high inequality in the youngest age cohort, on the other hand, is due to the large variance in (estimated) years at work, which is dominated by current age and age of entry into the labour force. The lower inequality of SSA than of SSLW among the retired population indicates that an annuity-based social security system leads to less inequality in retirement benefits than the current system.

Human capital wealth is distributed more equally within the younger three age cohorts than over the whole population. The reason for this is that human capital wealth, by construction, is age dependent and, in particular, depends on the number of years remaining in the work life. Except for the first age cohort, the inequality in human capital wealth increases with age, due to both the increasing inequality in annual labour earnings with age and the increasing *relative* variance in years left to work.

Inequality in the distribution of household lifetime wealth increases steadily across age cohort (line 9). The Gini coefficient for HLW is 0.33 for the youngest age cohort, considerably smaller than the 0.51 Gini coefficient for the full population, and reaches 0.56 or 0.57 for the elderly cohort. In contrast, the Gini coefficient for HDW declines between the first two age cohorts, rises substantially between the second and fourth, and then falls between the fourth and fifth. The difference in age patterns is due primarily to the differential effect of human capital wealth on overall wealth inequality across age groups, since human capital wealth declines with age. For the youngest age cohort, the addition of human capital wealth to HDWX causes the Gini coefficient to fall from 0.70 to 0.35, or by 0.35 points (see line 8). For the 35–44 and 45–54 age groups, the resultant drop is 0.32 and 0.33 points, respectively. For the 55–64 age group, the Gini coefficient falls by 0.20 points; and for the elderly cohort there is virtually no effect (as expected).

The addition of social security wealth to HDWX also results in a reduction in wealth inequality within age cohort. However, the reduction in inequality is smaller for the three youngest age cohorts than that occasioned by the addition of human capital wealth and larger for the oldest two cohorts. Moreover, the degree of reduction in age cohort wealth inequality from the addition of SSLW to HDWX is generally related to the relative magnitude of SSLW in household lifetime wealth (see Table 9.5). The major exception is for the elderly, where the reduction in the Gini coefficient from the addition of social security wealth is the smallest, despite the fact that SSLW is a high proportion of total wealth for the elderly. The likely reason for this is a strong positive correlation between social security wealth and traditional wealth among the elderly.

The upward trend in inequality in household lifetime wealth across age cohorts can now be explained. The trend follows that of traditional household wealth except for the first and last age cohort. For the youngest cohort, the relative magnitude of human capital is the largest of any age cohort, which results in the largest reduction in the Gini coefficient from the addition of human capital to HDWX of any of the cohorts. For the oldest age cohort, the apparent positive correlation of SSLW with traditional wealth causes a much smaller reduction in inequality from the addition of SSLW to HDWX than in the second oldest cohort. This, coupled with the absence of any human capital wealth among the elderly, results in the highest degree of total wealth inequality in this age cohort. In contrast, the age pattern in Gini coefficients for household accumulations (line 10) directly mirrors that of traditional wealth, and the inclusion of social security accumulations with HDWX causes a reduction in the Gini coefficient that is relatively small and unvarying across age cohorts.

VI. Conclusion

The results of the analysis generally support those of Feldstein's 1976 study. Social security wealth is found to be more equally distributed than traditional household wealth. The Gini coefficient for the latter is 0.73, whereas Gini coefficients for social security lifetime wealth range from 0.43 to 0.55, depending on the assumptions used to generate social security wealth. Moreover, the addition of social security wealth to traditional household wealth causes a marked reduction in measured wealth inequality. However, the degree of reduction depends strongly on the assumptions used to generate estimates of household social security wealth. Whereas the Gini coefficient for household disposable wealth is 0.73, the Gini coefficient for household disposable wealth and social security lifetime wealth ranges from 0.49 to 0.61 in the limited set of simulation reported in this paper. In comparison, Feldstein calculated a reduction in the Gini coefficient from 0.72 to 0.51 from the addition of social security wealth.[25]

Pension lifetime wealth is found to be more unequally distributed than disposable wealth but much smaller in magnitude. Its inclusion in the household portfolio thus has a minimal effect on measured inequality.

The rationale for including social security wealth in the household portfolio also necessitates the inclusion of human capital wealth. Human capital wealth is found to dominate in magnitude all the other elements of household lifetime wealth. It is distributed more equally than traditional wealth but less equally than social security wealth. The addition of human capital wealth to disposable wealth causes a decline in the Gini coefficient from 0.73 to about 0.55. This reduction is found to be insensitive to the assumptions used to generate human capital wealth. The further addition of social security wealth causes the Gini coefficient to fall to about 0.50. It thus appears that it is the equalizing influence of human capital wealth, rather than social security wealth, that reduces the inequality of lifetime wealth over disposable wealth.

Further analysis using a decomposition of the coefficient of variation statistic seems to corroborate this. There are only two important elements that contribute to overall inequality in household lifetime wealth. The first is disposable wealth because of its high degree of inequality and despite its relatively small magnitude. The other is human capital, because of its high magnitude and despite its relatively small degree of inequality. Social security wealth contributes little to both because its inequality is low and because its relative magnitude is low. Moreover, the coefficients of covariation between the various components are also uniformly low.

The effects of social security wealth and human capital wealth on total wealth inequality are different within age cohort than within the full sample. Inequality in the distribution of traditional wealth is found to be almost as great within age cohort as within the whole population. The Gini coefficient for traditional wealth is higher for families under 35 than for families between 35 and 44 year of age, then increases over the next two age cohorts, and then declines for elderly families. In contrast, inequality in household lifetime wealth is considerably lower for families under 35 than for all families, increases uniformly with age across age cohorts, and is somewhat higher for elderly families than for the full population.

The difference in age pattern is due to the diminishing importance of human capital wealth in the household portfolio as a cohort ages. The reduction in measured wealth inequality from the addition of human capital to disposable wealth is particularly pronounced for the youngest age cohort. As its effect wears off with age, so does the diminution in measured inequality. Social security wealth, on the other hand, increases in importance with age, and its effect on inequality is greater than that of human capital for the two oldest age cohorts. However, the reduction in measured inequality from the addition of social security wealth to disposable wealth is significantly lower for the elderly than for the 55–64 age cohort, apparently because of a strong position correlation between social security and disposable wealth among the elderly.

A similar set of calculations was also made for social security accumulations. Social security accumulations is a hypothetical concept of social security wealth which shows what social security entitlements would be if they were strictly based on actual social security contributions. Aggregate SSA is considerably smaller than aggregate SSLW and the consequent reduction in measured inequality from the addition of SSA to disposable wealth considerably smaller, with the Gini coefficient falling from 0.73 to 0.67. As a result, it appears that the large distributional effect of SSLW on measured inequality is due primarily to legislative fiat, and this effect will very likely diminish over time due to demographic changes.

Two other general inferences can also be made from the results of this study. First, according to Feldstein (1976), a major reason why the current fungible wealth distribution is so unequal is that middle- and low-income workers are saving less than they would otherwise, because they expect to receive future social security (and pension) benefits. Yet my results indicate almost no (negative) correlation between social security wealth and fungible wealth, which suggests that the two are *not* substitutes. Second, Feldstein (1974) argued that, for similar reasons as above, social security wealth may have significantly depressed the aggregate savings of households. Yet my results indicate that social security wealth is quite unimportant for the upper wealth groups, who likely account for the bulk of household savings.

Endnotes

1. New York University. I would like to express my gratitude to Lars Osberg, Marcia Marley, and others present at the conference for their helpful comments.

2. Technically, this is referred to as 'gross social security wealth', since future contributions are not subtracted from expected benefits. His calculation of SSW uses the current social security benefit formula as the basis of the calculation. Each male earner is ranked in the distribution of labour earnings and his basic benefit is calculated based on his percentile ranking in the distribution of labour earnings. Thus, a man who was in the thirty-ninth percentile of the 1962 distribution of men's earnings is assigned the thirty-ninth percentile in the distribution of basic benefits as his base benefit B. This base benefit level is then adjusted by a factor $(1 + g)^T$, where g is the rate of growth of the social security benefit level for new retirees and T is the number of years to retirement (that is, to age 65). After age 65, the basic social security benefit is assumed to grow at a slower rate, g'. The family's SSW is then computed as the sum of the actuarial present values of (a) the man's basic retirement benefit, (b) his wife's retirement benefit while the husband is alive, and (c) his wife's survivor benefit after he is deceased. In the case of an unmarried man, SSW is given by

$$\text{SSW} = B \sum_{a=65}^{100} (1+g)^T (1+g')^{a-65} (1+d)^{-(a-A_c)} m_{c,a}$$

where d is the discount rate, A_c is his current age, and $m_{c,a}$ is the probability of a man age A_c surviving to age a.

3. This should be qualified since many companies used their workers' pension funds as a source of capital, particularly before the passage of the Erisa act in 1974. The Erisa act eliminated most of these abuses.

4. Actually, the projected Medicare and Medicaid payments are so large that in future years they probably cannot be reasonably ignored. The computation of the present value of income from such programmes might be called 'medi-wealth'.

5. More correctly, the current market value reflects current *expectations* about future income flows. For my purposes here, I shall ignore this distinction.

6. The only exception is defined contribution pension plans. In these plans, benefits depend directly on contributions. The capital value of such a plan would equal the accumulated contributions to date, since increased benefits from future contributions would simply offset future contributions.

7. This is very different than for marketable forms of wealth. For these, the current market value reflects people's *expectations* about the future; for pension and social security wealth, their value depends on the *actual* future macro-economic conditions.

8. It should be noted that I subtract both the employee and employer contributions into the systems in computing net pension and social security wealth. For this, I am making the standard assumption that the full incidence of social security taxes falls on the employee. The employer contribution, in other words, is part of worker compensation. A related issue is that one might argue that other forms of taxes, particularly income taxes, should also be netted from labour earnings in computing human capital. However, in a neo-classical world, one could counter by arguing that income and related taxes are paid by households in exchange for contemporaneous government services, such as education or defence.

9. This assumes, of course, that other forms of household savings behaviour would be unaffected by this new institutional treatment of social security contributions.

10. My basic methodology here, as in the other imputations described in this paper, is to understate the concentration of each asset in the household balance sheet when relevant information is missing.

11. Data on the number of covered workers from 1969 to 1977 and the number of beneficiaries from 1969 to 1980 were obtained from the 1980 statistical supplement of the *Social Security Bulletin* (Tables 30 and 49). Projections through the year 2050 were obtained from *Long-Range Cost Estimates for OASDI* (HEW Publications No. 78-11524, June 1978, Tables 3a, 3b, 9a, and 9b).

12. In this scenario, equation (9.4) used in computing $GSSLW_w$ must be altered slightly, since the value g^* will vary from year to year.

13. The difference between $SSLW_b$ and SSA_b might most helpfully be thought of as a pure government transfer. This difference is not necessarily positive and, in fact, is very likely to be negative for younger age cohorts today (particularly their upper income members).

14. Technically, HRW should include life insurance reserve wealth (LIRW), instead of its cash surrender value (LIDW). The difference between the reserves and the cash surrender value represents the accumulation of equity by insurance companies from undistributed profits. These residual reserves could be viewed either as part of the net worth of insurance companies and therefore part of the assets of the enterprise sector or as assets held in trust (that is, as a mutual fund) for the benefit of policy holders (some insurance companies are, in fact, called mutual life insurance companies). The dollar difference between LIDW and LIRW was quite small in 1969, with the former totalling $106.0 billion and the latter $117.8 billion. For convenience, I use only LIDW in the computation of household wealth.

15. This is likewise true for (net) PLW, since covered workers are assigned the liability for future pension contributions, as well as the (discounted) value of future benefits. However, average gross pension lifetime wealth (GPLW), which is defined as the (discounted) value of future benefits only, is about equal between pension beneficiaries and covered workers. As a result, the Gini coefficient for GPLW among holders only is 0.37, in comparison to a corresponding value of 0.75 among holders of (net) PLW.

16. On the other hand, the Gini coefficient for GSSLW does increase with g^* over the range from zero to 0.03. In fact, under Scenario A assumptions, the Gini coefficients for GSSLW are almost identical with those for SSLW, for g^* equal to 0.01, 0.02, and 0.03. The result may at first seem surprising since younger age cohorts must pay social security contributions into the system for a longer period of time than older age cohorts and their total liability to the system (SSCW) will be correspondingly greater. However, as long as g^* is greater than r^*, which is the case in these three simulations, the present value of the expected annual social security benefit for a young worker in the nth percentile of the earnings distribution will be greater than that for an older worker in the nth percentile. As a result, GSSLW is greater for the younger worker than the older one.

17. Moreover, the Gini coefficient for GSSLW under Scenario B falls as k^* increases from zero to 0.01 and then rises as k^* increases from 0.01 to 0.03.

18. The Gini coefficients are computed on the basis of household labour earnings for all households, including those with no wage earners.

19. The Gini coefficient for HK is almost invariant across values of k^*. In the formula used to compute HK, annual earnings are essentially weighted by the number of years left in the working life multiplied by a factor involving the exponential term $(1 + k^* - r^*)$. The higher k^* is, the greater becomes the estimated value of HK of younger age cohorts relative to older age cohorts. The apparent effect is that the increase in the standard deviation of HK is offset by the increase in its mean value.

20. Actually, SSLW computed under Scenario B and HDWX tend to be positively correlated across age cohort, because both increase at about the same rate with age until about age 55. However, SSLW and HDWX tend to be negatively correlated within age cohort. The explanation for this is as follows. First, *gross* SSLW is positively correlated with labour earnings and hence with HDWX within age cohort. Second, social security liabilities (SSCC) are greater for those with higher labour earnings than those with lower earnings within age cohort. As a result, for certain assumed values of k^*, (net) SSLW may actually be smaller for those with higher labour earnings than those with lower earnings, because future liabilities dominate future benefits. Indeed, net SSLW can be negative for the upper income families.

21. The low correlation of SSA and HDWX can be accounted for by the same two factors which explain the low correlation between SSLW and HDWX.

22. Human capital wealth and SSLW computed under Scenario A are positively correlated because both are strongly correlated with labour earnings. However, HK and SSLW computed under Scenario B are largely uncorrelated because (net) SSLW may be uncorrelated or even negatively correlated with labour earnings (see note 16 for more details).

23. Technically, I have used HDWP in the decompositions, where HDWP is defined as the sum of HDWX and pension lifetime wealth. Since PLW is only 4 per cent of HDWX in total, the distribution of HDWP is almost completely dominated by that of HDWX.

24. Comparisons of Gini coefficients across age cohorts are not strictly legitimate, since the age span is greater for the first and last age cohort than for the middle four. It should be noted that the Gini coefficient for HDW is 0.72 among all families under 65 of age.

25. There are three other differences in methodology, which are found to make a minor difference in results. First, Feldstein used the 1962 Survey of Financial Characteristics of Consumers (SFCC). The SFCC omits pension rights, consumer durables (except automobiles), and household inventories as part of household assets (see Projector and Weiss (1966) for a description of the data). These exclusions are found to slightly bias upward the estimate of household wealth concentration and thereby slightly bias upward the measured reduction in inequality from the addition of social security wealth.

Second, Feldstein included only those families with a man between the ages of 35 and 64 in his sampling frame. Using my sample, I find that the distribution of HDW is slightly less for the 35–64 age cohort than for the full population (the Gini coefficient is 0.70, compared to 0.73). The Gini coefficient for SSLW ranges from 7 to 22 per cent less for the 35–64 age cohort than for the full sample, depending on the assumptions used. Moreover, the ratio of aggregate SSLW to disposable wealth is about 10 per cent higher in the 35–64 age group than in the whole sample. As a result, the addition of SSLW to disposable wealth causes a slightly greater reduction (about 2 per cent) in the Gini coefficient for the 35–64 age group than for the whole sample.

Third, Feldstein included gross social security wealth in the household portfolio rather than net social security wealth. The Gini coefficient for GSSLW is about 8 per cent lower than SSLW for the whole sample. Moreover, its aggregate value is about 27 per cent higher than the aggregate value of SSLW. As a result, the addition of GSSLW to HDW causes a 5 per cent or so greater reduction in the Gini coefficient than the addition of SSLW.

References

Feldstein, M. 'Social Security, Induced Retirement, and Aggregate Capital Accumulation', *Journal of Political Economy*, 82 (Sept/Oct 1974), 905–26.

—— 'Social Security and the Distribution of Wealth', *Journal of the American Statistical Association*, 71 (Dec 1976), 800–07.

Kotlikoff, L.J., Smith, D.E. *Pensions in the American Economy* (Chicago, 1983).

President's Commission on Pension Policy, 'Pension Coverage in the United States.' Mimeo (1980a).

—— 'Preliminary Findings on a Nationwide Survey on Retirement Income Issues.' Mimeo (1980b).

Projector, D., Weiss, G. *Survey of Financial Characteristics of Consumers* (Federal Reserve Board Technical Papers, 1966).

Ruggles, R., Ruggles, N. 'Integrated Economic Accounts for the United States, 1947–1980', *Survey of Current Business*, 62 (May 1982), 1–53.

Skolnik, A. 'Private Pension Plans, 1950–74', *Social Security Bulletin*, 39 (June 1976), 3–17.

Wolff, E.N. 'Estimates of the 1969 Size Distribution of Household Wealth in the US from a Synthetic Database.' In: Smith, J. ed. *Modeling the Distribution and Intergenerational Transmission of Wealth* (Chicago, 1980).

—— 'The Size Distribution of Household Disposable Wealth in the United States', *Review of Income and Wealth*, 29 (June 1983), 125–46.

10

The Influence of Relative Prices on the Distribution of Wealth and the Measurement of Inheritance

C. D. Harbury and D. M. W. N. Hitchens

Introduction

Wealth is measured in money terms. Prices therefore enter into its calculation. Our interest in this chapter is in whether, and to what extent, price changes affect the observed size distribution of wealth. The chapter is in two parts. The first considers the influence of changing relative prices on the distribution of personal wealth over time. The second part is devoted to a consideration of the effect of price changes on the measurement of inheritance as a determinant of inequality.

I. Relative Prices and Changes in the Size Distribution of Personal Wealth

Table 10.1 starts by considering the long-term trend in the shares of the top 1, 5, and 10 per cent of personal wealth holders in Britain. Changes in relative prices may help to explain such changing shares

Table 10.1. *Distribution of personal wealth in Britain 1911–1980 (selected years)*

Share	1911	1923	1938	1950	1960	1970	1980
Top 1%	69	61	55	47	34	30	23
5%	87	82	77	74	59	54	43
10%	92	89	85	–	72	69	58

Sources: 1911—Revell (1965); 1923-70—Atkinson and Harrison (1978); 1980 —Inland Revenue Statistics (1982).

Table 10.2. *United Kingdom Asset composition of personal wealth by range of net wealth; 1973[a] (per cent of total)*

Asset/Liability	Range of net wealth (lower limit)						
	£5,000	£10,000	£20,000	£50,000	£100,000	£200,000	TOTAL
Physical assets:							
Dwellings	59.4	54.6	37.2	21.4	15.2	8.0	38.2
Land	0.4	1.1	4.4	7.5	10.8	15.2	4.3
Other buildings	0.3	0.7	1.6	1.4	1.9	1.2	0.9
Household goods	3.8	2.7	2.5	2.6	2.4	3.2	3.3
Trade assets	1.3	2.0	3.2	3.6	2.4	1.8	2.1
Financial assets:							
Listed ordinary shares	1.3	2.9	10.8	23.4	31.9	34.2	11.0
Other company securities	0.8	1.9	5.8	11.4	14.8	19.4	5.9
Life policies	20.1	16.7	13.2	6.8	3.0	1.3	14.3
Building society deposits	6.3	8.7	10.0	7.2	4.2	0.9	7.2
Listed UK government securities	0.4	0.5	1.5	2.3	3.1	3.4	1.3
Cash and bank deposits	5.1	5.6	6.5	7.8	7.4	6.1	6.6
National savings	4.9	4.2	2.9	1.7	1.1	0.9	4.3
Other assets	8.4	8.3	8.6	9.4	7.8	10.2	10.0
Liabilities:							
Personal debts	-2.4	-2.9	-4.2	-4.5	-5.2	-4.6	-3.7
Property debts	-10.0	-7.2	-4.4	-2.0	-0.8	-1.3	-5.7
Net worth	100.0	100.0	100.0	100.0	100.0	100.0	100.0

Source: Inland Revenue Statistics.
a. 1973 was selected as a mid-year, one used as a watershed in an important study to be discussed.

as a result of two well-known facts: (a) that wealth holders in different size classes hold very different proportions of their wealth in the various types of assets available to them, and (b) that the prices of such assets diverge, sometimes substantially, over time.

The asset composition of personal wealth in the UK by range of net wealth is set out in Table 10.2 for 1973. It can be seen that the disparity in holdings is very considerable. Typically, as one can see, the rich favour company securities and land while the lower wealth holders, hardly surprisingly, tend to hold the bulk of their assets in the form of dwellings, with a second important category consisting of life assurance policies.

Major interest attaches to four classes of asset; dwellings, land, and company and government securities. The highest wealth size class held nearly three-quarters of their total assets in the last two categories. The next two richest classes held about 60 per cent and 45 per cent respectively in the same assets. At the lower end of the distribution, in contrast, we find dwellings accounting for over half the total.

The very different asset portfolios of the various wealth size classes shown in Table 10.2 may be considered against the background of differential price movements of the main assets shown in Fig. 10.1. These, it can be seen, are very considerable. The price of land rose by a multiple of almost thirteen during the decades of the 1960s and 1970s, that of dwellings by about ten, while the FT all share index (equities) rose a mere two and a half fold and the index of fixed interest securities sank to approximately half its level by the end of the period. All this occurred while the index of consumer prices had risen more than fivefold.

Prima facie, with such very different price movements and asset portfolios of wealth groups, one might expect significant effects on the degree of inequality in Britain during the 20 years following 1960. This, it may be argued further, is in spite of the fact that the two asset groups with the most rapid price increases were held by top and bottom wealth groups (land and dwellings respectively). However, the course of the various price indices shown in Fig. 10.1 is still far from steady.

1. Regression Analysis

We therefore set out to test the hypothesis that relative prices

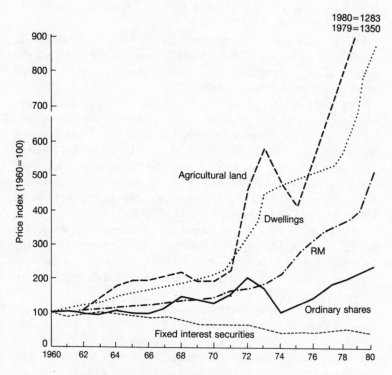

Fig. 10.1   *Trends in prices of selected assets*

Source: Diamond (1979) extended to 1980.

affected the degree of inequality, using standard multiple regression analysis. As dependent variables we took in turn the shares of a number of percentiles of the population of wealth holders, cumulatively measured from the top—for example, the share of the top 1 per cent of wealth holders in total personal wealth, the next 2–5 per cent, the top 5 per cent, and so on. The independent variables employed in the regressions were the various price indices displayed in Fig. 10.1, namely the FT/Actuaries index of ordinary shares[1] (SHAR), the FT/Actuaries index of fixed interest securities[2] (FIX), The Department of the Environment second-hand house price index (HOUS), and the Ministry of Agriculture and Fisheries total land price index (LAND).[3] The equation to be estimated was of the form

$$W_x = a + b_1 T + b_2 S + b_3 F + b_4 H + b_5 L + e$$

where W_x is the share of the xth percentile in the wealth distribution, T is a time trend, and S, F, H, and L are the indices of the price of shares, fixed interest securities, houses, and land respectively.[4] Additionally, a dummy variable (T) was introduced dividing the period into pre- and post-1972. The reason for this was the price shock affecting oil and commodity prices the following year and the subsequent collapse of ordinary shares on the London Stock Exchange, when the FT/Actuaries all share index halved between 1972 and 1974. It was also because the Diamond Commission (1979) (using a quite different method) reported to have found a distinct difference in the determinants of inequality in Britain between 1960 and 1972 on the one hand and 1972 and 1976 on the other, doubtless due at least in part to the price movements just referred to.[5] In the event, however, the dummy came out as not statistically significantly different from zero in every single one of the estimations, so it has not been included in the report of the results of the analysis presented here.

The model was estimated using as the dependent variable W_x, the share of wealth of the top 1 per cent, 2–5 per cent, 6–10 per cent, 11–20 per cent, and 21–50 per cent. Additionally the cumulative percentages of the top 1, 5, 10, 20, and 50 per cent were used. The independent variables were the four price indices referred to above, and time and the dummy variable. Table 10.3 shows the results of the regressions using the separate price indices for different wealth shares. The most general conclusion which can be drawn from the table is that only three of the twenty price index coefficients are statistically significant. When regressions were run on a cumulative dependent variable no price index (except that shown for the top 1 per cent) was significant.[6] The coefficient for time in many of the estimations was however significant.

The results of the first set of regressions can be regarded as no more than inconclusive of whether price movements affect inequality. For this reason it was decided to weight the four price indices (and here additionally making an allowance for cash), thereby constructing an asset price index. Two sets of weights were chosen, one for 1960 the other for 1975, that were based on the published data on the asset composition of estates. Difficulties in matching the data to the asset composition of percentile shares decided that the

Table 10.3. *Regression results using different price indices*[a]

	1%	2-5%	6-10%	11-20%	21-50%
Constant	33.79	24.8	14.47	25.93	5.89
	(8.12)	(5.4)	(5.0)	(7.65)	(0.97)
F	0.015	0.019	-0.014	-0.067	0.0098
	(0.41)	(0.48)	(-0.53)	(-2.23)*	(0.18)
S	0.030	-0.00322	0.0023	-0.016	-0.013
	(3.02)*	(-0.29)	(0.32)	(-2.03)*	(-0.87)
H	-0.002	-0.00192	0.0019	-0.0049	0.0059
	(0.38)	(-0.32)	(0.49)	(-1.10)	(0.73)
L	0.00082	-0.00268	-0.0043	-0.00087	0.0022
	(0.25)	(-0.73)	(-1.87)	(-0.32)	(0.45)
T	-0.92	0.0207	0.21	0.53	0.093
	(-4.9)	(0.10)	(1.59)	(3.50)	(0.34)
R^2	0.98	0.83	0.75	0.95	0.77
DW	2.72	2.73	1.62	2.70	2.65

a. The figures in brackets are t-statistics.
* Statistically significant at the 5 per cent level.

Table 10.4.   *Regression using an asset price index*

$$W_1 = 22.86 + 12.88A - 0.66T \qquad R^2 = 0.97$$
$$\quad\;\; (7.33) \quad (4.76) \quad\;\; (15.59) \qquad\quad DW = 2.16$$

Notes: The asset price index has been weighted using 1960 weights.
Estimates using 1975 weights showed no materially different results.

analysis should be restricted to the share of the top 1 per cent. Table
10.4 shows the results. As before, the dummy variable separating
1960–72 from 1973–80 was insignificant. The asset price index is
however highly significant[7] suggesting that while the wealth share is
not significantly related to any particular price index it is to the
index weighted to represent the asset portfolio of that percentile.

The conclusions drawn from the tests described above should be
compared with those obtained by other workers in the field. Three
are especially relevant: those of Harrison (1981), Atkinson and
Harrison (1978), and the Royal Commission on the Distribution of
Income and Wealth (Diamond 1979).

Harrison (1981, pp. 77–85) ran regressions to try and explain
changing shares of the top 1 per cent, the next 4 per cent, and the
next 5 per cent for England and Wales in 1923–69. He too incorporated a house and a share price index as well as a time trend (also
used squared to allow for possible non-linearity) as explanatory
variables. He also included dummy variables for known breaks in
the data series between 1938 and 1950 and between 1959 and 1960,
a variable representing the proportion of owner occupiers in the
population, and a proxy for the level of estate duty. Harrison's
results, shown in Table 10.5, led him to conclude that the share and
house price indices, as well as the level of estate duty and the extent
of owner occupation had little explanatory power, the largest portion of the variance in wealth shares among the top groups being
due to the presence of the time variable—a conclusion which, it
must be added, Harrison himself had difficulty in accepting.

Atkinson and Harrison[8] used the same basic series for their
dependent variable, though restricted themselves to the share of the
top 1 per cent of the distribution. Their set of explanatory variables
comprised a share price index, 'popular' wealth (dwellings and
consumer durables) as a proportion of the remainder of personal
wealth, post-tax real dividend yields (net return), the rate of estate
duty paid by the top 1 per cent, and identical dummies to Harrison.

Table 10.5. *Regression results, England and Wales 1923–1969*[a]

Dependent variable	Constant	Share price index	House price index	Extent of owner occupation	Estate duty	Time	Time[b]	War dummy	Data change dummy	$\overline{R}^2$	DW
W_1	73.03 (62.23)	0.07 (2.85)	-0.06 (2.47)			-0.57 (14.33)			-4.07 (3.13)	0.98	2.28
W_{5-1}	3.73 (0.64)	0.03 (1.86)	0.10 (2.04)	0.68 (2.03)	-0.56 (1.71)	0.64 (3.47)	-0.01 (2.97)	3.51 (2.88)	-1.64 (1.59)	0.82	3.08
W_{10-5}	-5.37 (1.16)	-0.05 (2.31)	0.08 (3.25)			0.69 (2.88)	-0.008 (2.53)		4.26 (4.42)	0.82	1.64

Note:
a. The figures in brackets are t-statistics.
b. The estimates for 1970 to 1973 were not used in the regressions because of their preliminary nature.
Source: Harrison (1976) p. 80.

Table 10.6. Regression equations for the share of the top 1 per cent

Equation	Constant	Dummy variables D1	D2	Time T	Share price π	$\log \pi$	'Popular' wealth PW	Net return RR	Estate duty ED	$\bar{R}^2$	SE	DW (four gaps)
Chapter 6	60.6	−2.91 (1.6)	−6.90 (7.1)	−0.42 (6.5)	—	—	—	—	—	0.983	1.42	2.26
A	4.12	−0.022 (0.5)	−0.201 (7.7)	−0.0097 (5.6)	—	—	—	—	—	0.977	0.0381	2.23
B	4.10	−0.017 (0.3)	−0.235 (5.4)	−0.0089 (4.2)	0.0014 (2.6)	—	−0.151 (2.18)	—	—	0.982	0.0344	2.19
C	4.12	−0.035 (0.6)	−0.223 (6.4)	−0.0097 (3.5)	—	0.057 (1.1)	−0.066 (1.6)	—	—	0.978	0.0377	2.22
D	4.10	−0.017 (0.3)	−0.237 (8.0)	−0.0088 (4.0)	0.0014 (2.6)	—	−0.149 (2.7)	0.042 (0.2)	—	0.981	0.0350	2.18
E	4.08	−0.025 (0.5)	−0.200 (5.1)	−0.0022 (0.4)	0.0016 (2.9)	—	0.064 (0.7)	—	−0.024 (1.3)	0.982	0.0339	2.13
F	4.07	−0.034 (6.8)	−0.192 (6.1)	—	0.0016 (3.0)	—	0.041 (0.7)	—	−0.030 (4.5)	0.983	0.0334	2.09

Note: The dependent variable is $\log_e W_1$, except in the equation from chapter 6 where it is W_1.
The figures in brackets are t-statistics.

Source: Atkinson and Harrison (1978) p. 236.

Their results, shown in Table 10.6, produced two estimated equations (*B* and *F*) which provided reasonable fits, but embodied rather different explanations of the declining share of the top 1 per cent of wealth holders. One attributed it to the upward share in the proportion of the 'popular wealth' variable coupled with the share price index and an exogenous time trend. The other equation pointed up the level of estate duty as well as the share price index.

2. *The Work of the Diamond Commission*

The third and final study concerned with quantifying the influence of price changes on inequality was that conducted by the Royal Commission on the Distribution of Income and Wealth. Its estimation of the effect of prices on distribution was conceptually and methodologically different from that of the other studies discussed above (including our own). Its procedure can be likened to that of partitioning value changes in economic aggregates into price and quantity changes. Starting with the totals of asset values of different types for the personal sector derived from estate multiplier methods at two dates, they apply price indices to each asset group in order to evaluate asset quantities adjusted for price changes. There is a choice of course, between base and current weights, corresponding to Laspeyre and Paasche, and both are employed.

Having obtained the totals for each asset class, as described above, the method next requires the allocation separately of the price (or quantity) changes of each asset to each wealth size class. The next step is to calculate the percentile shares of wealth, given the separate effects (of price/quantity changes) for each asset. There are many problems involved in the method, not least is that the detailed application necessarily involves a step-by-step procedure. Whenever someone is taken down from one size class of wealth to another, by scaling down to allow for the price change in one asset, he or she may move into a different percentile share (taking, as it were, all his other assets with him). The ordering of the steps, which is essentially arbitrary, can effect the net results. In spite of this problem and others of different types, fully recognized by the Commission, their results are interesting. Table 10.7 is divided into two periods separated by the year 1972, a date chosen when the ordinary share price index was at a peak. In the earlier of the two periods, from 1960 to 1972, as far as the top percentile of the

Table 10.7. *Contributions to changes in percentile shares Great Britain 1960–1976*

	Top 1%		2–5 per cent from the top		6–20 per cent from the top	
	1960–72	1972–76	1960–72	1972–76	1960–72	1972–76
Assets						
Cash assets						
Quantity increase	− 1.8	− 0.4	− 0.2	+ 0.5	+ 0.5	− 0.1
Policies						
Quantity increase	− 3.8	− 0.8	− 1.5	− 1.5	+ 1.1	—
Goods						
Quantity increase	− 0.5	—	—	—	—	—
Price increase	− 1.7	− 0.2	− 0.2	− 0.5	+ 0.6	− 0.3
Personal debts						
Quantity increase	− 0.5	—	+ 0.2	—	+ 0.1	—
Stocks						
Quantity increase	+ 0.5	+ 0.4	+ 0.1	+ 0.7	− 0.1	− 0.3
Price decrease	− 0.3	− 0.3	+ 0.1	− 0.2	+ 0.1	+ 0.3
Ordinary shares						
Quantity increase	+ 1.0	+ 0.2	—	+ 0.5	− 0.3	+ 0.1
Price increase	+ 6.4	− 2.5	+ 0.5	− 1.5	− 2.3	+ 0.5
Dwellings (gross)						
Quantity increase	− 0.9	− 0.1	− 0.4	—	+ 0.7	—
Price increase	− 6.0	− 2.3	− 2.4	− 1.2	+ 2.8	+ 1.0

Table 10.7. (*Cont*)

	Top 1%		2–5 per cent from the top		6–20 per cent from the top	
Mortgages						
Quantity increase	+ 0.9	+ 0.3	+ 0.6	+ 0.2	– 0.6	– 0.1
Land						
Quantity decrease	—	+ 0.4	—	—	—	– 0.2
Price increase	+ 0.9	+ 0.1	+ 0.4	+ 0.5	– 0.5	– 0.2
Total						
Quantity changes	– 5.1	—	– 1.2	+ 0.4	+ 1.4	– 0.6
Price changes	– 0.7	– 5.2	– 1.6	– 2.9	+ 0.7	+ 1.3
Total change in wealth shares	– 5.8	– 5.2	– 2.8	– 2.5	+ 2.1	+ 0.7

Sources: Royal Commission on the Distribution of Income and Wealth (Diamond, 1979) pp. 129–30.

distribution of wealth holders is concerned, the findings were that the largest price movements, of houses and equities, virtually offset each other, so that the influence of relative prices over the period did not explain more than a very small amount of the declining share of the top 1 per cent in total personal wealth. The (smaller) falling share of the next richest 2–5 per cent of persons was estimated to be due slightly more to price than to quantity changes, while for the next wealthiest 6–20 per cent (whose share had *risen*), quantity changes were about twice as important as price changes.

In a much shorter second period, 1972–6, in contrast, the research results for all three wealth size classes were that price changes were the dominant influence—chiefly again that of dwellings and ordinary shares. Indeed, as can be seen from the table, the falling share of the top 1 per cent (of 5.2 percentage points) is attributed, net, entirely to price changes.

3. Conclusions

What is one to make of the evidence surveyed, including the regression analysis of Atkinson and others and our own attempts to update them, and the results using the different approach of the Diamond Commission? They do not all tell the same story. The reason we think is due to the methodology of each approach which suffers from unavoidable deficiencies, given the present state of knowledge. The regression analysis is clearly not ideal[9] and the Diamond Commission approach suffers from its own technicalities.[10] There is therefore need for a good deal of further research which may reveal the nature and direction of any biases which result from existing methods, and should improve understanding of the importance of relative price changes on the inequality of wealth distribution in Britain.

As far as longer term considerations are concerned, relative price movements do indeed seem to have played a part in redistributing wealth, but their effect is rather slight, partly, we submit, because the trend in inequality has been continuous, but that of prices more sporadic. In the regression analyses of Atkinson and Harrison and Harrison and ourselves, the time variable tends to explain the largest portion of the variance in wealth shares. This variable encompasses, no doubt, a variety of 'real' influences not separately included in the analyses. We would do no more than hypothesize that they include the influence of taxes both on earned income as well as on capital and dividends[11] which are essentially long-term operators, but affect the ability of persons both to accumulate fortunes and to pass them on to the next generation. We wonder also if the growth of large-scale corporate enterprise during the present century may not have inhibited the opportunities for private individuals to amass large fortunes.[12]

Finally, one ought to consider an important matter which has not so far been mentioned. This is the extent to which asset holders adjust their portfolios as asset prices change. As far as those at the bottom of the distribution are concerned, there is very little opportunity for them to do so. If assets consist very largely of a dwelling, household goods, minimum life policies to cover a mortgage, and highly liquid assets of cash and building society deposits, there is little scope for changing the portfolio. Individuals may try to move up to increasingly better houses as the price of dwellings mounts rapidly but one suspects this is more common among middle and upper wealth size brackets because of the high transactions costs of moving.

At the other end of the distribution, in contrast, the scope for asset switching within portfolios is much greater. The highest wealth bracket (shown in Table 10.2) held about two-thirds of its wealth in financial assets. One would expect some persons to have switched out of equities, for example, as prices fell dramatically in 1972–3, or made a profit on a falling market. The better informed, or better advised, would even perhaps have been able to anticipate the market collapse. The smallest shareholder on the other hand may have been 'locked into' the market because of higher transactions costs. Unfortunately there is no evidence of which we are aware to support or refute this hypothesis. Research might be helpful, but it is no simple task to design a study which would put a quantitative handle on it.

II. The Effect of Price Changes on the Measurement of Inheritance

We turn now to consider a conceptually different effect of changing relative prices—that of the way they enter into the measurement of inheritance.

Attempts have been made using a number of techniques to quantify the contribution of inheritance to the degree of inequality in the distribution of personal wealth in Britain. Most use aggregate data, but one method has been that of analysing the estates left by matched pairs of individuals of different generations of the same family hereafter referred to (incompletely) for convenience as 'fathers' and 'sons'. The method involves comparing the wealth of people at different points of time and calls, inter alia, for adjustments to allow for changing prices. Such adjustments may assume considerable importance because the intergenerational span between the deaths of father and son may be great. In the study conducted by the present authors of more than 1,500 paired estates, the mean intergeneration span was rather less than 40 years, though in some cases it was as long as 80 years. In such circumstances it is clear that allowances must be made for price changes.

The standard technique used in such cases is to apply an index number of the cost of living. This method is unsatisfactory for a number of reasons.

The first is the fairly obvious one that the weights used for the calculation of the UK index of retail prices are based on average family expenditure habits, whereas, of course, the appropriate weights should be those related to expenditure of each wealth class. However, one must also question whether a price index of consumer goods and services is one that should be applied to wealth and, more especially to that which is inherited. Such would doubtless be right if bequests were immediately spent on current consumption, which, particularly when the amount involved is small, could be a fact. In other cases, the index of retail prices would not be appropriate for rendering wealth at different points of time comparable.

1. Motives for Holding Wealth

In order to determine the proper index for deflationary purposes it may be argued that it is necessary to understand the use made of an inheritance and, in principle, to know the utility functions of beneficiaries. Two motives for holding wealth may be distinguished other than that for the purpose of consumption. These may be referred to as a retention motive and an income motive.

In the former case, the assumption is that wealth holders wish to hold on to their wealth in order, for example, to pass it on to the next generation or to maintain its capital value either for the power that it brings or for security reasons. For such inheritors the prices that should be held constant are those of the assets in the estate they acquire. In the latter case, the income motive, the different assumption is made that the inheritance is desired for the income that can be derived from it.

It is hardly necessary to point out that it is impossible in practice to use the appropriate index for all intergenerational comparisons in a study such as the one referred to. In the first place information is not available in the UK probate records (other than in Scotland) on the asset structure of estates. Secondly the attitudes of persons sampled in the field work cannot be ascertained, even by questionnaire, since, by the time even 'sons' ' wealth is known, they are by definition dead! We might imagine, nevertheless, that most, if not all, individuals in the higher wealth brackets have utility functions which contain mixes of consumption, retention, and income motives. It seems, however, important to investigate the approximate sensitivity that use of each index might make to the analysis of the relationship between the estates of fathers and sons. It might, in principle, be great. Consider, for example, two inheritors, one of whom was entirely concerned with the capital value of his assets while the other was totally preoccupied with obtaining an income from them. Suppose also we were living in a world of constant prices for all goods, services, and assets other than those of bonds, whose price is inversely related to the rate of interest. The asset price index would then move in the opposite direction to a yield price index, exactly offsetting it.

Fortunately, the assumptions of the simple model discussed in the previous paragraph are not realized in practice. People hold many different kinds of asset other than bonds and their yields are not all inversely associated with their prices. We constructed three price index numbers to allow for long-term changes in price levels when estimating the quantitative importance of inheritance and comparing the results of applying them with each other and with those based on the retail price index. Two of the three have already been described, the asset price index and the yield price index, the third index we assembled, which we term a 'relative wealth index' is different in nature and requires a word of explanation.

The intention behind the use of the relative wealth index is to hold constant, not the real value of the assets, the yield, or the purchasing power of a first generation estate, but its relative position in the distribution of personal wealth. Suppose two sons died in year z and that all prices, including interest rates, were constant between their deaths and the earlier death of their fathers. Further, assume both sons were associated with fathers who left, say £250,000. Father A died in year x and father B in year y. The only difference between them was that the distribution of wealth was more unequal in year x than in year y. Then, for some purposes it might be reasonable to quantify inheritance differently for the two of them in so far as one of the fathers was *relatively* richer than the other because he was nearer the top of the wealth distribution of his day.

An index number was therefore called for which could be used as a benchmark against which a father's estate could be measured. Any parameter of the wealth distribution could have been adopted, but the decision was taken to use minimum level of wealth needed by an individual to secure a place in the top 10 per cent of the distribution at a particular time.

2. Indices employed

The methods of construction of the four price indices are described below. They are designed to test, above all, the sensitivity of conclusions about the quantitative importance of inheritance, rather than to proxy very closely the ideals implied by the previous discussion about motives. It should be remembered too that it was desirable to extend the analysis back as far as possible (in the event to 1900).

2.1 Retail Price Index (RPI)   The longest series available was that of Jefferys and Walters (1956) which was extended forward into the official index of the Department of Employment.

2.2 Asset Price Index (API)   The API was the most complex of those used here. The method of construction is basically similar to that of Sandford and Wright (1969). Sub-indices were compiled for a number of groups of assets and used to construct an overall weighted average API. Two major problems were encountered. The first was the choice of assets to include in the index. The second was a problem of weighting the sub-indices. The weights to use for any estate should, of course, be decided by its portfolio. However, this information is not available and the proxy weights employed were derived from data published by the Inland Revenue relating to the asset structure of estates by size class.

Assets were placed into one of four groups following the method of Sandford and Wright. The first group contains 'near cash' assets. They consist of cash, balances at clearing banks, trustee and post office accounts, mortgage loans, ordinary life policies, farming stock, trade assets of individuals, household goods, government securities, preference and debenture shares. The grouping is based on the assumption that all assets included had maintained a fairly constant monetary value. The second group consists of quoted and unquoted ordinary shares. The third group covers realty including land. The final group comprises residential and industrial buildings and miscellaneous property rights.

For the first group of items, by assumption, there are no price changes to be accounted for. The price index for the second group is that of industrial ordinary shares. The sources over the period are the London and Cambridge Economic Service (1970) updated by the FT/Actuaries Index. The index of groups covering land and miscellaneous realty is based on the price of agricultural land values.

The index for the last group of assets, from 1900 to 1969, consisting of residential and industrial buildings, is that compiled by the London and Cambridge Economic Service on a sample of existing houses sold with vacant possession. From 1970 the data source is the Nationwide Building Society's index numbers of existing dwellings sold with vacant possession.

The final step in the construction of the index was to obtain data on the asset structure of individual estates over the period 1900–73 to use as weights for the four sub-indices.

2.3 Yield Price Index (YPI)   In contrast to the rather complex API, a relatively simple basis was used for the YPI. This was partly because of the lengthy work of data collection which would have been necessary to produce sub-indices for incorporation into an overall index reflecting the movement of yields of assets of different types. However, there is some justification for holding a degree of confidence that long-term yields from various financial assets tend to keep more or less in line with each other as a result of market forces. Hence a single consistent asset was used to derive the YPI. It is the yield on undated government securities, Consols, adjusted for changes in the general level of the prices of consumer goods and services by means of the RPI.

2.4 Relative Wealth Index (RWI)   As explained earlier, the RWI is not a price index proper, but an index designed to enable comparisons to be made between estates at different points of time when not only prices but also the distribution of wealth differs. The end-product of applying the RWI is to compare the relative positions of the wealth distribution of the fathers of sets of inheritors.

The first step was to decide on the benchmark against which the wealth of any given father might be compared. This could in principle be any parameter of the distribution such as mean or median wealth, but the greater interest in the proportions of the wealthy with antecedents in the high wealth groups implied that a more appropriate benchmark would be the minimum wealth needed for inclusion in the top 10 per cent of the distribution in any particular year.

The minimum wealth of the top 10 per cent was not directly observable from any statistical source. It was necessary to estimate, first, mean adult population wealth, This also involved making an assumption of the shape of the wealth distribution itself which was that it approximated to the log normal.[13] Using the method of Prais (1976) it is then possible to estimate the standard deviation from data on population shares in personal wealth and to derive a series for the minimum wealth of the top 10 per cent which was smoothed by a 3-year moving average to yield the RWI.[14]

3. Results

The sensitivity of analysis of the estates of matched pairs of fathers and sons to the different indices can be observed with reference to three samples of top male wealth leavers (falling approximately into the top 0.1 per cent of the wealth distribution) for the years 1956–7, 1965, and 1973. The estates of fathers were *de*flated by the reciprocals of the RPI, API, YPI, and RWI, the course of which are plotted in the graph Fig. 10.2.

We may first briefly examine the difference between results using the RPI against those leaving fathers' estates in current prices (see Table 10.8). Since it is immediately apparent that the difference is

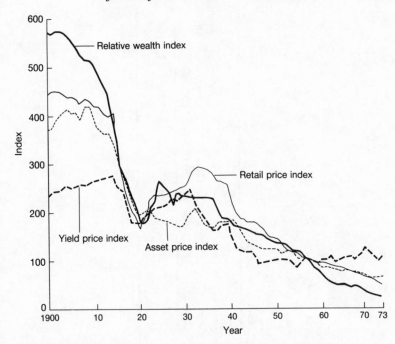

Fig. 10.2 *A graphical comparison of the relationship between four price indices, 1900–1973 (base year 1956–1957)*

Note: The index numbers are those used to inflate estates of those dying before 1956–7 (and to deflate estates of those dying after 1956–7) in order to value them at the prices ruling in the average of those years. For example, an estate valued at £100,000 in 1920, when the index was 200, would be revalued at £200,000 in 1956–7 prices.

considerable, the results are given for the largest sample with 530 cases. It can be seen that the percentages of top wealth leavers of 1956–7 who were preceded by rich fathers would be anything from *ten to twice* as high for fathers worth six figures or more if their wealth is measured in constant purchasing power rather than at current prices.

Comparison of the effects of using each of the three indices RPI, API, and YPI is shown in Table 10.9. It can be seen that these differences are markedly less than those in Table 10.8. This suggests that it is more important to make some adjustment for changes in the general level of prices than to bother too much about how

Table 10.8. *Estates of top male wealth leavers 1956–7 (cumulative percentages)*

	Size of father's estate						
	Over £1,000,000	Over £500,000	Over £250,000	Over £100,000	Over £50,000	Over £25,000	All
At current prices	1	5	12	28	42	57	100
At constant prices	10	20	34	52	58	69	100

Table 10.9. *Estates of fathers of top male wealth leavers, 1956–7, 1965, and 1973, adjusted by three price indices (Base 1956–7)*

Size of father's estates: cumulative percentages

Index	Sample	Over £1,000,000	Over £500,000	Over £250,000	Over £100,000	Over £50,000	Over £25,000	Over £10,000	Over £5,000	Over £1,000	All	Sample Size
RPI	1956–7	9	20	35	55	67	72	79	82	88	100	430
API	1956–7	7	17	32	51	64	70	78	81	88	100	430
YPI	1956–7	5	15	28	50	62	70	77	80	88	100	430
RPI	1965	5	13	24	47	60	74	83	88	91	100	77
API	1965	4	11	29	45	64	76	85	91	96	100	55
YPI	1965	1	7	17	33	46	59	71	81	86	100	118
RPI	1973	6	14	22	40	51	62	76	79	84	100	101
API	1973	3	9	19	37	47	60	72	78	84	100	101
YPI	1973	6	9	20	38	49	59	70	78	84	100	101

Note: RPI is the Retail Price Index, API the Asset Price Index, and YPI the Yield Price Index.

Source: Harbury and Hitchens (1979, p. 66).

Table 10.10.   *Estates of top male wealth leavers 1956–7, 1965, and 1973*

	Percentages of fathers with wealth in		
	Top 1%	Top 5%	Top 10%
1956–7	71	81	87
1965	74	84	91
1973	60	79	82

exactly to standardize for them, though it may be added that in almost all cases the retail price index valued fathers' estates the highest, followed by the assets price index and the yield price index.

Table 10.10 brings in the relative wealth index. This cannot be compared on a strict basis with results obtained by using RPI, API, and YPI. However the results are interesting in their own right. The table shows that 82 per cent, 91 per cent, and 87 per cent of the fathers of the top wealth leavers of 1973, 1965, and 1956/7 were preceded by fathers whose wealth, at their death, put them in the top 10 per cent of the wealth distribution of their day, while 60 per cent, 74 per cent, and 71 per cent of them were within the top percentile.

Although comparisons with the effects of deflating by other price indices is not strictly possible, the percentages shown in Table 10.10 for the top 1 per cent, 5 per cent, and 10 per cent are similar to fathers' estates in excess of £25,000, £5,000, and £1,000. This implies that if one seeks to define a rich father as one whose wealth was in the top 1 per cent of his day then it implies the same proportion as those who were preceded by fathers with estates in excess of £25,000.

4. Growth Rates

There is one further method of allowing for the influence of changing price levels which may be used to compare the estates of fathers and sons at widely separated points of time, which does not incorporate index numbers directly, but can have certain advantages. It is related conceptually to asset yields.

The technique requires the calculation of compound interest growth rates over intergeneration spans, with fathers' estate taking the role of P and sons' estate that of A in the formula $A = Pr^t$. If it were possible to estimate t in terms of the active economic life of the son and compare the computed r with some indicator of the average rate of return on inherited assets, one could distinguish dissipators and accumulators among inheritors. We calculated growth rates for the sample of wealth leavers referred to earlier, using as the proxy for t, the span in years between death of father and of son. The results are set out in Table 10.11 for each of three sample years. Since the data relating to sons tell us that they were engaged in a wide variety of trades and industries with distinctive financial outcomes in the different time spans, it was not practical to compare their growth rates, one by one, with the most appropriate indicator. An attempt was made, however, to provide some general standard of comparison, comprising the rate of return on portfolios of equities and fixed interest securities. Series are available covering nearly 50 years (by Merrett and Sykes (1966)), which show that a single lump sum would have grown before tax at compound rates of 8 per cent for equities and 0.07 per cent for fixed interest securities taking both income streams and capital growth into account. This is not the place to discuss the results in detail, but if one examines the distribution of growth rates in Table 10.11 with an 8 per cent watershed in mind as separating the self-made from inheritors one might conclude that approximately a third of the sample of top wealth leavers were self-made and the remaining two-thirds were inheritors; a conclusion not too different from those reached by other methods of allowing for changes in the level of prices.

5. Conclusions

We have been concerned in the second section of this chapter with the special problem of the effect of changing prices on the measurement of inheritance. It was suggested that, at the conceptual level, there was no ideal way of applying a price index because of the relevance of the varied motives for holding wealth by different individuals. Three price indices were constructed and applied, together with a consumer price index, to the data to test the sensitivity of the estimates to the quantification of inheritance. We concluded that some allowance is essential, but that the orders of magnitude of differences when comparing results using the four indices are not really substantial. It ought perhaps, to be added that data

Table 10.11.   Compound interest growth rates between fathers' and sons' estates, Top wealth leavers of 1956-7, 1965, and 1973 (constant prices)

Sample year	Cumulative percentages growth rate equal to or greater than %												Less than 1	Sample size
	20	15	10	9	8	7	6	5	4	3	2	1		
1973	18	22	28	31	33	36	39	45	47	54	63	68	100	108
1965	9	10*	18	21	26	28	30	37	38	46	53	61	100	94
1956-7	10*	15	20	21*	24	26*	29*	31*	36*	39*	43*	52*	100	532

* Statistically significantly different from the 1973 sample at the 5 per cent level.
Source: Harbury and Hitchens (1979, p. 60).

deficiencies of other kinds not referred to in this chapter suggest that the major expenditure of time and effort would be better applied to improving the quality of the data than constructing more elaborate indices. The only exception to this conclusion relates to the possibility of computing compound interest growth rates by industrial classification. The official Standard Industrial Classification (SIC) minimum list heading is available for the great majority of sons and a smaller majority of fathers in the sample data. Moreover, quite high proportions of wealthy sons seem to have remained in the same line of business as their fathers—58 per cent on average and as high as 75 per cent or more in as many as seven of the eighteen SIC classes employed.[15] A further improvement might arise if the estimates for those in the top wealth brackets were based on an asset price index, while it might be sensible to use the RPI as the main deflator for those in the lower part of the distribution to whom a consumption motive might appear more appropriate. For middle of the range wealth holders, some mix of the yield and retail price indices should be considered.

Endnotes

1. Ordinary shares: Actuaries Investment Index (ordinary shares) (to 1962), FT/Act. All-share index (1963 onwards).
2. Fixed Interest Securities: Actuaries Investment Index (Debentures) (to 1962), FT/Act. Fixed Interest Securities (Debenture and Loan Stocks) (20 years to maturity) Index (1963 onwards).
3. Sandford (to 1965) Ministry of Agriculture 1965 onwards.
4. The equation was specified in linear form rather than log-linear. It is worth recording that Atkinson and Harrison (1978) found similar results between the two formulations when engaged in a comparable exercise.
5. See Diamond (1979) p. 131.
6. We selected as our independent variables the share and house price indices for a separate analysis. Only the share price index was statistically significantly related to the wealth of the top 1 per cent. In the cases of the other percentile shares the house price index was the only significant coefficient but had the 'wrong' sign. It is of some further interest to note that the ratio of the share price index to the house price index was also tried and proved significant in the case of the top percentile but no other percentile.

   A further separate analysis was conducted over a longer period, 1923–80, using Atkinson and Harrisons' (1978) data. In this case the share of the top 1 per cent was regressed on that of the share and house price indexes for 40 years in that period for which data were available. The share price index was statistically significant.

7. It should be noted that the same analysis was undertaken for the longer period 1923–80 and yielded virtually identical results.

8. See Atkinson and Harrison (1978, pp. 235–40), Diamond (1979, pp. 127–31 and 192–7), and, also, Tomkins and Lovering (1978).

9. The regression equations that were estimated (see pp. 251–3), for example, include a price component of wealth on both sides. While it would be preferable to regress relative prices on the quantity of wealth, there is no inherent reason to suspect that the validity of the econometric estimation on this account alone (any more than there would be for suspecting it in equations which try to explain expenditure on the demand for a commodity in terms of incomes and relative prices). Of course, there are many simultaneous relations in the economy which one hopes may be taken into account in a full study that may one day be made, but at this stage, as in the early stages of demand analysis, the procedure used seems to us an acceptable means of proceeding.

10. The Diamond Commission presented their estimates with 'strong reservations'. Among the reasons for this is the problem of partitioning price and quantity changes which occur simultaneously, but which can only be estimated procedurely on a step-by-step basis, with the clear possibility that the ordering of the steps will influence the results (see Report No. 7 p. 127).

11. Atkinson and Harrison (1978) and Harrison (1981) both included an estate duty variable among their explanatory variables. The latter reported that estate duty appeared to have little effect on the distribution of wealth. The former found in one of their six equations that it did.

12. This is a possible explanation of a finding, using one technique, that inheritance may have been becoming more important an explanation of (declining) inequality in the UK. See Harbury and Hitchens (1979).

13. Data were also computed on the assumption of a Pareto distribution with little material difference in the outcome of the analysis.

14. Given the mean $\overline{w}$ and variance σ of the distribution the minimum wealth of the top 10 per cent may then be estimated as follows:

$$\log w_{\min 10\%} = \mu + 1.282\sigma$$

where $\log w_{\min 10\%}$ is the logarithm of the required minimum; μ is the log of median wealth; and 1.28σ is the size of the standard deviation which is added (in logs) to the median to give a level of wealth above which all persons holding that wealth are in the top 10 per cent of the wealth distribution. When only $\overline{w}$ and σ are known the median μ may be obtained from the following relationship:

$$\mu = \overline{w}e^{-\sigma^2/2}$$

15. Readers may consider that this and other results reported earlier suggest a certain stability in the structure of British society. There is evidence to confirm this in many studies. For instance Stanworth and Giddens (1974) state 'Our data do not indicate that there has occurred a process of increasing "openness" of recruitment to the chairs of the largest corporations'. However, there is much evidence that some aspects of the class structure may be changing in some ways. The situation is exceedingly complex and one should be wary about drawing conclusions from a few pieces of evidence. More research is certainly needed.

For anyone who is inclined to try out alternative models, the data which we collected and used in Part II of this chapter are publicly available from the Archives of the Economic and Social Research Council (ESRC).

References

Atkinson, A.B., Harrison, A.J. *Distribution of Personal Wealth in Britain* (Cambridge, 1978).

Harbury, C.D., Hitchens, D.M.W.N. *Inheritance and Wealth Inequality in Britain* (London, 1979).

Harrison, A.J. 'Trends over time in the Distribution of Wealth.' In: Jones, A. *Economics and Equality* (Oxford, 1976).

Heath, A. ed. *Social Mobility* (Glasgow, 1981).

Jefferys, J.B., Walters, D. 'National Income and Expenditure of the UK 1870–1952', *International Association for Research in Income and Wealth*, Series V (London, 1956).

Lampman, R.J. *The Share of Top Wealth Holders in National Wealth 1922–1956* (Princeton, New Jersey, 1962).

London and Cambridge Economic Service *The British Economy, Key Statistics 1900–1970* (Times Newspapers Ltd., London 1970).

Merrett, A.J., Sykes, A. 'Return on Equities and Fixed Interest Securities', *District Bank Review*, 158 (1966), 29–44.

Prais, S.J. *The Evolution of Giant Firms in Britain: A Study of the Growth of Concentration in Manufacturing Industry in Britain, 1909–1970* (Cambridge, 1976).

Revell, J.R.S. *Changes in the Social Distribution of Property in Britain during the Twentieth Century*, Third International Conference of Economic History (Munich, 1965).

Royal Commission on the Distribution of Income and Wealth (Diamond) Report No. 7 Cmnd 7595 (1979).

Sandford, C.T., Wright, P.M. 'Estate Duty, Inflation and Capital Gains', *The Banker* 119, (1969).

Stanworth, P., Giddens, A. *Elites and Power in British Society* (Cambridge, 1974).

Tomkins, C., Lovering, J. 'Price Changes, "Fixed-price assets" and the Personal Distribution of Wealth', No. 7, Discussion Papers in Business Research, Finance, Accounting and Industrial Economics, University of Bath (1978).

Wedgwood, J. *The Economics of Inheritance* (London, 1929).

INDEX

adequacy (of income) 2–3, 19–20, 94, 179, 186, 191

age:
  and human capital 226, 233–4, 239–40, 242
  and pension wealth 230–3
  and portfolio composition 102, 103–5, 116
  and social security wealth 224, 226, 233–4, 237–40, 242
  and wealth accumulation 127–8
  and wealth inequality 21, 22, 35, 102–3, 115–16, 121–2, 129–30, 131–5, 137–8, 237–40, 242
  earnings profiles 187
  income profiles 100–2, 127
  wealth profiles 7, 10, 13–14, 16, 43–4, 99–102, 105, 115–16, 128–9, 137, 164, 165, 230–4

aged *see* elderly

altruism 158–9

annuities 18, 94, 163, 181, 196

apartments:
  houses 54, 55, 63
  owner-occupied 53–4
  price of 65, 66

asset prices 22–3, 45, 65–7, 250–61, 263, 264–5, 266, 267, 270

asset substitutability 163

Atkinson, A.B. 29, 32, 33, 38, 41, 171, 254, 260, 274 n.

automobiles 54, 96, 98, 195

balance sheets *see* household balance sheets

bank accounts (deposits) 11, 54, 57, 65, 66, 67, 213, 265

Becker, G. 158, 174 n.

Belgium 18, 153

bequests 23, 158, 159, 162, 164, 165
  motive 158, 163, 165, 171, 172, 262–3

Bernheim, B. 161

'biens de famille' 162

Blinder, A. 158

bonds 3, 4, 11, 12, 18, 53–4, 57, 67, 80, 99, 144, 164, 192, 213
  corporate 123, 124
  municipal 123
  price of 66
  short-term 163
  state and local 6, 15, 83, 122
  US federal 6, 123, 124
  US savings 99

Brumberg, R. 7, 127–8

business equity 3, 4, 5, 10, 11, 14, 18, 45, 55, 56, 57, 70, 82, 96, 98–9, 164, 192, 213

Canada:
  income inequality 19–20, 187–90
  income replacement ratios 196–206
  joint distribution of earnings and wealth 194
  retirement income system 179, 186
  wealth inequality 18, 19–20, 153, 193–4

Canada and Quebec Pension Plan (C/QPP) 182, 184, 186, 187, 192, 193, 199

Canada Pension Plan 187

capital gains 18, 98, 164

cars *see* automobiles

cash (on hand) 3, 5, 18, 82, 99, 162, 163, 195, 261, 265

Census Bureau (US) 97, 220

Central Statistical Office (UK) 41

Centre de Recherche sur L'Épargne (CREP) 144

certificates of deposit 99

checking accounts 3, 18, 99, 163, 195

claims 54, 55

consumer durables 3, 4, 5, 6, 14, 15,

POINT LOMA NAZARENE COLLEGE
RYAN LIBRARY